Handbook of Behavioral Assessment *edited by Ant[...]*
    Henry E. Adams

Counseling and Psychotherapy: A Behavioral App[...]

Dimensions of Personality *edited by Harvey London [...] Exner, Jr.*

The Mental Health Industry: A Cultural Phenomenon *by Peter A. Magaro, Robert Gripp,*
    David McDowell, and Ivan W. Miller III

Nonverbal Communication: The State of the Art *by Robert G. Harper, Arthur N. Weins, and*
    Joseph D. Matarazzo

Alcoholism and Treatment *by David J. Armor, J. Michael Polich, and Harriet B. Stambul*

A Biodevelopmental Approach to Clinical Child Psychology: Cognitive Controls and Cognitive
    Control Theory *by Sebastiano Santostefano*

Handbook of Infant Development *edited by Joy D. Osofsky*

Understanding the Rape Victim: A Synthesis of Research Findings *by Sedelle Katz and*
    Mary Ann Mazur

Childhood Pathology and Later Adjustment: The Question of Prediction *by Loretta K. Cass and*
    Carolyn B. Thomas

Intelligent Testing with the WISC-R *by Alan S. Kaufman*

Adaptation in Schizophrenia: The Theory of Segmental Set *by David Shakow*

Psychotherapy: An Eclectic Approach *by Sol L. Garfield*

Handbook of Minimal Brain Dysfunctions *edited by Herbert E. Rie and Ellen D. Rie*

Handbook of Behavioral Interventions: A Clinical Guide *edited by Alan Goldstein and Edna B. Foa*

Art Psychotherapy *by Harriet Wadeson*

Handbook of Adolescent Psychology *edited by Joseph Adelson*

Psychotherapy Supervision: Theory, Research and Practice *edited by Allen K. Hess*

Psychology and Psychiatry in Courts and Corrections: Controversy and Change *by*
    Ellsworth A. Fersch, Jr.

Restricted Environmental Stimulation: Research and Clinical Applications *by Peter Suedfeld*

Personal Construct Psychology: Psychotherapy and Personality *edited by Alvin W. Landfield and*
    Larry M. Leitner

Mothers, Grandmothers, and Daughters: Personality and Child Care in Three-Generation Families
    by Bertram J. Cohler and Henry U. Grunebaum

Further Explorations in Personality *edited by A.I. Rabin, Joel Aronoff, Andrew M. Barclay, and*
    Robert A. Zucker

Hypnosis and Relaxation: Modern Verification of an Old Equation *by*
    William E. Edmonston, Jr.

Handbook of Clinical Behavior Therapy *edited by Samuel M. Turner, Karen S. Calhoun, and*
    Henry E. Adams

Handbook of Clinical Neuropsychology *edited by Susan B. Filskov and Thomas J. Boll*

The Course of Alcoholism: Four Years After Treatment *by J. Michael Polich, David J. Armor, and*
    Harriet B. Braiker

Handbook of Innovative Psychotherapies *edited by Raymond J. Corsini*

The Role of the Father in Child Development (Second Edition) *edited by Michael E. Lamb*

Behavioral Medicine: Clinical Applications *by Susan S. Pinkerton, Howard Hughes, and*
    W.W. Wenrich

Handbook for the Practice of Pediatric Psychology *edited by June M. Tuma*

Change Through Interaction: Social Psychological Processes of Counseling and Psychotherapy *by*
    Stanley R. Strong and Charles D. Claiborn

Drugs and Behavior (Second Edition) *by Fred Leavitt*

(*continued on back*)

THE PSYCHOSOCIAL WORLDS
OF THE ADOLESCENT

To Bill —

a combination of very
good friend and highly
respected colleague —

with admiration —

Vivian

THE PSYCHOSOCIAL WORLDS OF THE ADOLESCENT: PUBLIC AND PRIVATE

VIVIAN CENTER SELTZER

University of Pennsylvania

1989

A WILEY-INTERSCIENCE PUBLICATION

JOHN WILEY & SONS

New York ● Chichester ● Brisbane ● Toronto ● Singapore

Library of Congress Cataloging in Publication Data:

Seltzer, Vivian Center.
    Psychosocial worlds of the adolescent : public and private /
Vivian Center Seltzer.
        p.   cm. – (Wiley series on personality processes)
    Bibliography: p.
    ISBN 0-471-63258-9
        1. Adolescence. 2. Self. 3. Peer groups. 4. Socialization. 5. Identity.
    I. Title. II. Series.
    HQ793.S428   1989
    155.5–dc20   89-5710
                                                      CIP

Printed in the United States of America

10 9 8 7 6 5 4 3 2 1

This book is dedicated to my "adolescent peer"
Anna Shure Simon
of blessed memory
and to the adolescent years
we so energetically engaged, side by side

Series Preface

This series of books is addressed to behavioral scientists interested in the nature of human personality. Its scope should prove pertinent to personality theorists and researchers as well as to clinicians concerned with applying an understanding of personality processes to the amelioration of emotional difficulties in living. To this end, the series provides a scholarly integration of theoretical formulations, empirical data, and practical recommendations.

Six major aspects of studying and learning about human personality can be designated: personality theory, personality structure and dynamics, personality development, personality assessment, personality change, and personality adjustment. In exploring these aspects of personality, the books in the series discuss a number of distinct but related subject areas: the nature and implications of various theories of personality; personality characteristics that account for consistencies and variations in human behavior; the emergence of personality processes in children and adolescents; the use of interviewing and testing procedures to evaluate individual differences in personality; efforts to modify personality styles through psychotherapy, counseling, behavior therapy, and other methods of influence; and patterns of abnormal personality functioning that impair individual competence.

IRVING B. WEINER

University of South Florida
Tampa, Florida

Preface

"Who am I?" may be a universal question, but there is a difference in the meaning of the question as posed by the adult and by the child, particularly by the adolescent. Generally, the child finds his or her answer to the question through identifying with the attributes of Mom, Dad, and siblings. The adult may ask the question in a variety of new situations, whenever he or she experiences a deviation from the more familiar "self." But the adolescent asks this question at a time of few external referents and an undeveloped internal sense of self. Adolescence is an age of inquiry into the potentials of "self" and of decision-making as to which dimensions are possible or practical. It is an age of evolution of self, of cocoon into butterfly, and is perhaps the most intriguing of the developmental periods. It is, in pure form, a period of inquiry into "who am I?"

The exploration is characterized by trial and error as adulthood is sought while childhood is not quite abdicated. Externally observable behaviors range from participation in crowd activities to individual, idiosyncratic preferences and preoccupations. Adolescence is generally seen as an impressive period of growth, but one that is undiscernible and mystifying. Witness the myriad of social problem behaviors that appear so resistant to control.

Adolescents have long held a fascination for me. I have been involved in work with them from the very beginning of my professional life. At that time my efforts were with troubled adolescents. Later my interest shifted to the normatively progressing adolescent. Certain phenomena fascinated me, the most prominent of which were the large crowds within which most early adolescents travel and what appears an almost magnetic pull between them: adolescents have "to be together," sometimes forgoing spectacular opportunities. Examining this phenomenon over time led me to develop several theoretical constructs:

1. A psychological "peer arena" made up of many, many peer groups—both physically and psychologically encountered
2. A deep-structure, developmentally based "adolescent imperative" to be together with agemates
3. The dynamics of an "adolescent dialectic"—a pull between childhood and adulthood that characterizes the period
4. A uniquely adolescent type of social comparison, the "comparative act," which is functionally energized whenever adolescents are in each other's company
5. The central developmental position of the adolescent peer as the "relevant environmental other"
6. The concurrent "present and future" character of their mood
7. Both surface and deep-structure levels of motivation and behavior

This book explains these dynamics as well as others, some of which have been given new interpretations. It offers the reader theoretical connections by which to better grasp how the core developmental task of achieving a "sense of identity" directs adolescents' internal energies and fuels their behavior. The task is complex and taxing. What is crucial to understand is that the task is an ongoing subliminal activity, absorbing high levels of psychic energy.

Findings discussed in this book reveal dimensions of adolescent thought and behaviors that suggest effective practice with adolescents can no longer concentrate primarily on parent-child interactive dynamics and family history and processes. Much of adolescent energies seem to be expended coping with demands of daily functioning (e.g., school and personal responsibilities) and with psychosocial growth imperatives. In both areas, peers are the relevant others. They serve as cotravelers and as positive and negative models for both present and future matters. My intent was to bring the adolescent mental state alive with findings relating to favorite reference groups and persons and the areas of their influence; what interests adolescents most about each other; types and numbers of friends; the various ways in which adolescents meet, do or do not socialize, and select friends; and when and to what degree the dynamics of comparing self against peers are operative. This information will yield additional dimensions for understanding confusing and unexpected adolescent behaviors, some normative and some problematic.

It also appears that the use of clinical instruments, if geared to test how adolescents fare in peer interactional life, could shorten counseling and therapeutic hours. I developed the Peer Arena Batteries, whose individual instruments can be used alone or in tandem. They are suitable for a range of professional settings and can be administered, as fitting, to the adolescent and/or the appropriate environmental figure—parent, caretaker, teacher, minister, etc. If desired, data from more than one respondent can be compared for additional insights or perspectives.

Suggestions and strategies discussed in closing chapters bring theory and pragmatics together. Although clearly of use to educators and professionals in mental and physical health, the content of the book is useful to any individual whose academic field, professional interest, or target area is adolescence and adolescents.

To understand the multifaceted dimensions of the impact adolescents have on one another's psychosocial growth and actions, the importance adolescents hold for one another, and, thus, the imperative they experience to be together, is to be well on the road to understanding adolescence. I trust that this book will bring the reader some steps closer to that end.

VIVIAN CENTER SELTZER

Philadelphia, Pennsylvania
September 1989

Acknowledgments

It seems appropriate to note at this time that the theoretical frame of my work in the field of adolescence—a blend of developmental and social psychology—is an outcome of my graduate studies in the Department of Human Development at Bryn Mawr College, where "cross-fertilization" of theory was advocated and creativity encouraged. Specifically, I would like to mention the contributions of Dr. Emmy A. Pepitone, who introduced me to the field of social psychology and whose academic guidance was invaluable, and of Dr. Janet Hoopes, who expanded my horizons on adolescence.

I was very fortunate to have the cooperation of public and private school personnel in the communities of Long Island, N.Y., Canton, Ohio, and Philadelphia, Pa., who allowed me access to their students. I thank them as I do the students who responded to our inquiries. Several fine students of my own devoted long hours to accessing the samples and collecting the data: Diane Ellis, Vicki Ellis, Wendy Hoffman, Jane Rosenberg, and Brother David Trichtinger. I am deeply appreciative of their contributions. The following individuals have also been very helpful. My thanks go to Drs. Robert Spena and John Vafeas and to Maryann Florio and Charlie Pyrozees for their assistance with computer analyses; Dr. Morris Hamburg, Professor of Statistics and Operations Research of the Wharton School of the University of Pennsylvania for consultation on questions of statistical analysis; Ben Scheindlin and Robert Lebeau for help with computations and organizational tasks; Laurie McAdams for her assistance in typing early concept papers, and Lee Early for typing many drafts and the final manuscript. A special message of appreciation goes to my editor at Wiley, Herb Reich, for his editorial skill; I thank him for his expert help to me. I would like to acknowledge the contribution of the production staff of John Wiley. I would also like to acknowledge the support of grants received from the University of Pennsylvania Research Foundation, which helped to defray costs of analysis of the data.

V.C.S.

Contents

During most of adolescence, independence is sought, not possessed. To appear independent and in command of one's life is important. It reassures the adolescent that his or her secret instability does not show. Paradoxically, this same assumed demeanor on the part of agemates increases the adolescent's own anxiety about his or her own inner sense of tentativeness.

Introduction

This book is about the manner in which adolescents view and use their greater social world, the primary position and developmental value of the peer in it, their reciprocal psychosocial interactions, and how they operate for or against one another in accomplishing the psychosocial task of achievement of identity. It links surface-structure behavior and deep-structure developmental needs and discusses overt social behavior as a manifestation of this connection.

The approach of this book is that adolescent behavior can be understood only within the context of an organism in the growth process. The behavior cannot be taken at face value. Neither can we assume adolescents fully understand the forces motivating their behaviors or that they interpret them accurately to themselves or others. Behaviors are generally based on more than the external circumstances to which they are ascribed; behaviors are developmentally driven. They are derivatives of the adolescent imperative to capitalize on the gains of childhood and individuate into one's own person.

Stability in childhood is based on borrowing self descriptors from family and close friends. Physical puberty heralds a period of rapid growth and consolidation of biological, intellectual, and psychological components essential to identity formation. Before an adolescent becomes his own person, he must experiment with heredity and also incorporate social factors. The child, with all his uniqueness, has operated on a quasi-borrowed identity; the task of the rather long adolescent period in our complex Western society is to give back the borrowed identity and to construct one's own.

Our model for understanding adolescent behaviors and effectively working with them varies from traditional practice, which generally has

Our model for understanding adolescent behaviors and effectively working with them varies from traditional practice, which generally has been guided by psychoanalytic theory or variants thereof (see Chapter 1). These theories have held that overt adolescent behaviors can be attributed to dynamics of psychosexual development. External behaviors are held to reflect internal conflict between the superego and unacceptable drives stimulated by the id. The strength of this conflict is seen as energizing the erratic behaviors of adolescents. Opposite theoretical postures in the literature claim society's mores and values are determinant and that overt and subtle environmental reinforcements influence behavior. There are a number of positions in between (Chapter 1).

The position taken in this book is that, nature or nurture notwithstanding, adolescents experience similar developmental imperatives. They enter the period with diverse psychological conditions, but they share a state of uncertainty and a similar task: Each must discover what defines himself or herself as an individual and forge a direction in life. Each must understand the relative values of the attributes and skills identified as his or her own. This psychosocial task of adolescence, frequently referred to in Erikson's (1950) nomenclature as discovery of one's identity in love and in work, is a difficult, all-consuming task to be carried out over many years. Our approach concentrates far less attention on relationships between adolescent and non-peer figures than do other theoretical models. Non-agemates are viewed within a framework of how they support or complicate smooth psychosocial interactions with the crucial relevant other of the period—the peer. Emphasis on relationships of peer to peer and peer to peers is central to the model presented (Chapters 2, 3).

We will argue a divergent theoretical framework [an approach to adolescent development spelled out by the theory of dynamic functional interaction (DFI) (Seltzer, 1982)]—that the processes of adolescent interaction are the cardinal dynamics of adolescence and that effective relationships with and therapeutic treatment of the adolescent is based on a comprehensive knowledge of these dynamics, when and how they become active and whether they are functional or dysfunctional.

Psychological forces that surface in early adolescence act to stimulate strong desires to be with agemates. Agemates have information to offer one another about themselves and others. They prepare and practice together; they model, copy, compare, evaluate against, experiment with, and come to conclusions about one another. They model raw materials of innumerable attributes, characteristics, and skills. They try out many new roles on one another. To arrive at a true self-perception requires not only risk and trial, but sharp and persistent introspection to assess which qualities, talents, and abilities are really components of self, which can be developed, and which are unchangeable. Furthermore, the task is not complete without a sense of the relative marketability of each dimension relative to the cohort group with whom the adolescent will cooperate and compete in the travel through life (Chapter 4).

This book offers a delineation of the adolescent's larger social world and the socialization functions of the various individuals in it. It stresses the immediate relevance of agemates and how integral they are to psychosocial growth. The peer is seen to be the primary environmental figure, and psychosocial interactions with peers are viewed as core developmental dynamics. Adolescents repeatedly watch, listen, and learn. They are one another's audience, witnesses, and judges. Successful passage through the stage is a result of ample engagement of the growth challenges adolescents provide for one another. Maladaptations are responses to difficulties in navigating these developmental tasks (Chapter 10).

Empirical portions of the book offer data on the basic theoretical premises of how adolescents engage the larger social world—who the preferred reference groups/persons are and when they are called upon, the relative posture of peers as influence and comparison figures, the numbers of agemates they engage with and where they like to gather with them, and the nature of their public and private associations (Chapters 5, 6, 7, and 8).

Not all adolescents enter the period strong, and some experience intense trauma during the period. Some cannot successfully manage both daily tasks and developmental demands. Our look at maladaptations and problems is framed within a context of flight from painful responses to developmental peer arena interactions. We also consider the problems of the exceptional and the isolated adolescents. Special concerns about the impact of these circumstances on completing normative development are discussed with some interventions suggested (Chapter 11).

We next introduce practical tools to assess both normative and maladaptive functioning in two batteries of instruments appropriate for educational and clinical use by professionals. The first battery of tools elicits the adolescent's perception of his larger world and how he reaches out to its members. The second yields information on relations between adolescents and significant environmental others, as well as their respective attitudes (Chapters 12, 13).

The closing chapters offer developmentally focused perspectives, pragmatic suggestions, and some additional tools for professionals advising adolescents and parents; for professionals in educational settings who plan for, instruct, and counsel adolescents; and for professionals dealing with these youths in the health and mental health fields. A group therapy approach unique to adolescents—peer arena therapy—is recommended and presented (Chapters 14, 15, 16).

Adults negotiate the world armed with a sense of self. Adolescents negotiate it while in a condition of continuous change. Early unconscious experiences, prior events, and family relations are indeed contributing factors to adolescent behaviors, particularly with disturbed adolescents, but should not receive disproportionate attention. Of paramount influence on present functioning and behavior and on smooth progressive growth are the deep-structure growth dynamics, experienced with continuity and with intensity. Their overt manifestations are observable from early adolescence into maturity. To work with adolescents without the guiding principles an understanding of these dynamics affords is to chase shadows in the dark. The dynamics, the nature and character of the process, and *the place of the adolescent peer in it* form the subject matter of this book.

PART ONE

A Historical Overview

Adolescence is more than an extended period of change. It is an interval of continuous changing. It is an interlude of life that has held more fascination than answers. Since introduction of the term *adolescence* early in the century, theorists of human growth and development have searched to understand the forces that direct and affect the course of the stage. This introductory section selects from the major currents of thought about the adolescent period to provide background for discussions of the central dynamics of adolescence and the empirical data that follow in subsequent chapters.

CHAPTER 1

Tasks and Challenges of Adolescence: Divergent Views

It may be helpful to begin with a brief historic overview of selected areas of major thought on the period of adolescence. Inherent is the question of the relative impact on development of that which comes with one at birth (nature) versus the circumstances of the societal milieu (nurture). Adolescence is a period of growth during which the offspring changes from child to mature adult, from one happily dependent on parents and elders to an individual fully capable of independent living and decision-making. During the process many changes occur on the biological, intellectual, emotional, and social levels (Tanner, 1972; Piaget, 1972; Freud, A., 1936), and these changes take a long time. In Western society, the onset of puberty, which marks the biological beginning of adolescence, is starting earlier and the duration of the entire adolescent period is growing longer. For some who marry after high school and take jobs immediately, rather than prolong education, the period of adolescence is shorter. They quickly become self-supporting and, many times, begin a family of their own and conduct adult lives quite early. But for most who go through college or otherwise postpone independence, adolescence does not end until the mid-20s.

Present-day thought generally acknowledges that a combination of nature and nurture contributes to human growth and to the development of personality. What controversy remains of old theoretical differences lies with the issue of which is the major force. This dilemma is reflected in the literature on adolescence, which is replete with theoretical postures (Muus, 1982). At one end of the continuum are those thinkers who claim that personality develops in a sequence of internally predestined steps irrespective of environmental conditions. The timing of the unfolding may differ, but the sequence remains the same. These proponents are regarded as "stage theorists." Included within this broad category are seminal thinkers in both the emotional (Freud, S., 1905) and the intellectual (Piaget, 1952) domains of development.

G. Stanley Hall (1916), who is considered the father of adolescence, compares the developmental stage of adolescence to the turbulent, transitional period of the last decades of the eighteenth century, characterized by "Sturm und Drang." He sees adolescence as a unique time of "storm and stress," quite unlike the ups and downs of the other developmental periods.

Only a decade later a view quite opposed to Hall's was aired, and the controversy between nature and nurture, which has lasted over half a century since, was begun. Leta Hollingsworth (1928), an anthropologist, refutes the notion of specific developmental stages. She suggests that growth takes place imperceptibly, not dramatically. Furthermore, she disagrees with the notion of universal growth patterns and, as an anthropologist, points to their culture-specific nature. Support for Hollingsworth's position comes from two famous anthropologists, Margaret Mead (1928) and Ruth Benedict (1938), who contributed important cross- cultural findings. They hold strongly to the position that adolescent behavior must be viewed directly in relation to the culture in which the person lives.

Among the more influential contributors to the debates were those of the psychoanalytic school. Those of the Freudian tradition consider that adolescence is the last of five psychosexual periods of emotional development. It is characterized as normally turbulent; the adolescent must reindividuate himself and achieve emotional separation from parents. This necessitates managing strong libidinal drives stimulated by the advent of puberty and initially misdirected to parents. The task of the period includes redirecting these drives to suitable environmental others (Freud, S., 1905; Freud, A., 1936, 1958).

Margaret Mead (1942) in particular rejects the psychoanalytic notion that onset of puberty precipitates upheaval within the system and that erratic overt behavior should be expected. She feels that the manner in which the particular society looks upon developmental milestones is influential. Different societies stress different points of development and label them good or evil; corresponding behaviors then follow. Ruth

Benedict (1938), who also stresses the responsibility of the culture, investigated whether the culture's mores allowed development to be smooth and continuous or whether customs of the culture created sharp change in attitudes and actions at certain points (e.g., expecting sexual relationships to be open and loving in adulthood, while sex is hidden and forbidden in childhood). Benedict calls these disconnected actions and attitudes "discontinuities" in a culture and contends that they, not the physical changes of maturation, provide the stress leading to the extremes in behavior.

Conversely, the prominent psychoanalytic thinker Anna Freud (1936, 1958) lends support to Hall's position of adolescence as a unique stage. She argues that adolescent behaviors may at time become so extreme they resemble psychosis. Anna Freud picks up from Sigmund Freud's acclaimed position (1905) that the first five years of childhood are the most formative for personality development. She attributes the vicissitudes of the adolescent period to unacceptable, unconscious libidinous drives whose intensity manifests itself in the highly erratic behavior of teens. Because of the unconscious battle raging within the individual between unacceptable drives and societally admissible outlets, the adolescent is subject to extremes of emotion and resulting turbulent behaviors. The turmoil confuses the adolescent and those about him. These behaviors have often been reduced to the now-popular simplified concept of "rebellion." It is based on the connection psychoanalysis draws between inner dynamics and overt behaviors.

While the controversy continues over whether adolescence is a unique stage or one like any other period of development, recent theorists no longer align their views as strictly nature-based (biological forces stimulate the vicissitudes of behavior) versus nurture-based (impact of the society/culture and its mores and values are responsible for the behavior). There is now a continuum of views. Although many theorists prefer to be at either end of the continuum, all do not deny the influence of the other pole. Anna Freud remains consistent with Sigmund Freud's psychoanalytic teaching in her position that equilibrium in adolescence is unnatural. The libidinous impulses of childhood, dormant through the elementary school years, reawaken unconscious desires for the parent of the opposite sex, which resurface with greater biological maturation. Defenses are weak relative to the strength of the desire, and the raging conflict manifests itself in tumultuous behaviors. Thus, equilibrium is seen as developmentally inappropriate; conflict and turmoil are seen as natural. New defenses, previously unnecessary, come to the aid of adolescents to hold anxiety in check.

Anna Freud (1936) holds two defenses to be prominent in adolescents: asceticism and intellectualization. Asceticism defends against instinctual desires for all forms of comfort. Such rejection of worldly comforts masks the drive for satisfaction of unacceptable sexual desires since all sensual or sensory pleasures are rejected. The second defense, intellectualization, represents the adolescent's fight to resist strong instinctual needs to see/touch/feel/enjoy. He or she turns to abstract theoretical interests and rejects concrete involvements. Both defense mechanisms mask potent desires. Guilt over the unacceptable drive is turned inward— and, thus, anxiety is reduced. Ironically, adolescents who can handle the raw drive and do not need a high degree of defensive protection may appear on the surface to be more disturbed than those who do not assume the defenses. Strange and erratic behaviors cause them to appear very different or even transformed to family members who know them best. Accordingly, parents/caretakers become alarmed, adding familial stress to personal stress. Nevertheless, Anna Freud contends that this upsetting behavior bodes well for the development of a full adult personality. Those who act in a bizarre fashion for a time until they work through the conflict pass into maturity fully developed. Her concern is greater for those who may not mature because their emotional stamina does not allow them to endure the vicissitudes of instinct. To Anna Freud, lack of turmoil is not a sign of stability but a sign of arrested energies.

Peter Blos (1962, 1970) also sees turmoil in adolescence as part of a normal progression toward becoming adult. He views the stage as having five parts: preadolescence, early adolescence, adolescence proper, late adolescence, and post-adolescence. Peter Blos too is a proponent of psychoanalytic theory and equates normal development with successful resolution of the five psychosexual phases of Freud. Blos connects the turmoil and stress of adolescence with a period that occurs at about age three, when the child must psychologically separate from the mother in order to move out to others. Although the adolescent is to separate again in order to achieve worldly independence, there is a big psychological difference between the two tasks. At age three, in order to deal with the pain and anxiety of leaving Mother from time to time, the child's task is to *internalize* the mother—to psychologically keep her with him. In adolescence, a decade later, in order to separate from the mother, who has heretofore been internalized, the adolescent has to shed what now feels like a part of him. To do so is to feel as if a piece is missing. Thus, the adolescent experiences psychological instability and indecision.

This withdrawal and striving for a stable independence causes many emotional ups and downs. According to Blos, the path is not only difficult, but long. Blos contends that in preadolescence the child withdraws deep love from the parent and carries fantasies of an ideal other within. The enormous emotion bound up in earliest relationships with parents cannot just be "turned off." Blos suggests the conception of the "ego ideal" as a helper. The adolescent chooses someone just like himself to whom he can transfer the love withdrawn from parents, which he has had to handle within himself and which has become burdensome. This new emotional tie helps him weather the difficulties of the transition to psychological independence and maturity. [Blos's theory deals primarily with the adolescent male, for which he has been criticized. His later work (1970) places somewhat more emphasis on females. The adolescent girl, unlike the male, transfers her love and dependency to a "crush" on an older person.]

Back-and-forth psychological movement continues over Blos's next two stages, but eventually disengagement from childhood ties and identifications does occur. The adolescent works out his own identity. The last stage, transition to adulthood, is devoted to polishing rough edges, finalizing a sense of one's own person, and establishing life goals. When psychosexual development is successfully completed, it is manifested in healthy functioning. However, matters do not always go smoothly. Dependent on a number of factors (e.g., characteristics of the adolescent, level of stability, and complications of the new and old relationships), the adolescent may suffer serious malfunctions. Blos would contend that one or more of the five stages were not successfully resolved. The intermediate transfer of affection from parents to peers and models was not adequate. Hence, the processes necessary for sexual identification and heterosexual life were not exercised. The psychological task of transferring deep, sexualized emotion from parents is incomplete. Outside appearances often do not tell the entire story. The individual may appear to go on to adulthood but in reality is handicapped psychosocially.

Neither Anna Freud nor Peter Blos deal with the impact of the peer society and its values on the course of adolescent development. This task has fallen to thinkers who are dissatisfied with the separation of nature from nurture. Although this second group of theorists subscribe to biological determinants of behavior and support Freud's structural theory of id, ego, and superego, they feel the model is incomplete without stressing influence of environmental factors on the individual. These psychosocial theorists bridge the gap between those who believe that what is endowed at birth is paramount and those who adhere to the power of the immediate environment.

The most influential of the modern thinkers on adolescence, Erik Erikson, points out the fallacy of disconnecting a theory of behavior and development from the culture/society in which the growth took place and from the behavior that was acted out (1950). Consequently, his work concentrates less on the genesis and dynamics of distortions and more on the connection between maladaptive functioning and the maladies of society. His well-known contributions argue that a sense of wholeness in adulthood is based on the psychological integration of past, present, and future. This synthesis of past, present, and future involves determining those characteristics that are trait—not state, updating them in the present, and connecting them to planning for future functioning as an adult member of society. He introduced the concept of achievement of a sense of identity—a sense of "who I am," in gender and in work.

A major factor for the adolescent to deal with is a high level of self-awareness as she compares herself with others her own age. Erikson strongly emphasizes that the self-judgments eventually arrived at by an adolescent are heavily influenced by what she gleans are the impressions others have of her. How others regard her is heavily influenced by current values and norms of agemates—the general crowd.

Thus, Erikson establishes as a cornerstone of his theoretical approach that an adolescent cannot develop separate from his or her society. Close peer association is essential since teens need to be aware of the norms and values agemates hold as they work out their own developmental tasks. Erikson feels that real understanding of adolescent conflict must include an awareness of the peer-dominated nature of social values. Erik Erikson's contributions to understanding adolescence are major. He highlights the peer as an important figure and the peer group as a setting for experimentation, role play, and psychosocial development. He does not spell out the mechanics of this development.

Of pertinence to our brief review of selected perspectives is Irene Josselyn's emphasis on a dimension of Erikson's views. Erikson's formulation argues that the adolescent takes future aspirations into consideration as he works out his adolescent conflicts and tries to integrate past, present, and future. Josselyn emphasizes in her work the emotional component of "pressure" as adolescents view the future (1952). She contends that the adolescent's need to define goals is stressful. Knowing that goals are necessary and not yet having them is tension-producing. This tension may be manifested as disorganization. Adults may be particularly troubled by this behavior since they would like to see the energy that appears scattered to be channeled. But the adolescent is not able to focus without more self-knowledge. Ironically, adults wish their adolescents to do what they are not yet developmentally able to accomplish. Time to grow is necessary.

More contemporary work applies a pragmatic approach to the adolescent period. For example, Ruthellen Josselson (1980) also argues that adolescence is a second try at individuation and sees completion of identity as occurring when the adolescent is free of the archaic superego of Freudian tradition. But she also includes freedom from dependence on the perceptions and judgments (actual or imagined) of the significant persons in the social environment — specifically, parents *and* peers. Josselson organizes the long stage of adolescence according to growth tasks, not chronologically. Early and middle adolescence is a time when the youth searches out "who I am." During this time, the adolescent can comfortably remain a satellite of his or her parents. But when the growth task changes from "who I am " to "who I shall become," both Josselyn and Josselson agree that pressure to reach the nebulous but demanding goal is strongly felt and often is manifested in tension, disorganization, and/or more serious acting-out behaviors. Josselson too sees the adolescent task as managing issues of behavior, self-control, values, and self-esteem.

OTHER DOMAINS OF DEVELOPMENT

Up to this point this brief overview has focused on theorists reflecting the emphasis in the literature on affective development. However, the literature has also examined the impact of physical components of development, for example, the rate and timing of physical growth (Tanner, 1972), adolescent body image (Schonfeld, 1969), and perceptions and consequences of early or late maturation (Clausen, 1975; Mussen & Jones, 1957). Biology and affect come together in the work of Petersen and Taylor (1980) and Richards and Petersen (1987), who look at pubertal change in relation to psychological development. They provide a context for an organized scrutiny of relationships between biological change, modification of psychological systems in the individual, and the effects of variations in socialization and sociocultural factors. They include parents and peers among the variables that potentially influence adolescent ideation about biological changes and their subjective meaning or affective significance.

Lawrence Kohlberg (1976), who observed the preoccupation of adolescents with formulating ideals for bringing order and value to their lives, investigated moral development in the adolescent within a framework of moral judgment, not conduct. Building on stage notions of development, he formulated a typology of definitive and universal levels of development in moral thought, each with two stages. Each stage represents a higher cognitive organization than the one before, taking into account everything in the preceding stage but with new distinctions and organizations. The stages represent an invariant developmental sequence. Building on Piaget's notion of the development of abstract thought in adolescence (discussion to follow), Kohlberg defines the third level generally reached in adolescence as one in which the moral conceptualizations are not necessarily applied systems but can exist independently and in juxtaposition to conflicting moral statements—abstract and ethical rather than concrete, with an awareness of the relativism of personal values and opinions.

Piaget sees adolescence as the final period of intellectual development, when the child moves from an ability to abstract only on concrete images to an ability to abstract on abstractions (Piaget & Inhelder, 1969). This ability is a function of the construction of new intellectual structures that allow mental manipulations of 16 different varieties. It is based on a new ability to hold these varieties of manipulations in mind as one tries out a number of combinations and permutations. They suggest that prior to adolescence, intellectual activity is involved initially with sensorimotor equipment and later with achievement of the ability to abstract the concrete image. The final achievement of formal operational thought enables the adolescent not only to conceptualize his own thoughts, but also to conceptualize the thoughts of others. In this initial period of cognitive broadening, however, there is a failure to distinguish one's own acts from those of another. The adolescent, therefore, assumes that others are as obsessed with his behavior as he is. He develops a sense of an "imaginary audience," cognizant of all his activities and thoughts. At the same time, newly felt powers embolden a "personal fable" of uniqueness and immortality, which gives rise to behaviors reflecting increasing power and ability. Thus, on the one hand the adolescent feels limited by being in the limelight; on the other, a new sense of freedom and power makes reality secondary to possibility (Elkind, 1967).

Piagetian theory further contends that the adolescent is caught in this egocentrism. Thus, the cognitive task of the period is to "decenter" and thereby complete the gradual move away from egocentrism, which had its origins in the omnipotence of infancy. Decentering involves a process of continual cognitive refocusing of perspective and the acquisition of multiple perspectives (1972). Feedback from peers helps, and the peer groups offer the available settings in which to work at this task. The final stage is manifested in a clear perception of reality and the adolescent's place in it. Objectivity is enlarged, and there is a true understanding of reciprocity. Cognitive growth has enabled the adolescent release from egocentricity. The world no longer revolves in his image; he is but a part.

Another body of theorists do not consider adolescence a discrete stage. Rather, they suggest a "continuity of development," which places adolescence as one of several periods along the continuum of growth. They hold that the behaviors in this period are not subject to new internal forces but are consistent with prior behaviors (Offer, 1969; Offer & Offer, 1975; Masterson, 1968). Thus, for the child who had a turbulent childhood, adolescence might be more stormy than for the child who did not. They also stress the impact of present experience on behaviors.

They are closer to the notions of cultural pluralists (mentioned earlier), who place even more emphasis on societal factors.

The extreme end of the continuum reflects the positions of behaviorist psychology (Watson, 1925; Thorndike, 1932; Hull, 1943) applied to human social behavior, which holds that behavior is a function of the reinforcement contingencies of the immediate parenting generation and the mores and customs of the general society. They suggest that conditioning agents are both overt and covert (Skinner, 1972). The child learns by experiencing immediate positive reinforcements and by cultural encouragements (Bandura, 1964; Dollard & Miller, 1950). Quite a bit of responsibility is placed on the parenting generation (Sears, 1957) and on the values and structure of the culture (Bandura & Walters, 1963; Bandura, 1964). Varying social philosophies are reinforced by governmental structures and policies, particularly through the educational system (Bronfenbrenner, 1970). An intermediate position is that of interactionism, which recognizes the combined forces of the biological and the physical. It is concerned with the interactive effects from both internal and external sources. David Ausubel (Ausubel, 1954; Ausubel & Sullivan, 1970) regards the adolescent transition period as one of thorough reorganization of the personality structure, deriving from a shift in the adolescent's biosocial status. He perceives the peer group as filling a societal gap. He contends that since urban culture is not organized to offer the adolescent the opportunity to gain the external status he or she needs to cease being a satellite of parents, the peer group serves this function. If cultural unavailability of adult status is extreme, personality maturation is retarded. Exposure to peers only for an overextended time results in reduced standards.

Along with this range of adolescent theory, a social force beginning in the 1950s but achieving notoriety in the 1960s brought an impact on adolescent socialization (Goodman, 1956; Friedenberg, 1959). Although they were actually a small minority, the impact of the peer protest groups resounded in various parts of the nation. As the 1950s turned into the 1960s, it became increasingly difficult to think about the adolescent without thinking of peers and peer group associations. These groups espoused new political philosophies in defiance of older generational policies and politics. Some saw these protests as group manifestations of adolescent rebellion; others considered the behaviors not as opposition to parents, but as carrying unexpressed ideologies of their parents forward. In other words, to some thinkers these behaviors appeared more continuous with those of the parenting generation than directed against it (Keniston, 1965, 1971).

No matter what the basis of the motivation, this protest activity established group action as normative for adolescents. It is in this milieu that John Coleman's notion of "adolescent society" finds its historical underpinnings. Coleman introduced the notion of an "adolescent society" as being a society of youth quite apart from that of their parents (1961). This society has its own set of mores, social prescriptions, and social roles. Male leaders are generally early maturers, socially adept, and engaged in athletics. Female leaders are social leaders. Coleman's unique contribution was a conceptualization of an age-defined structural adolescent society coexisting with other generations. As the 1970s progressed, adolescents turned more to self-serving needs than to societal concerns. This politically conservative trend intensified in the 1980s, with increased individualistic orientations in adolescents.

Theorists agree that the peer group phenomenon is a dominant force in adolescence (Erikson, 1963; Costanzo, 1970; Dunphy, 1980; Newman & Newman, 1976). They vary as to the import they accord its impact and the functions it serves. Theoretical formulations of the functions the peer group serves vary in their emphases among serving affective environmental functions as an island apart (Coleman, 1980; Josselyn, 1952; Ausubel, 1954); as the only arena provided by an otherwise rejecting society (Friedenberg, 1959; Goodman, 1956); as a way station on the path to maturity (Keniston, 1965); as an atmosphere in which reversion to childhood ways is acceptable (Gesell, Ilg, & Ames, 1956); as a family substitute in which libido can be transferred in the process of sexual identity resolution (analytic theorists); or as a haven away from external pressures (Erikson, 1968b). The peer group is also regarded as serving interactional functions, as an arena for social play and experimentation (Erikson, 1968a; Piaget, 1972; Ausubel, Montemayer, & Svajian, 1977). It has also been presented as a place to work out self-definition (Friedenberg, 1959) and identity (Erikson, 1968a), as an arena in which to become free of egocentric thought (Inhelder & Piaget, 1958), and as a subsociety that can serve the needs of a transition period, with interests and responsibility far removed from real responsibility (Coleman, 1961). It has been characterized as an ever-present "group under the couch" (Redl, 1974). It is as if every adolescent action passes through a peer group anticipated-response filter, as if it were a structural piece of the adolescent's mental functioning. Each adolescent acts as both subject and object.

However, notions of whether peers serve as an escape hatch or provide a safe haven in which to try out adult functioning have given way to concerns about serious problem behaviors. For example, the impact of "peer pressure" on adolescent drinking (Jessor & Jessor, 1977); drug taking (Kandel, 1973); sexual acting out, promiscuity, and pregnancies (Furstenberg, 1976); and suicide (DeCatanzaro, 1981) is of primary concern. Thus, the role that peers play during adolescence has gone beyond being an interesting theoretical issue. Peers in peer groups may be the most crucial phenomenon to understand about adolescent growth and behavior, adaptation and maladaptation, and behavioral problems.

Having briefly surveyed a number of different positions on the period of adolescence and the forces that influence the behaviors of adolescents, we now turn to a closer look at the many sides of adolescent socialization habits, behaviors, interests, and concerns—a look at peers in peer arena groups.

PART TWO

An Alternative Orientation

This section offers an overview of an alternative approach to interpreting adolescent behavior. Chapters 2 and 3 examine familiar concepts as developmental clues: conformity, other adolescents as social preference, the nature of adolescent friendships, the rate of development, etc. They present a bird's eye view of adolescent thought and experience and explain how they are manifested in the adolescent's conduct. Confusing and contradictory actions are interpreted as overt disclosures of deep-structure growth imperatives. Chapter 4 addresses in some depth the central psychological dynamic of the adolescent period—the comparative act—and how it impacts and directs behaviors. It also focuses on the setting of the peer arena.

CHAPTER 2

Unique Aspects of Adolescence

Perhaps we should think of adolescence as comprising four processes of change, each a monumental, complex system in itself and each affecting the others. In the physical, emotional, and intellectual domains of change, the adolescent is host to change over which he or she has little control. The socialization domain allows room for more conscious involvement. It is no less complex and no less dramatic than other domains of change, but the cumulative modifications that are taking place make the task of development uneven, taxing, and at times utterly confusing. It is in this state of tension caused by constant change that the process of establishing self-definition takes place.

Relationships that exist among adolescents have a number of unique aspects. They are a product of adolescents' parallel development and the thrust of the period to discover one's individuality at the same time one is identifying similarities to others.

FRAMEWORKLESSNESS

Frameworklessness, a rather cumbersome term, best describes the psychosocial situation of the early adolescent. During these years the new adolescent feels driven to find agemates in the same state of frameworklessness, who understand the condition and are experiencing it at the same time. Prior to the onset of puberty, when abrupt changing begins, the child does not lack for a psychosocial framework. It is provided by parents and elders. During this period expansion and growth take place within a context of the familiar. However, with the advent of adolescence comes a sense of expansive emotional and intellectual energies that can rise and ebb as development demands. Thus, adolescence includes a period of living in a "no man's land," of being on unfamiliar, unsteady ground, having left childhood yet remaining far from adulthood. The adolescent has been referred to as "a marginal man" (Lewin, 1951). The allure of the adult world calls, and the vision of independence intoxicates; yet the safety of childhood, still close, beckons. Neither role fits; the one is outgrown, the second not yet attainable. Cognitive expansions incrementally broaden horizons, but concrete skills have yet to be developed, and opportunities must be sought. Each individual must make the passage independently while cognizant that agemates are seeking the same goal simultaneously. Confusion coexists with challenge, accomplishment coexists with anxiety, exhilaration coexists with sadness, new freedoms coexist with new responsibilities.

The adolescent crowd is unique because of the identical psychosocial condition of its members. They share the excitement and challenge of forthcoming maturity, which brings with it the necessity to find an interim framework; they must replace the now-uncomfortable parameters set by parents and elders. Since they experience only "potential," adolescents crave new guides and guideposts. Thus, although familiar mentors are available, they are not chosen. Instead, adolescents select each other as their counselors. Most do not recognize that their guides share a condition of frameworklessness. It is the chemistry of this mutual need that makes peers so important in helping to establish a framework from which further development can proceed.

THE DOMAINS AND IDIOSYNCRATIC RATE OF ADOLESCENT CHANGE

Adolescent growth in the physical domain is observable visually. Developmental change in the emotional and intellectual domains and the integration of all three in social functioning become apparent in the nature of adolescents' behavior. Along the road to maturity, there is no uniform cadence of progress across growth domains. One individual's profile of growth at any one time is unlike his or her profile at any other. For example, at one point in the process, physical development may be ahead of intellectual development; the reverse may be true a short time later. Different parallel and inverse relations of this type exist among all four domains of development during the growth period. Integrated development occurs on occasion during the developmental period, and then the uneven course renews itself. Final integration of the domains heralds the end of the period. The adolescent becomes an adult.

At times outward manifestations of this uneven growth can be confusing, not only to the adolescent but to interested elders, parents, and teachers. Premature remediation efforts are sometimes taken to address a problem where none exists. For example, premature supplementary help educationally or socially may be the response of parental over-concern because the slower pace of intellectual or social growth is not as well understood as is slower physical growth. The latter is observable and acceptable in our society. The former is elusive and is viewed as cause for concern, particularly when it is inconsistent with physical spurts. Alternatively, premature concern may exist over what appear to be overintellectual interests at the expense of social experimentation and social ease. Either of these may be a valid concern, but more often such development reflects the uneven nature of growth domains.

Not only is uneven development of concern to parents, teachers, and elders, it causes considerable concern to the adolescent. The adolescent develops to full physical, emotional, and cognitive stature by the time she reaches maturity and adulthood, as do her peers. However, they do so in very different patterns. Not only is the cadence of the change different, but the interactive effects of the four domains add additional variation. Physical growth is most apparent; intellectual growth is apparent based on "what I am learning to do in school"; emotional growth is experienced in terms of internal signals; social growth is revealed intermittently in higher levels of comfort in heretofore-stressful social conditions. The similarity adolescents experience lies in the series of change in the four domains of development, but their day-to-day manifestations never mesh.

Thus, what exacerbates the mysteries experienced in "self" is the fact that agemates don't change at the same rate. The absence of reassurance is keenly felt. Furthermore, changes are not only unpredictable, but they can often be surprising or even alarming. When a close friend suddenly exhibits attitudes or interests that seem quite foreign to those familiar with him or her, not only is a type of loss experienced, but the temporary stability of feeling similar to another is threatened. In adolescence the major involvement with peers displaces attachment to parents, causing friends to be looked to as dependable anchors. When they appear unfamiliar, the individual must expend added energies to regroup and to find replacements who will be experienced as familiar and dependable.

PEERSHIP, NOT FRIENDSHIP

Peership is an important and uniquely adolescent relationship. It is indispensable to growth and development during the adolescent period. Adolescent peers generously give to one another, and they also freely take. They psychologically borrow characteristics from one another to "try out" (Seltzer, 1982); they use one another as sounding boards for their own varying views and strong opinions. They imitate one another and take joy in being imitated. Peers offer themselves freely to be used as models representing the attainable and the unattainable, the possible and the unreachable, and even the despised. Peers extend themselves to being both soulmates and competitors. They are ever eager to try out new experiences together and to spend hours of time digesting the nuances of the happening. They feel good when they feel needed. It reinforces their own reality and counters sensations of instability and irrelevance.

Adolescents share various conditions:

1. Each is in transition between childhood and adulthood, being no longer child and not yet adult.
2. Each experiences biological, intellectual, and emotional changes, all of which give rise to changes in social personality and overt actions.
3. Because of the quantity and frequency of these changes, each is unpredictable and subject to ups and downs of moods that accompany their daily experiences.
4. The norm is fluctuation and excitement, *not* stability.
5. Each self-picture is in the process of formation.

Since the boundaries of "who I am" are not yet clear to the adolescent, true friendship cannot exist in adolescence. The nature of the adolescent's relationships with agemates is not the same as friendships at other times in the life span. Adolescent agemates are peers, not friends. *Peer* is a term that denotes a counterpart. Only when two selves are distinct can there be true exchange. An individual with a firm sense of "who I am" can transact with a second who also has a clear sense of "who I am." With an undeveloped sense of self, boundary lines between "you" and "I" are invisible. Thus, adolescent peership can be best thought of as preliminary to friendship.

Requirements and expectations in peership are different from those in friendship. The first requirement of peership is that the peer be *physically present*. The peer cannot fulfill the role of model and evaluation object if he or she is physically remote. Some peers serve only this function.

A second requirement of a peer is to act as a *sounding board*. This does not necessarily require listening or offering a pertinent response. The adolescent need is to talk and to feel heard, to have an audience. If there is a reply, generally the content of the reply is not seriously attended to. Responses of others are important only when the adolescent deliberately seeks to evaluate a dimension of self. The response, therefore, is most generally interpreted as a cue to continue speaking.

Psychosocial growth is self-motivated, self-monitored, and directed. Boundaries between peers are not clear. The adolescent grasps each available opportunity to try self out. Thus, he responds to another's problem as if he were the presenter. This condition of parallel play is not only apparent but generally acceptable to all players.

Two criteria for peership have been established so far: physical presence and participation in content of the developmental exercise. A third criterion is *flexibility*. Peership anticipates change as normative. Peers are all in a process of experimentation—studying one another, copying, and borrowing looks, behaviors, attitudes, opinions, etc. Therefore, frequent change in point of view or behavior is commented on but ruffles no feathers and is considered the norm.

The fourth criterion of peership is a *nonjudgmental stance*. After all, adolescence is a period of new discovery (courtesy of new biological and intellectual abilities and expansion of skills). Ongoing discovery and experimentation seek no constraints. Consistency and logic are not factors of importance. Each adolescent intuitively cooperates. He accepts that his opinions may change moments after they are expressed, either as a result of thinking through the implications of what has been said after hearing it out loud, in an effort to match the general spirit that has been generated in others, or in order to be in line with some additional piece of information. The freedom to experiment, learn, and change is given hearty support. Reciprocity is a defining characteristic of the group.

ALONE TOGETHER

The pubertal advance, which heralds an explosion in various growth domains, brings adolescents to a state of readiness to venture out from the safe environment of home, to tolerate distance and difference, and to seek new experiences by which to gather new information. Small groups at this point no longer suffice. The early adolescent wants to handle an abundance of thoughts and ideas. Therefore, it is necessary to be in close contact with lots of other agemates so as to be able to choose from a variety of abilities and characteristics for future experimentation. Adolescents do not need to interact verbally. They can just look and/or listen.

Adolescents wish to evaluate their own responses and behaviors relative to a range of other responses and behaviors. The basis for attraction to large groups is the variety of models available for observation. They gain information by comparing the behaviors and reactions of those in a similar condition of bodily change and social frameworklessness—their age peers.

These large groups of adolescents generally are not groups of close friends. They are there together, they participate in the same activities together, but they do not share the experience. It is an extension of the parallel play of childhood. They may have a few close friends, but generally at this early period even close friends spend more time "together with others" than they spend together alone. They take advantage of the hordes together and then verbally review the proceedings with a few.

In early adolescence each individual is at a different growth point in each of the four domains of development. Each individual's profile of developmental progression dictates different concerns. Thus, each imbibes what is relevant to his or her own development needs. Each privately serves his or her own distinct needs while on the surface participating in the group activity.

Throughout the large-group socialization period, we continue to see "small best friend groups" or a single "best friend." These relationships are of two types: (1) a "friend" of many years, who fills security and emotional reinforcement needs but not necessarily self-expansion functions, and (2) a new "friend," whose attractiveness is based on manifestations of characteristics that are to be copied. Closeness to this new person may also serve to fulfill fantasies of possessing the admired characteristics or of a "reflected glory" in the close association. Psychologically, the adolescent borrows the desired element and fantasizes that it his own. Borrowing promotes stability during the period of experimentation.

Generally, both types of friendship last only as long as the adolescent need continues. When the adolescent becomes more comfortable about self and is ready to reach out for greater diversity and to risk rejection, the "friendship" may dissolve or be put "on hold." Some "old" relationships do continue as youths experiment side by side, in parallel and not intimate relationship. With new relationships, if close contact with the individual who exhibits the desired attribute yields a conclusion that the attribute can indeed be developed on one's own, the adolescent may then be ready to terminate the relationship. Conversely, if the adolescent ascertains that the characteristic is dissonant or impossible to achieve, the relationship may also begin to lose its luster. Search for attributes that are more congruent or easily acquired may be the next step. If the adolescent continues to need close exposure in order to come to a decision, or if the perception of "reflected glory" continues to fill ego-enhancing needs, the adolescent will strive to maintain the relationship.

In sum, the early period of adolescent socialization is characterized by: (1) parallel play within very large group settings in order to access peer models and engage in experimenting and information collection, and (2) shuttling back and forth between a few close friends who serve either socioemotional support needs or the need to psychologically identify and "try on" the admired characteristics for goodness of fit.

Later in adolescence, there has been enough looking, listening, and trying out, and the need for many others offering large quantities of raw materials tapers off. Older adolescents spend more time with smaller groups. The developmental task of this period of late-middle and late adolescence differs. Older adolescents have arrived at a temporary notion of what elements make up self, of who they are and where they are going in life. Now one's marketplace value in future life is a primary consideration. Evaluations are most relevant if accomplished with a frame of "relative values." Relevant others are peers with whom one will be competing for goods, services, and societal status. Thus, developmental work in the latter states of the period does not require volume, as was the case for earlier periods.

What it does require is real similarity. With others perceived as similar, they work at determining the relative status and weights of their attributes and abilities. The small group functions as the arena in which to closely reexamine and then refine or dispense with the elements that were selected as "my own" and included in the temporary self structure (which is arrived at when the first stage of adolescence is concluded, at the end of late-middle adolescence.) The preference change from large groups to small groups is evidence that psychological growth of the first period, the primary peer arena period, has been completed. The secondary peer arena period is entered for final resolution on choice of personality elements functional to present and future. These can be integrated smoothly into clusters of self characteristics, which combine to complete a "sense of identity."

Finally, during both large- and small-group periods, the adolescent has "special friends" to whom he entrusts more secrets and with whom he spends more time. Generally, they serve the function of others with whom to talk about self. It is not until psychosocial maturity is actually achieved and the egocentricity of adolescence is diminished that the purpose of conversation ceases to be "I will talk about you but think about me in the same situation." When egocentricity is highly active, the adolescent continues to overvalue the prominence of self. He or she is central to all action—involving self and others. With completion of the adolescent period and achievement of psychosocial maturity, egocentricity declines, and true interrelating begins.

CHAPTER 3

Distinguishing Components of the Adolescent World

TRANSITIONAL STATUS

The road from birth to maturity is a series of transitions. Adolescence is but one of these transitions, though perhaps the most crucial since it necessitates separating from former guideposts and seeking independent functioning. Puberty heralds this new status. The adolescent absorbs bodily and intellectual changes that affect prior perceptions and free access to familiar figures for support. Relationships with traditional support figures must be transformed; new support figures must be acquired.

Not only is physical stature and functioning in transition, but so is intellectual, emotional, and social functioning. The adolescent's physical functioning changes dramatically, awkwardly, surprisingly. New growth of intellectual capacity is pronounced but erratic; he or she is discovering, learning, and changing his or her ideas continually. Emotional capacity is enlarged, sometimes overwhelming his or her ability to know what is happening. As all these different domains of growth progress at their own rates, the adolescent is thrust into a new social context of peers with whom he or she must socialize, at the same time handling his or her social relationships with the outside world, parents, and other adults that impact his or her daily life.

Since the adult generation no longer comfortably serves dependency needs, the adolescent experiences an aloneness in this state of transition until he or she makes contact with others going through the same experience. These are his or her peers, but, of course, their availability to him or her differs considerably from the generally unconditional support role of parents. Thus, the initial transition period of adolescence can be a period of considerable loneliness.

Transitional status is confusing not only to the adolescent, but to the adult. Is the offspring child, adult, or both? Relationships can become very confusing as roles and responsibilities change. Physical advance does not necessarily bring the corresponding intellectual, emotional, or social advance in tandem. Outward physical appearances deceive and confuse. Since size seems to be associated with maturity, not only may the youth be confused about just who he or she is, but so may parents and elders. And so may peers.

FLUCTUATING EMOTIONAL STATES

The needs of the beginning period of adolescence, when the child experiences puberty, differ from those of the middle and ending periods. It is crucial to remember that it is a *child* who becomes pubertous and begins the psychosocial path to adulthood. The many changes that accompany physical puberty include intellectual and emotional changes, which coalesce into a social awareness that the dependence of childhood must be left behind and independence sought. "Breaking away" is a difficult experience, and the sense of aloneness becomes painful. In a position of uncertainty individuals look to be with others who share that position of uncertainty (Schacter, 1959). Adolescents experience lack of stability and uncertainty in the full spectrum of developmental domains. Thus, they are especially prone to seek the comfort of being with others who are in a similar condition. This perceived similarity offers a sense of emotional support, which helps reduce the aloneness stemming from the new constraints they feel in relation to parents and the parent generation. Hence, adolescents in the beginning stage look for companions generally with few specifications other than similarity in stage of life.

The adolescent is keenly aware of self in relation to other and becomes psychologically preoccupied with comparison, assessment, and evaluation. Behaviors are judged by the success of their present impact. At this stage the adolescent is acutely aware of her relative standing with her peers. Many diverse others are desired as company since they are necessary to fill functions beyond support and alleviating aloneness. Peers become essential comparison objects (raw materials) against whom to evaluate self. The similarity of their developmental condition initially stabilized feelings of peculiarness and discomfort into "It must be OK because everyone else seems to be like me." Now the outcome of the comparisons made with agemates can stimulate either "feeling good" about oneself or "feeling bad."

Large numbers of others serve important purposes: (1) Large numbers provide a normal distribution of attributes for study rather than a skewed one. (2) Large numbers provide considerable certainty that the results of comparison yield valid conclusions (Radloff, 1966). Depending on the outcome of the comparison, comfort or pain results.

SIZE OF GROUPS AND DEVELOPMENT

Differences abound in adolescence and in adolescents. Differences exist among the different periods of adolescence just as they do among childhood, adolescence, and adulthood. A very different set of processes are at play in early adolescence than in middle adolescence or in late adolescence. Each individual progresses through the period at a different pace and struggles with different issues. The degree of comfort or difficulty experienced during the adolescent transition will be affected by the extent of psychological strengths present upon entering the period and life experiences during the period. It is easy for none. It is a shared but individual condition.

The early period is one of borrowed elements of personality—from parents, siblings, relatives, etc. Youngsters are essentially what they see. They have yet to develop the emotional and intellectual abilities that allow them to begin to forge out a sense of identity. The filling in of this empty slate is what has been referred to as the psychosocial task of adolescence—achievement of identity, the knowledge of "who I am" in gender and in work. When we ask a 9- or 10-year-old child what she is like, we generally get a rather short answer—perhaps a description of some of the things she likes to do; whether she is short or tall, fat or thin; or the color of her hair. When we speak to the same person 10 years later, we expect a rather full description of the individual's characteristics, values, relationships, likes and dislikes, career aspirations, etc. This fuller discourse is the product of years of education and experimentation about self and other, about the world and the place the individual is prepared to occupy in it.

The size of groups for adolescents also has a developmental meaning. As adolescents progress through the period, the number of others in their social group changes. As children, individuals play in small groups. The size of the group the adolescent seeks out differs dramatically from that of late childhood. Early developmental needs press for interaction with numerous others, not just a few. Since they are highly aware of their bodily changes and emotional discontinuities, early adolescents almost exclusively seek out agemates like themselves. They need psychoemotional support garnered from knowledge that they are of a like condition. Parents and elders, their former guides, no longer seem relevant. Hence, they look to similar others in a "frameworklessness" condition to serve two functions: (1) to provide evidence that the adolescent is but one of many in a similar condition, and (2) to serve as source material for gathering new information.

TIME FRAME: PRESENT VERSUS FUTURE ORIENTATION

A distinguishing characteristic between the child and the adolescent is that the adolescent moves away from operating primarily within a present time orientation, incorporating more and more of a future time orientation. Generally, adolescents are intense in their involvement in each time frame—intense both in their ongoing activities and in their concern about their future. Yet they appear able to psychologically manage the two time orientations as logic-tight compartments; they do not necessarily intrude upon one another. This is manifested in both childlike behavior and adultlike, serious concerns. One may follow the other rather directly, and the pattern reverses with equal ease.

Future orientation becomes more pronounced the more advanced the progress through adolescence. In early adolescence energies are occupied with new bodily, emotional, and cognitive changes, which heighten present orientation. Comparative acts are very much rooted in the present experience as the adolescent compares in order to reassure himself that the experienced changes are "happening to most everyone." The orientation is very much in the present, with past dependencies still evident.

As the adolescent experiences further growth of intellectual structures, the future comes more into focus. Future orientation takes its place alongside the present orientation. Increasingly, characteristics and abilities must meet not only present demands, but their outputs are also examined in light of their functional value for the future. Will they facilitate achievement of future goals? In other words, once early adolescence is completed, satisfaction of present needs alone is not sufficient. Future orientation begins to overlay all action. Comparative and evaluational activities must serve both present and future needs. The task of this new stage becomes more complex since effective present functioning is still enormously important. Status within the group, and reflected status within oneself, is still at stake, as is feared rejection from the group. The adolescent must incorporate future-related components into thinking and behavior *and* simultaneously maintain current functioning on a level that will sustain a positive ego image.

While the transition is gradual, it does not pass unnoticed. Dropping dimensions of personality that have served present social needs but are now perceived as dysfunctional to future concerns may change the adolescent in observable ways and decrease similarities to close peers. Cognitively, the adolescent may be aware of the pragmatic need for change but may not be emotionally ready to drop the security of similarity. A state of dissonance, both cognitive and emotional, arises and continues until the conflict is resolved. This condition of dissonance, of resolution with loss and gain, characterizes movement from the early to the middle period of adolescence. The future orientation grows stronger.

Clearly, total future orientation as a basis for actions and decision-making is as nonadaptive as an exclusively present orientation. The parallel alignment of future and present orientations remains strong in the middle and late periods of adolescence. The balance shifts from heavily present to moderately present to heavily future as decision-making for future life reaches a peak in later adolescence; then it moves back to a more even ratio of present/future as the adolescent identity crisis is resolved in ending adolescence. Blending of present and future orientations characterizes appropriate adult functioning.

Although well-functioning adults possess present/future orientation, there is a fundamental difference in how the overall orientation serves adolescents and adults. The future orientation of adults does not serve establishment of self. Future orientation comes into sharp focus when adults deal with refinement of personality characteristics and skills or effect a major change. They think of tomorrow in relation to *how it can improve today*. Adolescents think in reverse. They regard today in relation to how its impact will affect tomorrow. They think about which appearances and behaviors bring present-day successes, then they ponder whether these actions will be functional to the life goal being considered. The sequence of this dynamic of middle and late adolescence continues for many years until identity resolution is accomplished. Once the adolescent achieves identity, the dynamics of the present/future orientation take on the adult nature. The interplay of present and future is no longer dedicated to personality establishment and identity formation; rather, it is functional to the realities of adult life planning.

CONFORMITY AS A FUNCTION OF ACCESS TO RAW MATERIALS

Studies in conformity have demonstrated that group pressures operate on individuals to change their behavior to be congruent with that of the group. It is socially more comfortable to conform than to deviate. Conformity pressures operate on adolescents as well as on younger children and on adults (Costanzo & Shaw, 1966; Berenda, 1950; Asch, 1956). In adolescence, conformity serves needs to avoid rejection from the group just as it does in other periods of life. Conformity generally has a prosocial function but is often seen as lack of independent thought and action.

The crucial difference about conformity in the adolescent period sheds some light on why the adolescent is often accused of "blind obedience to peers." In adolescence, rejection from the group means reduced access to the raw materials of development. The concept of "raw materials" becomes more clear as we note four major functions peers in groups serve for adolescents:

1. The group constituency provides models for the adolescent as she thinks about herself and what she wants to be like now and in the future.

2. Being in the company of peers activates the adolescent imperative to engage in comparative acts, to compare, contrast, and evaluate characteristics of herself against those she is with.

3. The adolescent has the opportunity to demonstrate and evaluate her own attributes in comparison to this large range of peers as many times as necessary to come to some resolution on the relative merit of the quality or ability under scrutiny. The adolescent needs to associate with many, many others so that a sufficient variety of personality characteristics to compare with are modeled and a range of quality on the same attribute or characteristic is available for an in-depth view of how it can be adopted.

4. The group offers the adolescent more than just the chance to admire characteristics seen in another. It is an audience before whom she can experiment to see if she too possesses the characteristic— and she can evaluate the group response. (For example, she may believe she has a subtle sense of humor. But her attempts at humor may go unrecognized.) The group both models and monitors desired characteristics. The familiar "I wonder what my friends will think of it" captures in simple terms the process and the arena for trying out both familiar and newly desired characteristics and skills.

CONFORMITY PRESSURES AND PSYCHOSOCIAL ADVANCE

The following behavioral conditions signal psychosocial growth:

1. Movement away from the exclusively present orientation of early adolescence to the present/future orientation of middle and late adolescence, reflecting an appropriate level of cognitive advance and increased ego functioning, which facilitates more complex psychological activity.

2. The ability to integrate fantasy-level future aspirations with reality factors based on present experience and information gain.

3. Willingness to recognize the current behaviors that are functional to future aspirations and should be continued versus those that appear dysfunctional and should be discontinued.

4. Recognition that change of self-orientation necessitates alternation of friendship networks.

The last must be accomplished without losing access to the group.

However, conformity pressures from agemates to resist change may be very strong—strong enough to delay progress toward life's goals and psychosocial advance. Thus, there may be a period when the adolescent inhibits further experimentation with combinations of characteristics and behaviors that might better serve maturational purposes. It is also possible that the ego may be so vulnerable from difficulties encountered in the psychological growth process that the individual cannot risk losing the emotional peace that comes from similarity with the group. On the other hand, present success may be in jeopardy if present behaviors are eliminated in favor of more desired personality traits. If, because of these pressures, the adolescent continues to satisfy current needs too long at the expense of future development, resolution of a full identity will be in jeopardy.

The adolescent who can successfully handle peer relations and also successfully act to accommodate future needs will discover opportunities to achieve a "self" that serves the present well and also has potential to contribute to future aspirations.

CHANGES IN PACE AND FOCUS

The number of others needed for psychosocial growth purposes changes as the adolescent matures. Although socialization with large groups is appropriate to early and even middle adolescence, developmental work in the late period is accomplished with small groups of others considered similar in attributes and future aspirations. Prior psychological work has yielded a temporary self-structure, which now needs to be refined, consolidated, and integrated. Thus, new characteristics and abilities are no longer sought out and assessed. The later stages concentrate on assessing the fine points and relative value of the elements selected during the earlier periods.

Dynamics similar to those of the earlier period are used again in later stages. However, the cadence and the emphasis are different.

Slow, concentrated, and precise examination takes place. The goal is to solidify elements that are strong and functional for present and future effectiveness. They must also be flexible and able to cluster with sympathetic elements. Tryout ensues, with close attention paid to recount of experiences involving similar attributes by those perceived as very similar others.

In late adolescence, as the self moves closer and closer to closure, we see beginnings of intimacy and real relating. As a sense of "this is who I am" evolves, the adolescent becomes able to assimilate the meaning of "this is who *you* are." In the prior stage, needs or attributes of the other served only to stimulate further attention and inquiry into self. The posture of searching for self thus permeated (and in a sense contaminated) every relationship. True involvement with another did not occur. Now boundaries grow increasingly clear.

Once the adolescent reaches true closure on a set of integrated elements and establishes a sense of self, an "other" is truly conceptualized as separate. Now he may look for similar others. On the other hand, he may enormously enjoy the company of those clearly identified as quite different. Now developmental needs for exercise of the adolescent dialectic and its dynamics of comparison and evaluation do not stimulate relationships. Friendship and even intimacy can begin.

CHAPTER 4

Dynamic Centers of Adolescent Growth: Peer Arena and the Comparative Act

WHY ADOLESCENTS NEED TO BE TOGETHER

With new physical and intellectual advance, the adolescent is truly no longer a child. The need is strong to function as an independent person, capable of making one's own decisions and no longer subject to parental directives. An unstable inner sense of self compounds the importance of demonstrating new ability to the outside world. It is particularly important for adolescents to appear grown up to peers. How peers regard one is external feedback, which bolsters or deflates the insecure ego. Peer response offers a measuring stick at a time when few external guideposts exist.

One might ask why parents cannot supply this important information. First, the parent is the conflictual figure. The adolescent task is to loosen ties of dependency. Second, the adolescent world has vastly expanded. The parental portion of the psychological space is reduced. Room is made for newly relevant environmental figures, such as older siblings, who become more relevant for consultation and for modeling. Older relatives represent activities and opinions that begin to appear relevant. Professionals in the community, such as clergy, teachers, and politicians, are increasingly seen as avenues to information, not just as nice people who are a lot older. In other words, the contours of the social world begin to change.

Although agemates are also changing in appearance and in manner, they nevertheless remain the most similar. They are all in transition from childhood to adulthood. Each is evolving from dependent child to independent adult. Who better understands and accepts change than one who is similarly engaged? Accordingly, adolescents serve two functions for one another: (1) They react to changes in one another, and their reactions send important messages. (2) They serve as models. Older persons do not supply these functions. They cannot. They simply do not carry the current emotional relevance that the peer does.

The pubertal child, entering adolescence, experiences a drivelike motivation to be in the company of his peers. This "adolescent imperative" is a product of a number of psychosocial forces acting to create a magnetic attraction among peers. Social psychology research has demonstrated that under conditions of insecurity, fearfulness, and relative instability, individuals seek out others who are experiencing the same set of conditions (Schachter, 1959). There is comfort in being with others in a similar condition. Furthermore, they provide a range of behaviors with which each can compare his own (Radloff, 1966). If the individual does not deviate too far from the norm, it is comforting; knowledge that others are experiencing the same condition is reassuring (Wheeler, Kelley, Shaver, Jones, Goethals, Cooper, Robinson, Gruder, and Butzine, 1969).

The need to be together has an additional dimension beyond the reassurance of others in the "same boat" or the social need for exchange and fun. In an arena of peers agemates serve as models for one another. They reciprocally model, borrow, try out, compare, and contrast all aspects of themselves. The qualities sought in both self and others are mediated by the status accorded each characteristic by the whole group. Furthermore, talents and abilities can no longer exist independent of purpose. They must be functional to future goals and aspirations because the adolescent and his peers are negotiating toward a future adult world. Close contact between the adolescent and those individuals who will occupy the adult world with him is necessary to assess the present currency and future value of various attributes.

Adolescent independence seeking is a process full of paradox. Independence from the prior central environmental figure (the parent) is a major objective. In order to achieve this independence, adolescents become dependent on a different set of environmental figures, their peers. Attributes, abilities, and opinions of peers come to provide the nurturant fodder that parents and elders supplied in other forms in prior years. In contrast to childhood dependence, which is seen as acceptable and is therefore open and obvious, adolescent dependence is hidden. It is experienced subliminally. It is overtly handled by an increased tendency to see the parent as the other to be "released from." Conflict with parents provides a socially acceptable rationale for independence seeking. Parents offer a convenient cover. Actually, the struggle with dependence is no longer with parents. On a deep-structure level, psychological discomfort is stimulated by awareness of the dependence on peers. Engaging in "adult behaviors," expressing shocking values, and emphasizing independent action and decision-making reinforce impressions of independence and therefore ease the inner tension. Erroneous popular notions that "rebellion" against parents in adolescence is normative reinforce the cover. To the outside world this cover is of minimal significance. The real meaning of this cover is to the adolescents themselves, since it helps shroud the new dependence.

External factors also promote the masking of dependence from others and from oneself. Societal norms discourage dependence. In early years of life it is acceptable. As physical size and appearance change, societal tolerance of dependence decreases. Our national ethic values independence, and its ramifications are universally felt. Social pressures to be independent are felt even before the adolescent has evolved into a mature, fully developed entity.

Yet adolescents clearly manifest dependence on peers in their imperative to be together. Once this phenomenon is understood, issues of conformity, mood change, and miscellaneous other confusing behaviors come into sharp, new focus. The dependence is rooted in the developmental need to access one another's attributes for trial and error on one's own. Physical access to agemates offers an arena in which to engage in comparative acts involving characteristics, abilities, and opinions and to get feedback as well as new models for new aspirations and tryouts. It provides the preparation necessary to move into maturity and to take one's place as a contributing member of society. As one major context of adolescence, it offers a good roadmap with which to examine and interpret adolescent behavior.

THE COMPARATIVE ACT PROCESS

The central process of the comparative act is not a psychological process reserved for adolescents. Social comparison is active over the life span as individuals continue to refine their own selves, adjust to new environments, acquire attributes and talents they admire in others, rid themselves of attributes and talents that are absent in the value system of others they aspire to be with, etc. (Festinger, 1954). However, dynamics of the comparative acts of adolescents are different. They do not serve refinement of self, but *establishment* of self. Hence, the process is intense and all-encompassing. The goal is to set in place every characteristic of the self the individual is working to consolidate. These attributes must be of value in both present and future functioning and role assumptions. Thus, the number of characteristics on which adolescents compare daily is large. By way of example, adolescents compare on every feature of the face — eyes, nose, mouth, teeth, skin, eyelashes, eyebrows, mustache, beard, ears, hair, eyelids, smile, size of forehead, etc. When one recognizes how detailed the examination is on most features of the body, innumerable personality characteristics, and the abilities and skills of hundreds of other adolescents, the magnitude of psychological activity of adolescence comes into perspective.

This comparative activity is constantly "turned on" — in school, at social functions, at church, on the school bus or the way home, etc. It is subliminally active at all times and stimulated to frenetic action when the person is exposed to large numbers of peers. It begins in early adolescence and reaches a peak in the junior high and early high school years. This enormous amount of psychological activity culminates in consolidation of self elements by the end of high school, when a temporary self structure has been psychologically constructed.

At this point, the need for huge numbers recedes as the youth now enters into a refinement phase. Elements of the newly formulated temporary picture of self are now closely evaluated. Friendships may change as needs for comparisons with peers narrow. Type of peer, not quantity, is what is important to the dynamics of the second period. Vast amounts of raw materials are no longer necessary. Specialized comparisons with others perceived to be like one's own temporary self are engaged. Now comparison and evaluation with those who seem most like oneself take on more of a market-value orientation, replacing the emphasis on self-definition of the earlier evaluations. Final resolutions as to the worth of each self-selected element of self, integration of identified skills and abilities, and clustering of abilities and characteristics are completed at this point. Each characteristic included in the cluster had at one time been identified and "declared as one's own" after much time and pain For those who fully engaged adolescent identity seeking and risked trials and rejections, this period is one of rich integration and a stability never before experienced (Seltzer, 1982).

A BLANK SLATE TO BE FILLED

In early adolescence the slate of self is primarily blank. The adolescent needs many, many others to model raw materials and to respond to experiments with self. Some tryout is private and fantasy-prone; other tryouts are public and reality-based. Tens or even hundreds of characteristics may be compared and evaluated in one afternoon or evening contact. This activity is engaged again the next day, and the next day, and the next. Sorting, sifting, and replacing is the activity of adolescent development. Here, with others like themselves, they put new skills to the test to measure their currency and relative value. Without access to the group, the adolescent is severely hampered in carrying out the psychosocial tasks of development. Learning in the abstract offers new information but for the information to be functional, it must be *tried out with relevant others*. Parents and others offer outlets to share newly acquired information and skills. But for adolescents the current value of the skill or attribute is ascertained only through the response of the relevant other of this stage—the adolescent peer.

Denial of access to the models and the testing ground is intuitively feared by the adolescent and is to be avoided at all costs. Adolescents experience an emotional pull to be together. They all share the status of transition; they have similar emotional vicissitudes. All must prepare for the future; all must function well in the present, too. Hence, being "a member" of a group of agemates serves both cognitive developmental and support functions. If one were to lose access to adolescent peers, where would these essential functions be served?

In spite of exposure to classmates five days a week in school, where the dynamics of development play themselves out, adolescents never seem to tire of seeing each other, as well as others in after-school groups, evening assemblies, weekend activities, etc. The "adolescent imperative" to be with the group is very intense—drivelike. Conforming to adolescent group norms insures against loss of access to essential developmental raw material and to the arena for tryout.

SURFACE AND DEEP-STRUCTURE FUNCTIONING

What is experienced as a slavish dependence on continued contact with peers (the source of data) is not understood by the adolescent on a surface level but is experienced on subliminal level. On the surface-structure level, the adolescent attends a party to "be with the gang" and to be independent of family plans. At the gathering, the developmental comparative processes are working full-time. New insights are achieved; new directions for self-questioning and investigation may develop. Deliberate attempts may follow to acquire new talents or improve old ones or a decision may be made to drop specific pursuits because of disappointing comparative results. The opportunities for comparison, alteration, and reassessment are endless. Comparative acts are the unacknowledged psychological activity that goes on when adolescent peers get together. Part of the process may consist of overtly talking about attributes of "others" with close friends, but the remaining dynamics of the comparative act process—comparison with self and relative evaluations—are not open to others and are generally not even consciously acknowledged to self. (Later chapters will disclose findings that document the activity.)

Once we understand that the comparative act, with its evaluation and assessment process, is a continuous one in the life of the adolescent, we can begin to understand a number of adolescent behaviors. Enormous energies are expended in this "non-accountable" psychological activity. The adolescent may be buoyed by results and stimulated to further comparative acts, or he may be disillusioned and saddened. In the extreme, the latter condition may stimulate the adolescent to flee (see Chapter 10). Flight can be manifested in a number of ways; some loudly signal psychological danger, and others overtly mask it.

This major psychological activity, which demands continuing access to peers, is not widely understood. Thus, adolescent behavior has continued to mystify. Conformity is an excellent example. Conformity, discussed in Chapter 3, is generally attributed to serving needs of feeling comfortable as part of a group and being identified as a member of that group. But in adolescence a deep-structure need is being served in addition. Conformity for adolescents is an insurance policy against being rejected by the group. Rejection means eventual ejection from the group. Adolescents *cannot risk* not having continuing access to the group. The group is the source of developmental materials. Without access to enough peer groups, the adolescent will be deprived of essential ingredients of growth. Fortunately, most adolescents, particularly those in cities, do meet with groups of peers every day in school. The work to be accomplished requires as much active involvement as possible. Developing a rich self is promoted by interaction with as many varied alternative models as possible. The more exposure and involvement, the fuller will be the emerging personality.

It may not be inaccurate to conceive of the need for continuing access in order to exercise these developmental needs as approaching near-drive intensity. With this conceptualization we better understand why adolescents never seem to tire of being with one another. Looking beyond surface-structure behavior, it is not the overt social activity or the content of the event (e.g., a rock concert, a football game, a dance) that feeds the drive. It is *being with one another*—looking, listening, and resultant comparing. Adolescents report details of who was there, what they did and said, or what they wore in far greater detail than they describe the content of the event.

Development is serious business. There is a lot of ground to cover. Surface-structure activity offers a rationale for the deep-structure imperative to be together with age peers. Fueled by developmental needs, peer group interaction is hard work. Developmental dynamics are active beneath overt cavorting and merriment. Subliminally, duals with self and other may be in process. The intense and functional nature of adolescence is best conceptualized as an "arena" for growth and development.

THE ADOLESCENT MIND AND BEHAVIORS

The developmental position and task of the period impact the adolescent mind, which apprehends the social world differently than does the adult mind. The urgency of developmental information needs transforms every peer contact into an opportunity for additional self-assessment. This subliminal, constant activity is what differentiates the adolescent mindset about peers. Others are seen as separate only momentarily. Very quickly the adolescent superimposes self on other and begins to measure. Characteristics of others are the yardstick used to measure the value of one's own. Many measurements combine to compute an average against which the adolescent ascertains his or her general standing. With continuing availability, the adolescent can measure and remeasure against particularly relevant figures, either for higher aspiration purposes or to feel better about present status.

The need to discover and describe the self to oneself distinguishes adult and adolescent. The adult has already established his or her identity. Social comparisons are utilized in developing or refining an aspect of the self, not the whole self. Adults who have successfully completed adolescence are not drawn into automatic comparative acts that dissipate separateness between individuals. Adults usually interrelate; the adolescent absorbs the other temporarily as part of his or her own self until the comparative process is over. This is sometimes observable in what appears to be overabsorption in another (see Chapter 10).

Many of the idiosyncratic and sometimes even bizarre adolescent behaviors can be attributed to aspects of the comparative act process:

1. Behaviors that are experimental—tryout of a characteristic that appears admirable or is suspected of being negative. How the behaviors "fit" is being tested.
2. Behaviors stimulated by a loss of esteem as a result of comparison with one who is ascertained to be superior. We may see compensatory behavior in bravado or even a range of delinquent acts. It may also be manifested in forms of ingratiation or overachievement in other endeavors.
3. Conversely, behaviors stimulated by a very positive result of the deep-structure comparative act, which gives rise to overt displays of surprising joy, affection, openness, bravado, reckless certainty of self, etc.
4. A range of ups and downs of moods, sometimes occurring within a very short time.

Behavioral extremes can confuse adolescents themselves; they are uncertain why they respond so extremely. Results of comparative acts are experienced emotionally but not always cognitively interpreted. More often than not, behaviors are erroneously attributed to external circumstances, not to the impact or outcome of comparative acts. Thus, looking to external precipitating events to explain behavior can mislead and confuse parents and other adults who deal with adolescents. Further confusion may be added by the naive adolescent who attributes his acts to precipitators observable to him. For example, it may not be that excessive drinking by others at the party caused him to leave early, but rather that the yield from the comparative acts engaged was painful and increased insecurities. It may be that the adolescent who "altruistically" chose to babysit for her older sibling rather than go to the class play is ashamed that she could only buy cheap tickets; she thus escapes the pain of feeling inferior to other class members. Or perhaps the fantasy she is temporarily assuming of membership in an upper-class economic echelon would be dealt a hard blow, shattering other fantasized aspirations that she does not wish to give up. It is not unusual for adolescents to project internal pain onto an external circumstance since deep-structure imperatives, generally not cognitively apprehended or even accessible, are served. These imperatives are powerful; they direct emotion and action.

Of course, it is necessary to view surface adolescent behaviors as authentic. To attribute behaviors totally to deep-structure-level functioning is as wrong as it is to attribute it only to deep-seated historical origins. However, an awareness of the developmental dynamics of adolescence must always be primary. Adolescents are *individuals in process*. Viewing them outside of this context is misleading. If we were to examine toddler behavior without the context of an organism in development, we would find the behaviors impossible to tolerate. Since toddlers are tiny and adolescents are not, developmental-phase behavior is commonly attributed to the former and, if acknowledged at all, is "humored" in the latter.

PART THREE

Adolescent Social Interactional Life: Empirical Findings and Pragmatic Implications

This section reports findings of studies that empirically tested major hypotheses of the theory of dynamic functional interaction (Seltzer, 1982) on which the peer arena model of adolescent development and behavior is based. The first series of studies, which examined the adolescent social reference world, is discussed in Chapter 5. Findings on 800 adolescents as well as a trend analysis over a 10-year period are reported. The results provide a framework of interactional preferences, indicating the relative postures of powerful reference groups such as parents and discrete groups of peers. Chapter 6 reports findings of which attributes (in agemates) carry particular meaning to the adolescent and which do not. Some interesting male-female contrasts are revealed as well as developmental differences.

The following chapter discusses findings on private and public socialization practices and preferences of the adolescent. Also included are findings on the level of awareness adolescents have of their agemates in social situations and the degree to which they seek out agemates as a barometer of the value of their own attributes. Here too male-female contrasts are noted. Chapter 8 offers data on where adolescents first meet one another, the size of groups they prefer to participate in, and how much time they spend with close others. This chapter concludes with findings on how the perceived group evaluation compares with the adolescent self-rank. Engaging male-female differences are again disclosed.

The last chapter in this section summarizes findings to frame a panorama of the greater and smaller social worlds of the adolescent—the observable and the private. A sketch is drawn of a cognitively maturing individual dealing with a rather expansive social arena of generational others and, at the same time, of an adolescent who is with agemates on a regular basis and must balance casual relationships to remain part of a social scene while also meeting the imperative to fulfill individual growth demands. Commentary within the chapters incorporates the findings to broaden understanding of the adolescent social experience, its impact, and its vicissitudes.

CHAPTER 5

The Psychosocial Influence Field:
Adolescent Reference Groups

The adolescent is keenly aware that there is much he has to learn about negotiating the world preparatory to taking his place in it. Most attention is paid to his relevant group of others. It is with agemates that he will cooperate and compete all his life. But early along in adolescence, his observations reveal that they too are uninformed and unaware about many matters. It is a paradox. On the one hand, naivete on the part of his friends can be quite reassuring since it mirrors his own condition. On the other hand, he has to seek out sources of information and guidance. Fortunately, others are at hand.

New intellectual advances afford the adolescent an ability to hold certain factors constant in his mind while he varies others. Thus, the lives of members of the greater society can be understood in more complex terms than was the case in younger years. A simple example is the picture held by a child of a schoolteacher. For the child this individual is always visualized within the context of the school, yet it may be that the teacher is also an expert at discus throwing, biking, jewelry making, etc. The ability to hold a number of factors in mind while dealing with another set of factors allows the adolescent to conceptualize the teacher as athlete, artist, parent, etc. in addition to teacher. The adolescent can handle fuller pictures of the people in his world. At the same time, the world becomes more complex, interesting, and frightening, but also wondrous and full of possibility.

Thus, although the peer is the most relevant other, the adolescent becomes increasingly aware that the greater society is composed of a variety of reference individuals and groups through whom he can access a great deal of information—serious and frivolous—and who can also offer guidance in accessing additional information.

WHAT IS A REFERENCE GROUP?

The concept of a reference group was first developed by Hyman (1942) as he investigated self-ranking in relation to other figures, rather than in relation to an objective external criterion. Ted Newcomb (1958) found reference groups a valuable conceptual tool with which to investigate influences on political decision-making of Bennington College female students. A reference group framework enabled Sherif (1954), Stouffer and associates (1949), and Hartley (1968) to contribute to the understanding of relative deprivation. Their contributions introduced the notion that deprivation is not necessarily caused by objective facts, but that who else is better or worse off may be far more pertinent.

The peer group fits well the criteria of a reference group, so we include it among the reference groups the adolescent will turn to. A reference group can be either a membership group or a nonmembership group. It can be a positive or a negative reference group. It can provide a normative or a comparative function, or both. It may or may not be the primary reference group. In adolescence, peers in their various groups are important reference groups. Whether the peer group continues to be a reference group depends on a number of factors. Among them are individual needs, the social situation, social demands, and whether or not it is a source for secondary reinforcements. All these factors are active individually and interact with one another. Furthermore, the strength of each peer group is relative to the strengths of other groups or figures. For an accurate understanding of just how much psychological space the agemate occupies in the adolescent mental field, it is important to understand who else takes up space, how much, and in what arenas.

The literature on reference groups of adolescents appears almost nonexistent (Seltzer, 1980), reflecting a lag behind the extensive literature on adolescent intellectual, emotional, and social growth. What the literature does contain on whom adolescents consult on issues of importance to them focuses primarily on parents and peers, or parents versus peers.

The notion of "a peer group" is also confusing. On one hand, it is referred to as the immediate membership group only; on the other hand, it is used as a global term to encompass teens as a whole. Different kinds of peers have generally not been distinguished. That adolescents are different constitutionally and developmentally is made clear in the literature. But these differences seem to dissipate when the concept of peers and peer groups are discussed.

Furthermore, the fact that there are different types of peers and different types of peer groups apparently escaped notice of the investigators of the 1960s and the 1970s. Hence, prevailing notions were that adolescents consulted either with their parents or with what was a general and rather abstract notion of peers. A few years later, the notion that groups of peers are as different from one another as are all groups of adults was recognized, and the existence of a peer reference field, including many peer groups as well as a range of generational others, was documented (Seltzer, 1980). Later the concept of a "peer arena" was introduced into the literature (Seltzer, 1982). The "peer arena" is psychological rather than physically observable. It stands for any and all psychosocial interactions with any and all adolescents in any or all peer groups—face to face, in literature, in visual media, and even in fantasy. The notion of "peer arena" takes into consideration that an adolescent moves into, out of, and back into a number of peer groups at the same time and, furthermore, is not necessarily a member of each. Some that are accessed only visually serve as psychological peers or models.

THE ADOLESCENT REFERENCE GROUP INDEX

To understand how the adolescent utilizes the advice and the influence of his contemporaries, it would be necessary to also know if and to what degree he utilizes the influence of those reference groups who are not the same age. The literature prior to the 1980s did not contain any such measure. This void is most likely the result of the notion that the adolescent world is composed of two entities—parents and peers. In order to meet this need, the Adolescent Reference Group Index (ARGI) was constructed. Its design included specific questions and a choice of reference groups and figures the adolescent might turn to for opinions or advice before acting. Its conception was simple, as is its design. As the first attempt to incorporate the influence of the peer within a broader context of influence, it filled a necessary void in the literature. Reference groups included not only parents but other family members and generational groups in the greater social world. An understanding of how the adolescent organizes and uses his greater social world brings a more precise understanding of the relative power of adolescent peers and peer groups and of what their areas of influence are and are not.

After pilot testing, the first study utilizing the ARGI tested its basic premise—that the adolescent would elect to use a variety of reference groups in coming to a decision and not restrict herself to only parents or peers. The questions covered a number of different areas: moral, technical, leisure, future, and relationships. They were:

1. Should murderers who planned the murder in advance be given capital punishment?*
2. Should I get my hair cut?
3. Is taking a year off between high school and starting a serious job/college a good idea?
4. I am on the honor system. I see a close friend cheating on a test. Shall I report him?
5. Where is a good place to shop for a jacket?
6. Should marijuana (or any soft drugs) be legalized?
7. Should people live together before deciding whether to marry or not?
8. What qualities are important to look for in other people and to develop myself?
9. What should I do with a day off from school next week?
10. What job/college should I try to get into, and why is it important?

An 11th, perceptual question was:

11. On most matters, whom would you consult?

The instrument offered 13 reference groups conceived to cover the range of adolescent socialization: older brothers and sisters, younger brothers and sisters, friends two to five years younger, friends two to five

---

*Amnesty for draft dodgers was the issue in the 1970s study.

years older, friends over five years older, media (literature, magazines, TV, etc.), minister/priest/rabbi, neighborhood friends of the same age, parents, older relatives, schoolmates of the same age, school personnel, and special friend (whom the subject was asked to specify). Peers were clustered into five distinct groups. Subjects were asked to select the reference groups they would consult before making a decision on how to proceed on each of the 10 issues. They were requested to indicate on the space next to each reference group the percent of influence that group would be accorded. All of the groups selected were to sum to 100% for each question. The 11th, summary question was included to obtain a generalized perceptual account of how influence is accorded. In the analysis, means for each reference group for each issue, as well as a grand mean for all issues, were calculated. The 11th question was not included with the other 10 in calculating the grand mean.

A number of studies were carried out over a 10-year period, beginning in 1974 and terminating in 1984. Included were adolescent males and females in grades 9–12 drawn from the city of Philadelphia and its suburbs and small communities in Long Island, New York. The data were analyzed in order to determine:

1. General influence power of each reference group
2. Specific areas of strong or weak influence for each group
3. Trends over a 10-year period
4. Male-female differences
5. Influence profile when selected groups are clustered
6. Whether or not age makes a difference in influence choices—a developmental analysis

The reader will note in forthcoming analyses that samples of different sizes, age ranges, and gender composition are compared. Originally, the intent was to present only findings on a large, mixed-sex sample of 732 in grades 9–12 (a composite of four subsamples) in the 1980s study. However, when findings from the large sample were compared with those from the sample of the original study (66 12th-grade males) of a decade earlier, major findings were very similar. One of the subsamples in the 1980s study (93 12th-grade males) was comparable to the original sample in gender and in size, although they reached the same age in two separate decades. Comparative findings for these two cohorts are also reported.

THE STUDIES

Our initial (1970s) study examined a small sample of 66 12th-grade boys in a Philadelphia high school. The school enrolled males from all parts of the city. The sample was primarily middle-class and white but included students representing the four races, four major religions, and a variety of ethnic and socioeconomic groups. The subjects completed the 20-minute ARGI questionnaire as one group in one sitting. We carried out a replication of the 1970s study in the 1980s, on a sample of 732 adolescents (564 males and 168 females). Of the students who participated, 326 were high school students in public schools in Long Island, New York, and suburban Philadelphia. The majority were of the Protestant or Jewish faith. Four hundred and six were students in an all-male Philadelphia Catholic high school. The sample was primarily white and of middle- or working-class background. All racial groups were represented, as were business, professional, and working-class backgrounds. All questionnaires were filled out in homeroom classrooms during the homeroom period.

The hypotheses that (1) subjects would utilize a number of reference groups rather than just parents and peers, (2) the influence of parents and peers would remain strong, and (3) previously unreported groups would be utilized, were all strongly supported in all studies. We also hypothesized that (4) certain issues would be clearly "peer" issues and other issues would be clearly "parental" issues. This too was supported by the data of all studies. Findings are displayed in Table 5.1, which presents the mean percentage of influence accorded each reference group on each issue, as well as the grand mean percentage for all issues for the 1980s sample of 732. Since this sample size differed considerably from the 66 members of the 1970s study, no comparative analysis was undertaken. A comparative analysis was carried out with the subsample of 93 12th-grade males, who were enrolled in the Philadelphia Catholic high school. The majority of the group was middle-class, white, and

Catholic. Other religions and racial groups were also represented. Table 5.2 presents these comparative findings, which are discussed in the following section.

TREND ANALYSIS

How affected are adolescents by "the times"? To what extent will their behaviors withstand changing fads? A t-test analysis was carried out on the findings of the two studies on similar samples completed 10 years apart to determine if significant differences existed as to whose influence was sought out. Table 5.3 displays data on both the grand mean percent of influence attributed to each group and the findings on significance of difference. Findings from the 1970s accorded major strength of influence to parents, older siblings, and specific groups of peers. There were dramatically weak groups, too—younger siblings and younger friends. We predicted that there would be more stability than change in the reference group selections, notwithstanding changing times. We predicated our hypothesis on the characteristics and needs of the stage as being universal. Our hypothesis was supported. Findings reveal that 7 of the 13 categories of reference group showed no significant difference over the 10-year span in the amount of influence adolescents accorded them. A glance at Table 5.3 reveals a most interesting phenomenon: With one exception, those reference groups that were most popular and those that were barely used showed no significant difference in how much influence they were accorded between the two studies. They were: younger brothers and sisters, friends two to five years younger, neighborhood friends of the same age, parents, schoolmates of the same age, school personnel, and special friend.

The groups that did show significant differences were midrange influence groups, of (1980s) ranks 4, 6, 8, 9, and 10.5. In the 1980s, significantly *less* influence went to friends two to five years older, friends over five years older, and the media. Significantly *more* influence went to older brothers and sisters, older relatives, and clergy. Increased use of clergy may be explained by accessibility; the majority of the sample were students in a Catholic school. However, use of clergy increased by only one rank. Apparently, clergy do not occupy an important niche

TABLE 5.1. Percent of Influence Accorded Each Reference Group per Issue (1980s): Means, Standard Deviations, Grand Mean.

Reference group	Capital punishment		Haircut		Year off		Honor system		Jacket	
	M	SD	M	SD	M	SD	M	SD	M	SD
Older brothers/sisters	9.99	18.63	12.75	25.62	14.92	23.26	12.82	30.62	16.75	24.42
Younger brothers/sisters	1.08	6.21	3.46	14.12	0.91	7.39	1.58	11.19	1.77	8.11
Friends 2–5 years younger	0.69	4.22	0.91	5.21	0.66	4.28	1.04	6.97	1.05	5.26
Friends 2–5 years older	4.69	12.86	5.17	15.02	4.83	13.71	4.35	14.71	6.64	16.10
Friends + 5 years older	3.17	10.18	1.79	8.80	4.17	11.94	2.17	9.69	2.53	8.92
Media	12.67	25.96	1.93	10.84	1.68	7.32	0.48	4.78	6.99	17.72
Clergy	9.15	20.77	0.64	6.41	1.65	8.76	4.39	17.97	0.44	4.65
Neighbors same age	4.10	13.17	7.20	20.79	2.37	10.23	5.46	20.47	10.28	20.73
Parents	30.97	31.94	31.59	39.82	42.90	33.14	20.01	36.62	23.74	27.23
Older relatives	6.38	14.39	2.82	10.86	5.23	12.83	2.64	13.34	2.82	10.01
Schoolmates same age	6.56	15.80	15.01	28.53	4.78	12.07	26.35	47.88	16.64	23.32
School personnel	4.95	13.93	1.07	6.79	10.73	21.29	8.33	26.78	0.58	4.53
Special friend	5.11	14.78	15.62	31.57	4.81	15.18	10.24	30.68	9.72	20.61

$N = 732$

Reference group	Marijuana		Live together		Qualities		Day off		Job/college		Grand means		Most matters	
	M	SD	M	SD	M	SD	M	SD	M	SD	M	SD	M	SD
Older brothers/sisters	13.99	26.01	13.07	24.79	14.13	22.58	7.42	17.28	14.91	23.74	13.13	2.88	15.38	24.76
Younger brothers/sisters	0.78	5.99	0.89	7.68	1.12	6.10	1.21	5.88	0.52	5.60	1.29	0.64	1.35	8.16
Friends 2–5 years younger	1.16	6.88	0.85	6.05	1.01	6.59	1.76	10.87	0.70	4.93	0.94	0.32	0.71	5.36
Friends 2–5 years older	5.95	17.39	5.15	14.82	5.20	13.71	6.95	19.86	3.69	10.62	5.28	1.07	4.19	13.65
Friends + 5 years older	3.44	11.41	6.18	16.60	3.90	12.26	1.83	8.22	4.05	11.51	3.40	1.28	2.01	8.34
Media	11.36	27.68	2.83	11.65	1.85	8.51	2.93	12.81	3.02	10.19	4.69	2.99	0.94	5.64
Clergy	5.27	17.63	11.82	26.29	5.44	15.92	0.41	5.91	1.74	9.05	4.10	3.63	2.41	11.57
Neighbors same age	7.13	19.51	2.93	10.80	4.71	14.34	15.50	31.08	2.06	9.71	6.10	3.85	5.92	17.29
Parents	22.08	33.77	30.53	35.05	33.18	32.72	12.28	23.18	42.57	32.50	29.19	9.83	38.49	35.71
Older relatives	4.24	13.15	5.61	15.21	6.28	15.92	1.59	9.10	5.10	14.26	4.34	1.71	3.26	11.29
Schoolmates same age	14.28	26.61	6.52	16.46	9.63	19.94	24.43	37.14	3.72	10.90	12.43	6.62	8.83	18.99
School personnel	3.43	12.62	1.57	7.66	3.82	14.37	1.19	8.92	13.61	22.60	4.92	4.27	2.36	10.44
Special friend	6.53	18.82	11.76	27.09	9.72	21.89	22.32	35.33	4.15	13.25	9.85	4.91	14.23	26.06

N = 732

TABLE 5.2. Mean Percent of Influence Accorded Reference Groups by Adolescent Males, According to Decade.

Reference group	Amnesty/capital punishment		Haircut		Year off		Honor system		Jacket	
	1970s	1980s	1970s	1980s	1970s	1980s	1970s	1980s	1970s	1980s
Older brothers/sisters	9.89	11.39	9.39	11.50	13.67	12.70	9.03	9.13	9.35	12.97
Younger brothers/sisters	1.24	1.19	5.61	2.43	0.61	0.70	0.75	1.15	3.12	2.55
Friends 2–5 years younger	0.93	1.36	1.62	1.43	0.71	0.84	0.86	1.48	0.90	1.90
Friends 2–5 years older	9.89	6.88	6.36	5.79	10.61	8.65	6.67	3.93	8.94	6.95
Friends +5 years older	4.33	4.25	1.51	2.68	6.53	4.15	2.04	2.40	2.61	2.83
Media	26.26	10.97	1.19	0.91	4.39	1.52	1.29	0.75	7.84	9.67
Clergy	4.02	9.85	0.43	0.05	1.22	1.70	1.72	6.47	0.00	0.25
Neighbors same age	5.15	6.48	10.57	11.95	4.29	4.09	7.74	9.71	16.18	15.44
Parents	18.33	25.50	29.23	22.14	30.31	40.34	15.27	11.06	22.61	13.27
Older relatives	2.68	4.25	1.51	4.73	2.45	4.43	0.32	0.83	1.71	3.00
Schoolmates same age	9.99	8.19	13.70	12.54	6.33	6.10	37.10	27.80	20.10	20.23
School personnel	5.15	3.10	0.32	1.96	15.10	10.04	9.35	15.17	0.10	0.00
Special friend	2.06	6.60	18.66	21.89	2.45	5.36	7.74	10.23	6.53	10.97

1970s: *N* = 66
1980s: *N* = 93

Reference group	Marijuana		Live together		Qualities		Day off		Job/college		Grand means		Most matters	
	1970s	1980s	1970s	1980s	1970s	1980s	1970s	1980s	1970s	1980s	1970s	1980s	1970s	1980s
Older brothers/sisters	10.43	10.79	10.57	11.08	10.15	10.93	4.47	4.95	10.89	12.69	9.84	10.90	12.61	12.79
Younger brothers/sisters	0.73	1.33	0.92	0.51	1.22	1.06	1.81	1.69	0.50	0.49	1.66	1.29	1.42	1.24
Friends 2–5 years younger	1.36	1.33	1.03	0.64	1.52	1.28	1.60	1.47	0.81	0.69	1.14	1.23	0.71	0.56
Friends 2–5 years older	7.61	6.65	6.06	5.90	7.11	5.45	5.54	6.05	6.55	4.29	7.56	6.12	5.90	4.49
Friends +5 years older	8.13	3.74	10.16	8.63	7.31	4.54	0.53	2.39	5.34	4.58	4.87	4.10	2.44	2.83
Media	21.90	13.74	5.75	2.39	3.65	1.86	4.79	1.27	6.85	4.81	8.39	4.99	5.29	0.95
Clergy	4.38	5.22	7.60	14.26	4.67	6.32	0.00	0.64	0.60	2.45	2.49	4.80	1.12	1.90
Neighbors same age	10.53	13.53	6.67	4.82	8.32	8.46	24.60	22.36	1.81	2.88	9.53	9.83	5.19	8.90
Parents	12.30	16.88	18.89	25.89	27.92	27.92	9.69	7.29	26.01	34.96	21.14	22.96	35.20	37.06
Older relatives	1.25	3.48	2.05	5.86	4.16	6.90	0.21	1.43	3.63	4.64	2.07	4.05	2.14	4.13
Schoolmates same age	14.70	14.98	9.45	4.96	10.56	9.36	19.49	23.72	8.87	3.76	14.92	12.71	9.36	7.24
School personnel	3.23	2.57	1.95	2.21	3.65	5.00	0.85	0.42	25.40	18.74	6.63	5.79	3.66	1.99
Special friend	3.34	6.04	19.10	12.86	9.14	11.53	26.30	26.32	2.72	5.03	9.74	11.36	15.06	15.92

1970s: N = 66
1980s: N = 93

TABLE 5.3. Significance of Difference in Influence Accorded 13 Reference Groups.

Reference group	1970s			1980s			t	Significance
	Mean	SD	Rank	Mean	SD	Rank		
Older brothers/sisters	9.84	2.36	3	10.90	2.65	4	2.73	.01
Younger brothers/sisters	1.66	1.54	12	1.29	0.66	12	-1.72	NS
Friends 2–5 years younger	1.14	0.31	13	1.23	0.33	13	1.73	NS
Friends 2–5 years older	7.56	1.85	7	6.12	1.54	6	-5.16	-00.1*
Friends + 5 years older	4.87	3.18	9	4.10	1.87	10.5	-2.00	-.05*
Media	8.39	8.51	6	4.99	4.52	8	-3.18	-.01*
Clergy	2.49	2.56	10	4.80	4.41	9	3.80	.001
Neighbors of same age	9.53	6.46	5	9.83	5.29	5	0.34	NS
Parents	21.14	7.38	1	22.96	10.58	1	1.16	NS
Older relatives	2.07	1.33	11	4.05	1.87	10.5	7.37	.001
Schoolmates same age	14.92	8.51	2	12.71	6.62	2	-1.85	NS
School personnel	6.63	8.21	8	5.79	5.62	7	-0.76	NS
Special friend	9.74	8.21	4	11.36	5.73	3	1.43	NS

*Accorded less influence in 1980s.

1970s: N = 66

1980s: N = 93

in the adolescent world. Older siblings and older relatives may have been utilized in the 1980s in place of non–family members turned to in prior years and/or in place of media.

As mentioned, reference groups with no significant differences between the two periods ranked either at the top or bottom. Of the reference groups ranked in the top five, four showed no significant difference in the amount of influence accorded over the 10-year period: parents, schoolmates of the same age, special friend, and neighborhood friends of the same age. Parents and schoolmates of the same age ranked 1 and 2, respectively, in both studies (parents, 21.14 and 22.96, respectively; schoolmates of the same age, 14.92 and 12.71, respectively). Special friend and older siblings exchanged ranks 3 and 4. Neighborhood friends of the same age retained rank 5.

A glance at Tables 5.1 and 5.2 reveals the adolescent's pragmatic utilization of school personnel. They are seen as having information about future plans: schooling, jobs, and whether or not to take a year off before pursuing either one seriously. School personnel appear to be seen as employment counselors, not as general advisors. Equally fascinating is how teens seem to perceive younger individuals. Table 5.2, which displays an issue-by-issue analysis, reveals that in both samples (10 years apart) younger brothers and sisters were never accorded 2% or more influence on issues other than "Should I get my hair cut?" (5.61 and 2.43, respectively) and "Where should I go to get a jacket?" (3.12 and 2.55, respectively). In both studies, friends two to five years younger were never accorded more than 1.9% influence. Younger folk don't seem to matter much. They maintained their lowest-ranked positions (12 for younger siblings and 13 for younger friends) whereas older siblings ranked 3 and 4, respectively, in the two studies.

Findings on reference groups that did experience significant differences suggest an interesting trend. In spite of movement upward one rank, friends two to five years older were used significantly less in 1984, as were friends over five years older, whose rank dropped from 9 to 10.5. The drop of media influence from 6 to 8 may be explained by the substitution in the 1980s ARGI of capital punishment for amnesty, since amnesty was a 1970s and not a 1980s issue. Nevertheless, although capital punishment was conceptually related to the issue of amnesty, clearly it did not have the same relevance. The amnesty issue dealt with near-peers in the Vietnam era.

TABLE 5.4. Top Four Ranks of 13 Reference Groups on Ten Issues over 10-Year Span.

Reference groups	Amnesty/capital punishment 1970s	1980s	Haircut 1970s	1980s	Year off 1970s	1980s	Honor system 1970s	1980s	Jacket 1970s	1980s
Older brothers/sisters	4.5	3	4	4	3	2	4	3	4	2.5
Younger brothers/sisters										
Friends 2–5 years younger										
Friends 2–5 years older	4.5									
Friends + 5 years older										
Media	1	2								
Clergy		4								
Neighbors same age									3	
Parents	2	1	1	1	1	1	2	2	1	1
Older relatives										
Schoolmates same age	3		3	3			1	1	2	2.5
School personnel					2	3	3	4		
Special friends			2	2						

1970s: N = 66 (males).
1980s: N = 732 (564 males, 168 females).

Reference group	Marijuana 1970s	Marijuana 1980s	Live together 1970s	Live together 1980s	Qualities 1970s	Qualities 1980s	Day off 1970s	Day off 1980s	Job/college 1970s	Job/college 1980s	Most matters 1970s	Most matters 1980s
Older brothers/sisters	4.5	3	3	2	2.5	2			3	2	3	2
Younger brothers/sisters												
Friends 2–5 years younger												
Friends 2–5 years older												
Friends + 5 years older			4									
Media	1	4										
Clergy				3.5								
Neighbors same age	4.5	1	2	1	1	1	2	3				
Parents	3								1	1	1	1
Older relatives												
Schoolmates same age	2	2			2.5	3.5	3	1	2		4	
School personnel							1			3		4
Special friend			1	3.5		3.5		2			2	3

In sum, the comparative data support notions of adolescents seeking an environmental reference system for their development needs, not just one or two restricted groups. The data also reveal choices that reflect more stability than change over time.

ISSUE ANALYSIS AND PSYCHOSOCIAL GROWTH

Who is sought out and for what purpose presents another provocative dimension. Data of Tables 5.1 and 5.2 reveal reference group selections for consultation on specific issues. The findings help to effect a picture of how "others" fit into the adolescent's view of the immediate society and reinforce commonsense notions that while peers are very important to the adolescent, other figures are, too. The trend data, which disclose continuity rather than change, also reveal that in 10 issues, groups who ranked in the 1–4 range in the earlier data tended to remain in that range in the subsequent study (see Tables 5.2 and 5.4). For the issue of haircut, the ranks were identical across the 10-year span. A review of Table 5.4 shows parents, schoolmates of the same age, and older siblings to be reference groups that were highly ranked most frequently. Special friends ranked high for issues of leisure, appearance, and the specific issue that might affect them directly—living together before marriage. For specialized issues, adolescents accorded influence to experts. Overall, parents outranked all other groups.

Comparative data of the studies reinforce a conception of an adolescent who conceptualizes the question/issue and connects it to a source representing the necessary knowledge base. This activity reflects a state of cognitive integration—not imitation. For example, 1970s subjects consulted the media more than any other reference source for issues of amnesty and marijuana. At the time, amnesty for Vietnam deserters was a "hot issue." Effects of use of marijuana was a controversial issue in the medical literature. In the 1980s more was known about marijuana with less divided opinion, and capital punishment was not as relevant a moral issue. The data reflect this new situation and show a reduced use of media, with increased attention paid to other sources. A second example is buying a jacket. In both studies, when the adolescent wished to buy a jacket, his or her use of the media was minimal. Parents, older siblings, friends two to five years older, and two sets of favorite peers (schoolmates and neighborhood friends of the same age) ranked higher than did media on the issue of jacket. These data suggest a cognitively flexible individual who can evaluate relative importance of issues and select those reference persons or groups seen as having the most cogent information. Relatives and older friends represent pragmatism; agemates add information that is congruent with maintaining the desired conformity.

These data reinforce theoretical notions that the adolescent has at his disposal a variety of conceptual combinations and permutations unavailable in prior periods of development. The data reveal flexible cognitive appraisals and pertinent applications. These new abilities are evidenced in their choice of groups for help on each issue.

Table 5.4 provides rank and issue data on the top four influence groups over the 10-year span. On five issues, *parents* continued to be accorded the most influence: whether or not to get a haircut, whether or not to take a year off between high school and college/serious job, where to go to buy a jacket, what qualities to look for in others, and what job to take or which college to apply to. Parents ranked second to schoolmates at both times on whether or not to report a friend cheating, but they moved from second to first rank on questions of amnesty/capital punishment and if people should live together before marriage. The biggest change for parents over the 10-year period was the move from third place on "Should marijuana be legalized?" to first place. (In both the cases of capital punishment and marijuana, they took over first place from media.) What to do on a day off was the only question where parents did not appear in the first three ranks. This is clearly an issue of "peer relevance."

Over the 10-year span, *schoolmates of the same age* emerged as the second most powerful group. In both studies they achieved rank 1, 2, or 3 on six issues—rank 1 on reporting a friend cheating and rank 2 on legalizing marijuana. They ranked below parents and special friends on getting a haircut and just below parents on where to shop for a jacket. *Older siblings* also retained a strong influence position over time. In the earlier study, they were accorded ranks no less than 4 on 7 of the 10 issues. In the 1980s their influence rose. Their ranks improved to 2 or 3 for 6 of these 7 issues, and there was no issue where their influence declined. The earlier data introduced older siblings as a strong and previously unrecognized reference group. The later findings reinforce their strength. Later, we will discuss the additional power they yield as a swing group.

ADOLESCENTS AND DEPENDENCE: PERCEPTIONS OF INFLUENCE

The ARGI study further examined the issue of adolescence and independence. It is a natural state that parents are nurturers of children. This condition will naturally end as the adolescent enters maturity. But for peers to take on the importance they do in adolescence has no corollary in nature. Initially, adolescent peers provide mutual support due to their common condition of frameworklessness, their experiencing the changes of puberty, and their anticipation of a new status. However, when psychosocial development work takes on more intensity and peers become *the most relevant environmental figures for development*, the adolescent subtly begins a new dependence. What is experienced is a strong internal imperative to access agemates in order to look, listen, and borrow. Peers model data for the adolescent's own study as she works on what and how she wants to be. They offer the raw material necessary to hammer out a self. In order to retain this access, one must conform to group norms and values and participate in group-sanctioned activities. (Our model of adolescent development proposes that since the peer is the most important environmental figure for the adolescent, denial of access to peers constitutes developmental deprivation.) This "slavishness" may be hard to reconcile with the stated goal of the period —independent functioning. How can one claim growing independence from parents and relatives yet admit transferring dependence to another host? Ostensibly, eagerness to attend parties or gatherings is socially acceptable; it is "OK" to want to be together with peers. But it is not "OK" to be "led." A personal sense of psychological independence must be maintained in order to feel good about oneself. Thus, the adolescent experiences dissonance with this new brand of dependence and is uncomfortable. By contrast, dependence on parents is "comfortably uncomfortable" since the adolescent trusts that one day he will move beyond it into adulthood and independence.

TABLE 5.5. Actual Versus Perceived Influence Accorded 13 Reference Groups by Adolescents (Males Only).

	1970s			1980s		
Reference group	GM	MM	Direction	GM	MM	Direction
Older brothers/sisters	9.84	12.61	+	10.90	12.79	+
Younger brothers/sisters	1.66	1.42	0	1.29	1.24	0
Friends 2–5 years younger	1.14	0.71	–	1.23	0.56	–
Friends 2–5 years older	7.56	5.90	–	6.12	4.49	–
Friends +5 years older	4.87	2.44	–	4.10	2.83	–
Media	8.39	5.29	–	4.99	0.95	–
Clergy	2.49	1.12	–	4.80	1.90	–
Neighborhood agemates	9.53	5.19	–	9.83	8.90	–
Parents	21.14	35.20	+(14.08)*	22.96	37.06	+(14.10)*
Older relatives	2.07	2.14	0	4.05	4.13	0
School agemates	14.92	9.36	–(5.56)**	12.71	7.24	–(5.47)**
School personnel	6.63	3.66	–	5.79	1.99	–
Special friend	9.74	15.06	+(5.32)	11.36	15.92	+(4.56)

1970s: N = 66 (males) GM = Grand mean *Most overestimated
1980s: N = 93 (males) MM = "Most matters" **Most underestimated

65

TABLE 5.6. Actual Versus Perceived Influence Accorded 13 Reference Groups by Adolescents.

Reference group	1970s			1980s		
	GM	MM	Direction	GM	MM	Direction
Older brothers/sisters	9.84	12.61	+	13.13	15.38	+
Younger brothers/sisters	1.66	1.42	0	1.29	1.35	0
Friends 2–5 years younger	1.14	0.71	–	0.94	0.71	–
Friends 2–5 years older	7.56	5.90	–	5.28	4.19	–
Friends + 5 years older	4.87	2.44	–	3.40	2.01	–
Media	8.39	5.29	–	4.69	0.94	–(3.8)**
Clergy	2.49	1.12	–	4.10	2.41	–
Neighborhood agemates	9.53	5.19	–	6.10	5.92	–
Parents	21.14	35.20	+(14.08)*	29.19	38.49	+(9.3)*
Older relatives	2.07	2.14	0	4.34	3.26	–
School agemates	14.92	9.36	–(5.56)**	12.43	8.83	–(3.6)
School personnel	6.63	3.66	–	4.92	2.36	–
Special friend	9.74	15.06	+(5.32)	9.85	14.23	+(4.38)

1970s: N = 66 (males) GM = Grand mean *Most overestimated
1980s: N = 732 (males and females) MM = "Most matters" **Most underestimated

The 11th issue, "most matters," was designed to measure an impression. The adolescent is asked "On most matters, whom would you consult?" This question was inserted at the end in order to compare this response, which measures perceived (estimated) attributions of influence, with those revealing actual influence accorded on the 10 issues prior. Findings displayed in Table 5.5 reveal a great concordance over time. What is striking is the minimal difference between the sample years in both over- and underestimates. (Note that in both Tables 5.5 and 5.6 direction only is provided for all categories except those that were most striking, where actual differences are listed. Where differences were negligible, a 0 is entered as direction.) Furthermore, findings are the same, notwithstanding size of sample. (The comparisons of the two similar-size samples, Table 5.5, for both decades were reported to validate the findings from comparing the highly dissimilar sample sizes, Table 5.6.) Overestimates and underestimates of accorded influence were *identical* in Table 5.5 and showed one small difference in Table 5.6, in spite of the fact that the investigations were carried out 10 years apart. In all studies, influence of parents, older siblings, and special friends were overestimated. Parents are attributed the most influence (rank 1). Across the 10-year period they achieved either rank 1 or 2 with both cohorts on 8 of the 10 issues. The only issue for which their rank was below 3 was "what to do with a day off." Nonetheless, they were perceived as even more influential.

Only influence of younger siblings and of older relatives—two groups of low influence—were estimated accurately. The degree of influence of each of the eight remaining reference groups was underestimated. Among them were four of the five peer reference groups. What is fascinating is that in both decades, schoolmates of the same age were highly *underestimated*, and parents were the most highly *overestimated*.

FUNCTIONAL INCONSISTENCIES

What does all this tell us? Clearly, parents, siblings, and special friends are reference sources adolescents can acknowledge "privately" to be more acceptable as influence sources than are agemates. In fact, adolescents freely talk of how much parents "try" to influence, and at times they recoil in response to the perceived "burden." Paradoxically, during this period, on deep-structure-level functioning, they transfer psychological dependence from parents to peers. Findings that they attribute more influence than they actually accord to parents and less to agemates lend support to the theoretical assumption that the transfer of dependence is occurring. Adolescents find transition to independence and individuation socially acceptable, but not transfer of dependence to yet another. The data imply that, on a conscious level, this transfer is denied. We suggest that the strong influence exerted by peers is projected onto parents. It is psychologically safer to direct anger in response to challenged independence toward parents. They do not reject; peers might.

Adolescents make public statements of generational differences from parents. It may be that their target audience for these statements of independence are one another, and that they are pitched to maintain conformity with peers more than to reflect what is true for the adolescent. Implications are that parents take a good deal of the "rap" for adolescent dependence on peers and peer groups. Parents who do not actively encourage dependence in adolescent offspring are often confused by the rage that accompanies charges by the adolescent of continuing infantilization.

The adolescent's perception of the influence of older siblings is fascinating. They constitute a second "acceptable" group. The influence of older siblings was consistently overestimated in both decades' studies. Since older siblings technically are not "peers," it follows that feelings of inappropriate dependence would not be present. Neither are they of another generation. They represent a cross between the nurturance of parents and the camaraderie, competition, and relevance of peers. Consequently, influence from them is easier to acknowledge than is peer influence. They may also have some of the influence actually accorded peers projected onto them.

The third reference group whose perceived influence is overestimated is "special friend" (usually a friend of the opposite sex). For adolescents, a close relationship with one of the opposite gender is perceived as a symbol of maturation. Responsibilities as well as rights connected with this dyadic relationship are acceptable to other cohort members. Acknowledging the importance of the "special friend" is not dissonant with striving for independent thought and action. Clearly, selection of a love object is viewed as an independent action, not a group directive.

Thus, it is psychologically safe to privately attribute influence to a "special friend." It may even be ego-enhancing.

To understand all this one should bear in mind that the bottom-line emotional need of the adolescent is to enhance positive feelings about self. This perspective helps to understand the responses to discrepancies between the actual according of influence (as determined by responses to the 10 main issues) and the adolescent's general notion of amount of influence attributed. The first 10 questions called on objective, cognitive processes, the last on emotional interpretation. This ability to function comfortably with objectively illogical perceptions describes much of the inner dynamics of this stage of development. The developmental tasks of adolescence are completed when the individual is psychologically integrated, with few distortions. It is the product of hard-fought psychosocial development, which brings identifiable elements together into what we call "identity of self." Once the self is integrated, true independence is achieved. Dependence on others can more readily be acknowledged both publicly and privately because a self is experienced, discrete from other selves. The boundaries are clear, not confused.

CLUSTER DATA

The preceding analyses discussed findings on amount of influence accorded each of the 13 discrete reference groups. However, the social influence picture is not complete without an understanding of how influence postures are affected when the discrete groups combine into familiar clusters. Data analyzed according to social clusters provide some additional, interesting insights. The "peer group," which was dissected in the earlier analysis, is now reassembled into a peer cluster. This is based on our theoretical position that adolescents interact with peers in a number of group settings, giving rise to our construct of "peer arena," which refers to the psychosocial aggregate of any and all peer interactions in any and all peer groups. It includes all peers encountered—at various educational and religious institutions, in the neighborhood and its institutions, in the media (television, books, magazines), at rock concerts, at sports events, in volunteer groups, and in any other setting. All these interactions—physical, visual, auditory—become part of the psychosocial interactional world of the teenager. In the reference group study,

TABLE 5.7. Mean Percent of Influence, by Issue, of Reference Group Clusters, 1970s and 1980s.

| | Cluster | | | | | | | | | |
| | Parent | | Peer | | Sibling | | Authority | | Media | |
Issue	1970s	1980s	1970s	1980s	1970s	1980s	1970s	1980s	1970s	1980s
Capital punishment/amnesty	18.33	30.97	28.06	21.15	11.13	11.07	16.18	23.65	26.26	12.67
Haircut	29.23	31.59	50.91	43.91	15.00	16.19	3.77	7.51	1.19	1.93
Year off	30.31	42.90	24.39	17.45	14.28	15.83	25.30	21.58	4.39	1.68
Honor system	15.27	20.01	60.11	47.44	9.78	14.40	13.43	17.53	1.19	0.48
Jacket	22.61	23.74	52.65	44.33	12.47	18.52	4.42	6.37	7.84	6.99
Marijuana	12.30	22.08	37.54	35.05	11.16	14.77	16.99	16.38	21.90	11.36
Live together	18.89	30.53	42.31	27.21	11.49	13.96	21.66	25.18	5.75	2.83
Qualities	27.92	33.18	36.65	30.27	11.27	15.25	19.79	20.74	3.65	1.85
Day off	9.69	12.28	77.53	70.96	6.28	8.63	1.59	5.02	4.79	2.93
Jobs/college	26.01	42.87	20.76	14.32	11.30	15.43	34.97	24.50	6.85	3.02
Grand mean	21.06	29.02	43.09	35.21	11.42	14.41	15.81	16.85	8.38	4.47
Most matters	35.20	38.49	36.22	33.88	14.03	16.73	9.36	10.04	5.29	0.94

1970s: N = 66
1980s: N = 732

Note: Constituents of the clusters may be found in Tables 5.1 and 5.2.

adolescents encountered in these diverse groups were assigned to one of five discrete peer groups: schoolmates of the same age, neighborhood friends of the same age, friends two to five years older, friends two to five years younger, and special friend. They cluster into the broad category "peers." Our next series of analyses sought to recognize their combined force and to measure the extent of influence in aggregate. We compared the peer cluster with parents and other clusters, including a sibling cluster and an authority cluster (school personnel, clergy, older relatives, and friends over five years older). Media, like parents, was treated as an independent category.

Table 5.7 displays the cluster data findings on both 1970s and 1980s cohorts as to mean percent of influence accorded. Table 5.8 offers findings on rank. Examination of the tables reveals that in the earlier decade peers occupied more first-rank positions (8) than was the case 10 years later (5). Parents rose from one first-rank issue in the 1970s to five in the 1980s. Thus, the peer cluster lost the leading mean rank to parents in the 1980s. The peer cluster ranked first for both cohorts on the "peer" issues—"Should I report a friend cheating (honor system)?" and "Should marijuana be legalized?"—as well as in daily concerns such as getting a haircut, buying a jacket, and what to do with day off. For both cohorts parents occupied first place on the issue of whether to take a year off. The passage of time clearly had no impact on the adolescent's perception that this was a "parent" issue. The sibling cluster attained a rank no higher than 3 on any issue in either cohort. The power of the older sibling was reduced by the clustering with younger siblings, a weak influence group. The 1970s cohort attributed the authority cluster rank 1 on the job/college issue and rank 2 on two issues: living together before marriage and taking a year off before starting college or a serious job. But the influence picture in the 1980s changed. The 1980s cohort did not accord authority top rank on any issue. Rank 2 was achieved on capital punishment, on taking a year off, and on what job to take or college to attend, first place on the last issue being accorded to parents. On the whole, parents and peers remained the most utilized by both cohorts across the 10-year span, but parents gained in strength, and the influence of the peer cluster declined. With the exception of rank 2 (1970s) on marijuana and amnesty/capital punishment, the media did not occupy a position of major influence. The data imply that in matters where adolescents do not see personal contacts as having expertise, they do use the media.

TABLE 5.8. Ranking of Cluster Influence by Issue.

| | Cluster | | | | | | | | | |
| Issue | Parent | | Peer | | Sibling | | Authority | | Media | |
	1970s	1980s	1970s	1980s	1970s	1980s	1970s	1980s	1970s	1980s
Capital punishment/amnesty	3	1	1	3	5	5	4	2	2	4
Haircut	2	2	1	1	3	3	4	4	5	5
Year off	1	1	3	3	4	4	2	2	5	5
Honor system	2	2	1	1	4	4	3	3	5	5
Jacket	2	2	1	1	3	3	5	5	4	4
Marijuana	4	2	1	1	5	4	3	3	2	5
Live together	3	1	1	2	4	4	2	3	5	5
Qualities	2	1	1	2	4	4	3	3	5	5
Day off	2	2	1	1	3	3	5	4	4	5
Jobs/college	2	1	3	4	4	3	1	2	5	5
Mean rank	2.3	1.5	1.4	1.9	3.9	3.7	3.2	3.1	4.2	4.6
Ordered rank	2	1	1	2	4	4	3	3	5	5
Most matters	2	1	1	2	3	3	4	4	5	5

1970s: N = 66
1980s: N = 732

TABLE 5.9. Rank Order of Clusters for Each Issue.

Issue	Extended family*		Peer		Authority		Media	
	1970s	1980s	1970s	1980s	1970s	1980s	1970s	1980s
Capital punishment/amnesty	1	1	2	3	4	2	3	4
Haircut	2	1	1	2	3	3	4	4
Year off	1	1	3	3	2	2	4	4
Honor system	2	1	1	2	3	3	4	4
Jacket	2	2	1	1	4	4	3	3
Marijuana	2	1	1	2	4	3	3	4
Live together	2	1	1	2	3	3	4	4
Qualities	1	1	2	2	3	3	4	4
Day off	2	2	1	1	4	3	3	4
Jobs/college	1	1	3	2	2	3	4	4
Mean rank	1.6	1.2	1.6	2	3.2	2.9	3.6	3.9
Ordered rank	1.5	1	1.5	2	3	3	4	4
Most matters	1	1	2	2	3	3	4	4

1970s: $N = 66$
1980s: $N = 732$
*Parents and siblings

TABLE 5.10. Rank with Siblings and Peers Clustered (Extended Peer).

Issue	Extended peer		Parent		Authority		Media	
	1970s	1980s	1970s	1980s	1970s	1980s	1970s	1980s
Capital punishment/amnesty	1	1	2	2	4	3	3	4
Haircut	1	1	2	2	3	3	4	4
Year off	1	2	2	1	3	3	4	4
Honor system	1	1	2	2	3	3	4	4
Jacket	1	1	2	2	4	4	3	3
Marijuana	1	1	4	2	4	3	2	4
Live together	1	1	3	2	2	3	4	4
Qualities	1	1	2	2	3	3	4	4
Day off	1	1	2	2	3	3	4	4
Jobs/college	2	1	3	2	1	3	4	4
Mean rank	1.1	1.1	2.4	1.9	3	3.1	3.6	3.9
Ordered rank	1	1	2	2	3	3	4	4
Most matters	1	1	2	2	3	3	4	4

1970s: N = 66
1980s: N = 732

Pivotal Role of the Sibling

Siblings occupy an interesting position. On the one hand, they are family members and thus participants in socialization philosophies and practices of parents and elders of the family. Yet they are members of a different generation from parents. They are part of the same generational cohort as peers. Because they are members of "two worlds," they are a pivotal group with a unique power position. Their strength can be added to that of the parents or to that of those of their own generation. Table 5.8 presents ranks representing the influence accorded to discrete parent and sibling groups. Table 5.9 reveals changes in relative strength when influence accorded to siblings is added to that of parents to form an "extended family" cluster. A close look at the table reveals peers occupied the first influence position in the 1980s sample on the issue of legalization of marijuana. When influence accorded parents and siblings is clustered as family influence, peers are displaced to position 2. Note also the climb family took to rank 1 from rank 2 on haircut, living together, and honor system issues. With the added influence of their

TABLE 5.11. Comparison of Preferences When Siblings
Are Clustered with Parents and Peers (Percents).

Issue	Extended family*		Extended peer**	
	1970s	1980s	1970s	1980s
Capital punishment/amnesty	29.46	42.04	39.19	32.22
Haircut	44.23	77.78	65.91	60.10
Year off	44.59	58.73	38.67	33.28
Honor system	25.05	54.41	69.89	61.84
Jacket	35.08	42.26	65.12	62.85
Marijuana	23.46	36.85	48.70	49.82
Live together	30.38	44.49	53.80	41.17
Qualities	39.19	58.43	47.92	55.52
Day off	15.97	20.91	83.81	79.59
Job/college	37.31	58.00	32.06	50.03
Grand mean	32.66	43.61	55.41	49.02
Most matters	49.23	55.22	50.25	50.61

1970s: N = 66
1980s: N = 732
*Parents and siblings
**Peers and siblings

TABLE 5.12. Comparison of Preferences when Siblings are Clustered
with Parents and Peers (Ranks).

Issue	Extended family*		Extended peer**	
	1970s	1980s	1970s	1980s
Capital punishment/amnesty	2	1	1	2
Haircut	2	1	1	2
Year off	1	2	2	1
Honor system	2	2	1	1
Jacket	2	2	1	1
Marijuana	2	2	1	1
Live together	2	1	1	2
Qualities	2	1	1	2
Day off	2	2	1	1
Job/college	1	1	2	2
Mean rank	1.9	1.5	1.2	1.5
Ordered rank	2	1.5	1	1.5
Most matters	2	1	1	2

1970s: N = 66
1980s: N = 732
*Parents and siblings
**Peers and siblings

children, parents occupy first rank on 8 of the 10 issues. They were
second to the peer cluster only on issues of what to do with a day off
and what type of jacket to buy.

What happens when siblings are clustered with peers? Our next
analysis of 1980s data displays the pivotal influence power of siblings
when they are clustered with peers into an "extended peer" cluster (see
Table 5.10). Findings reveal that with addition of siblings, peer power
rose even more than did that of parents. The "extended peer" category
took nine first-place positions. The only issue for which parents (without
the addition of siblings) retained first place was whether or not to take
a year off before starting college or beginning a serious job. This table
displays data revealing that the 1970s sample also accorded the "extended
peer" cluster nine first-place ranks.

These data on two discrete samples examined 10 years apart reveal
similar findings. Siblings are an important group whose influence
must be seriously considered on issues of different "generational"
perspectives. They hold an important swing vote position. Tables 5.11
and 5.12 present a comparison of the family and the peer cluster when

sibling strength is added to each. The strength added to either parents or peers by clustering them with siblings assured a rank no less than the number 2 position in either decade.

BLOCK VERSUS DIFFERENTIATED PERCEPTIONS

Between-Group Analyses

As we try to capture a picture of the adolescent mind, it is important to know whether adolescents think in blocks. Do adolescents prefer specific reference groups and connect them globally with other reference groups? Or do they arrive at their influence-seeking decisions based on more objective, individualized perceptions? Inasmuch as the adolescent has matured sufficiently to hold discrete entities in mind and also conceptualize the whole, we hypothesized that the data would reveal a majority of statistically significant differences in how influence was attributed between the reference groups. In other words, we predicted that the reference field is individualized, not global, and that adolescents do not think in blocks.

To determine whether there were significant differences in how influence was accorded by the 1980s cohort of 732, the mean amount of influence accorded each reference group was compared with the mean amount accorded each of the other reference groups. For example, we tested if the influence accorded older brothers and sisters differed significantly from influence accorded to each of the 12 other reference groups. We followed this procedure with each group, comparing the influence each was accorded relative to all other groups. T-test analyses were performed for significance of differences. Findings revealed that with the exception of two instances, each reference group was attributed influence in an amount that was statistically different from any of the others. No significant differences were found between the amounts of influence accorded media and school personnel and in how clergy and older relatives were accorded influence. Adolescents were revealed to be highly discriminating.*

Findings on significant differences in amounts of influence accorded each reference group offer information on their relative standing with the adolescent. Some findings are of particular note. For example, with the

---

*Table 5.18 discloses male-female differences.

1980s cohort the amount of influence accorded parents was significantly greater than that accorded any other group. Older siblings emerged with strength. They were attributed significantly more influence than was any other reference group with the exception of parents. Schoolmates of the same age were attributed significantly more influence than any other group except for parents and siblings. The special friend was attributed significantly more than all other groups except the three just mentioned. Neighborhood friends were accorded significantly less influence than schoolmates of the same age or special friend. The findings illustrate the continuing relevance of family and of agemates who share daily experiences occurring in and in relation to a major social institution—the school. Growth in the desire for intimacy is implied by the fourth-place position accorded the special friend. Findings on younger folk again alert us to the pull toward maturity experienced by the adolescent. Younger siblings were attributed significantly less influence that that accorded any other group except younger friends. No group was accorded significantly less influence than younger friends.

Within-Group Differences

The next analysis examined whether the adolescents generally gave each group the same amount of influence, no matter what the issue, or let the issue determine the degree to which a specific reference group was sought out for consultation. We conducted t-tests for within-group differences on three major reference groups. Using the 1980s cohort of 732, t-tests were drawn between each of the 10 issues and the "most matters" issue for each of the three groups. For example, influence accorded to parents on "haircut" was compared to influence accorded parents on "where to find a jacket" and to each of the other issues. Then influence accorded to parents on where to find a jacket was compared to each of the remaining issues. In this manner 55 t-tests were carried out. For parents, 46 instances of significant differences were revealed (see Table 5.13) as to issue. This striking finding once again reveals the adolescent's ability to utilize individual initiative and judgment—an advanced cognitive state. Furthermore, when there was no significant difference, it did not appear to be related to whether the influence accorded was a high or low amount (see Tables 5.1 and 5.13). No statistically significant differences were

TABLE 5.13. Significant Differences in Influence of Parents among 11 Issues.

	Haircut	Year off	Honor system	Jacket	Marijuana	Live together	Qualities	Day off	Job/ college	Most matters
Capital punishment	-NS	-.001*	.001	.001	.001	NS	-NS	.001	-.001	-.001
Haircut		-.001	.001	.001	.001	NS	-NS	.001	-.001	-.001
Year off			.001	.001	.001	.001	.001	.001	NS	.01
Honor system				.05	NS	.001	.001	.001	.001	.001
Jacket					NS	.001	.001	.001	.001	.001
Marijuana						.001	.001	.001	.001	.001
Live together							NS	.001	.001	.001
Qualities								.001	.001	.01
Day off									.001	.001
Job/college										.05

*Minus (−) indicates column issue has less influence than row issue.

N = 732

found between capital punishment and the respective issues of haircut, living together, and qualities to look for in a person. Neither were there statistically significant differences in parent consultation between honor system and marijuana, jacket and marijuana, or taking a year off and advice on job/college.

Whether the issue made a difference in how much consultation was sought from *older brothers and sisters* was also examined. Here, the findings were quite different than for parents. Influence was far more even, with 25 statistically significant differences between the issues; 30 issue pairings showed no significant differences (see Table 5.14). These data clearly disclose that adolescents accord a broader influence to older siblings than they do to parents; it is more of a "block" response. In contrast, findings on how adolescents accord influence to schoolmates of the same age reveal little uniformity. As with parents, the issue is paramount. Only 7 instances of no significant difference were disclosed; 48 differences were statistically significant (see Table 5.15). What is quite intriguing is that, despite their position as the strongest single peer group, schoolmates are not allocated block areas of influence. The data reveal an *intellectual nonconformity*, which is independent of the behavioral conformity we witness daily. These data provide empirical evidence that the adolescent has begun to place important agemates into a psychosocial framework that is not intellectually rigid but responsive to external factors. They suggest an idiosyncratic intellectual utilization of peers for individual growth prerogatives.

As we look at the data of Table 5.15, we find interesting evidence of conceptual clustering—more evidence of cognitive advance. Noting examples where no statistically significant differences were disclosed may clarify: capital punishment and living together (both moral issues), taking a year off and which college/job to pursue (both future-oriented matters), honor system and day off (exclusive peer-interactional issues), and jacket and marijuana (again, both peer issues, but requiring pragmatic information). In these data we see evidence of an "ordering of the adolescent world." Individuation appears to be exercised.

Our data reveal a discriminating adolescent who thinks about each issue and seeks out the group who appears most pertinent to the specific issue. Table 5.16 shows the total numbers of significant differences in adolescent attribution of influence among the three important reference groups, dependent on topic. The data reflect the ability of the adolescent

TABLE 5.14. Significant Differences in Influence of Older Siblings among 11 Issues.

	Haircut	Year off	Honor system	Jacket	Marijuana	Live together	Qualities	Day off	Job/college	Most matters
Capital punishment	−.02*	−.001	−.05	−.001	−.001	−.01	−.001	.01	−.001	−.001
Haircut		NS	NS	−.01	NS	NS	NS	.001	NS	−.05
Year off			NS	NS	NS	NS	NS	.001	NS	NS
Honor system				−.01	NS	NS	NS	.001	NS	NS
Jacket					.05	.01	.02	.001	NS	NS
Marijuana						NS	NS	.001	NS	NS
Live together							NS	.001	NS	NS
Qualities								.001	NS	NS
Day off									−.001	−.001
Job/college										NS

*Minus (−) indicates column issue has less influence than row issue.

$N = 732$

TABLE 5.15. Significant Differences in Influence of Schoolmates among 11 Issues.

	Haircut	Year off	Honor system	Jacket	Marijuana	Live together	Qualities	Day off	Job/college	Most matters
Capital punishment	-.001*	.02	-.001	-.001	-.001	NS	-.01	-.001	.001	.02
Haircut		.001	-.001	NS	NS	.001	.001	-.001	.001	.001
Year off			-.001	-.001	-.001	-.05	-.001	-.001	NS	-.001
Honor system				.001	.001	.001	.001	NS	.001	.001
Jacket					NS	.001	.001	-.001	.001	.001
Marijuana						.001	.001	-.001	.001	.001
Live together							-.01	-.001	.001	-.02
Qualities								.001	.001	NS
Day off									.001	.001
Job/college										-.001

*Minus (−) indicates column issue has less influence than row issue.

$N = 732$

**TABLE 5.16. Numbers of Statistically Significant Differences
Between Issues According to Reference Group.**

Reference group	Statistically significant	Statistically nonsignificant
Parents	46	9
Siblings	25	30
Schoolmates of same age	48	7

to mentally refine the essence of the issue. Parents and schoolmates of the same age are utilized with considerable variation. This behavior exhibits a discriminative advance over childhood. An interesting implication from the data is that parents and schoolmates of the same age are better known to the adolescent than are older siblings, and this familiarity allows them to be utilized more flexibly. The older sibling is more remote in age than schoolmates. They are less accessible than parents since they are busy with their own lives and often quickly "dispense" advice. Hence, while they assume a strong psychological importance, the more blocklike pattern with which they are consulted implies less flexible use.

The question of whether there was a difference in the manner in which peers were sought out was examined next: schoolmates were compared to special friends and to neighborhood agemates. Were these groups sought out for the same matters?

Findings revealed more differences than similarity. Table 5.17 displays findings on schoolmates of the same age and neighborhood agemates. Statistically significant differences were revealed on *all* ten issues and on the "most matters" issue. There were *no* topics where influence was accorded similarly. Adolescents make a clear distinction between the two groups in terms of expertise and/or relevance. Findings on "honor system" reveal this attitude most dramatically; clearly, only schoolmates were seen as relevant.

A different pattern was revealed between schoolmates and special friends. A greater cognitive association is apparent than between schoolmates and neighborhood friends. Together they account for 22.28% of influence accorded to all reference groups, a figure 7% short of the amount of influence attributed to parents. Six issues revealed no significant difference: capital punishment, haircut, year off, qualities, day off, and job/college. Four issues (honor system, jacket, marijuana, and living together) were significantly different. Influence of schoolmates was significantly higher on honor system, where to shop for a jack-

TABLE 5.17. Significance of Differences in Influence Accorded
Pairs of Reference Groups According to Issue.

Issue	Schoolmates vs. neighbors same age	Schoolmates vs. special friend	Special friend vs. friends 2–5 years older	Schoolmates vs. friends 2–5 years older
Capital punishment	.01	NS	NS	.02
Haircut	.001	NS	.001	.001
Year off	.001	NS	NS	NS
Honor system	.001	.001	.001	.001
Jacket	.001	.001	.01	.001
Marijuana	.001	.001	NS	.001
Live together	.001	.001*	.001	NS
Qualities	.001	NS	.001	.001
Day off	.001	NS	.001	.001
Job/college	.01	NS	NS	NS
Most matters	.01	.001*	.001	.001
Grand mean	.001	.001	.001	.001

*Bottom reference group accorded more influence than top reference group.
N = 732

et, and marijuana legalization. But on whether individuals should live together before marriage, the special friend was accorded significantly more influence. This finding reflects the beginnings of intimacy with another and identification of "one-to-one" topics.

Inasmuch as having a special friend implies a more advanced and perhaps a future-related maturational level, we performed t-tests to examine how special friends and friends two to five years older were accorded influence on the 10 issues. Findings revealed that special friends were consulted significantly more on 6 of the 10 topics. What is of interest, however, is that two of the areas of no significant difference were indeed future-related (year off and job/college). (The other two were legal/moral matters, marijuana and capital punishment.) But on matters of daily relevance and personal morals, the two groups were consulted in significantly different amounts. These data reflect adolescents *in process* of maturing. Special friend may represent a transitional group from the peer group to a social arena of greater age variation.

The data comparing schoolmates and friends two to five years older offer an interesting footnote as to the powerful status of the schoolmate. Statistically significant differences in influence accorded occurred on 7 of the 10 issues. Two of the three issues where there were no statistically significant differences matched those for the comparison between special friends and friends two to five years older—year off and job/college. That schoolmates are accorded similar status as friends two to five years older on future-oriented issues is fascinating. Schoolmates' views appear to be as important as the views of those who may have "been there." Alternatively, this may represent a desire to check the accuracy of advice and opinions of agemates by comparing them with those of older friends. If so, information is thus gained that sheds light on the validity of views of the school peer. Their position may be enhanced if views are in concert with those of an "older, wiser" peer. If not, the adolescent may continue to further evaluate the schoolmate and readjust prior perceptions of schoolmate and, perhaps, of self. This is an example of the continuing action of the growth dynamics of the adolescent dialectic and the changes in perceptions and evaluations that are part of the process.

Clues to Developmental Progressions

The degree and manner in which the adolescent generally utilizes influence sources affords one avenue of appraising the cognitive developmental level of the adolescent. If the adolescent can compartmentalize a reference field and utilize it functionally for information and guidance, we are able to conclude that the processes of cognitive and emotional differentiation are progressing properly and that developmental integrations are occurring. This is very different from the child or very young adolescent who uses reference sources globally. The Adolescent Reference Group Index (ARGI) is an instrument to be used to access reference group information. It can be used in diagnosis and treatment planning. *Which* reference groups are selected, for *what* purposes, and *when* these selections take place offer diagnostic information about the adolescent's point and process of development. As a simple example, in early adolescence we expect emphasis on easily accessible peers and few reference sources beyond parents and relatives. Later in development, we expect a more differentiated use of peers and assume that the adolescent will reach into reference sources of the adult arena.

PARENTS AND PEERS: COMPLEMENTARY SPHERES

Although peers are very important on many matters, how to pursue a career or make a living is clearly an issue where the parent is considered expert. In fact, the data revealed that schoolmates (the third most influential group) were barely consulted on questions of job/college and whether to take a year off. Here parental influence was high.

How influence was accorded on qualities to look for in a person is of interest. Although parents were accorded significantly more influence on qualities than on the "peer issues" (honor system, jacket, marijuana, and day off), they were accorded significantly less influence on qualities than they were on the future-oriented issues (year off and job/college). Since no significant differences were revealed between qualities, capital punishment, and haircut, we are led to believe that "qualities" is seen as a combination peer-adult matter. One might ask why "haircut" is treated as neutral between parents and peers whereas where to buy a jacket appears to be a peer issue. First, shopping for clothes and making decisions about what to buy and how much to spend smacks of adulthood and independence. Attention to a changing body form is involved, and the manner in which that body form is displayed appears crucial. Second, clothing the body in a manner that does not deviate too much from the norm allows one to meld into the adolescent groups. Outward similarity serves as a protective mechanism allowing greater comfort with a new body experience. "Being like everyone else" is a form of security in this time of rapid change; hence the importance of peer guidance on what is preferable. Thus, style of dress serves twin functions. On the one hand, the adolescent clothes a changing body in a manner that adheres to group standards and brings comfortable similarity, if not praise. It says "I am part of this group." On the other hand, selecting one's clothes in consultation with peers is an outward display of independence from parents and maturation.[*] Shopping offers a rationale for venturing into new physical locations and interacting *as equals* with shopkeepers, clerks, etc. Hairstyle may be seen as more temporary and mutable than style of dress.

---

[*]See Chapter 6 for findings on clothes and maturity—two characteristics of high interest to adolescents.

Shopping carries different functions and purposes for adolescents than it does for other age groups, offering important opportunities that contribute to the course of social development. Hence, the outward rationale for shopping at a specific location is often difficult for generational others such as parents to understand. Logically, it may make no sense—the prices may be out of line, the merchandise may be of a poor quality, etc. It is helpful to the adult dealing with the adolescent to *always* bear in mind deep-structure motivation. A specific shop may provide the opportunity to try out a new and desired personality characteristic in a setting that is anonymous and safe, to act out a fantasy, to try out a new role, to experiment with how slow or fast money can be spent, etc. Depending on the developmental age of the adolescent, shopping may serve any number of different functions. Guidance from peers is helpful in determining where to go and how to negotiate these new experiences.

In sum, the data point to honor system, jacket purchase, marijuana legalization, and what to do with a day off as "peer issues." "Parent issues" are what college/job to look for and whether to take a year off before starting a serious job or college. Four issues cut across the peer/parent dichotomy: capital punishment, haircut, qualities to look for in a person, and whether to live together before marriage.

MALE-FEMALE DIFFERENCES

Males and females differ in the rate and course of biological development, which has implications for the rate and course of social development. Thus, we looked at whether male-female differences were present in the manner in which adolescents utilized the greater reference group field.

We looked at whether gender makes a difference in how influence is accorded the 13 reference groups irrespective of issue. A t-test analysis on the sample of 732 compared grand means of influence attributed by males to each of the 13 reference groups over all 10 issues with the grand mean attributions of females. Findings (see Table 5.18) revealed considerable difference between the sexes. Significant differences existed in the amounts of influence accorded 11 reference groups; only 2 reference groups were revealed to have no significant differences: friends two to five years older and school personnel, both mild influence sources. Most interesting is the direction the differences took. Males attributed

significantly more influence than did females to younger brothers and
sisters, friends two to five years younger, clergy, neighbors of the same
age, parents, and older relatives. Females attributed significantly more
influence than did males to older brothers and sisters, friends more
than five years older, media, schoolmates of the same age, and special
friend. Females turned more to older near peers, older siblings, and
older friends and less to parents and older relatives than did males.
The special friend may be older, too, but nonetheless represents a more
intimate than casual relationship. Boys sought out more counsel from
parents and older relatives *and* younger siblings and younger friends. The
finding that females substitute older contemporaries for family members
lends empirical support to the notion that females mature emotionally at
a more rapid rate than males.

We then analyzed the data to examine how each sex attributed influence to each of the 13 reference groups. We carried out 78 t-tests on
paired influence sources for a sample of 564 males and a second sample
of 168 females. Females were in grades 9–12 in Long Island, New York.
Males were drawn from grades 9–12 in Long Island and Philadelphia.
Findings revealed that neither sex used block attribution. For both males

TABLE 5.18. Significance of Difference in Influence Attribution
to 13 Reference Groups According to Sex.

Reference groups	t*	Significance	Higher usage
Older brothers/sisters	−3.65	.001	F
Younger brothers/sisters	5.67	.001	M
Friends 2–5 years younger	7.24	.001	M
Friends 2–5 years older	−0.09	NS	—
Friends +5 years older	−3.02	.01	F
Media	−2.35	.02	F
Clergy	6.54	.001	M
Neighbors same age	23.77	.001	M
Parents	2.95	.01	M
Older relatives	8.12	.001	M
Schoolmates same age	−10.73	.001	F
School personnel	1.85	NS	—
Special friend	−7.22	.001	F

*Positive value indicates males attributed more influence than did females.
N = 732 (564 males, 168 females)

and females there were 73 instances of significant differences and 5 instances of no significant differences. However, in no instance was a pair of influences showing insignificant difference the same for males and females.

Reference groups to whom males never attributed the same amount of influence as they did to a second reference group were: older siblings, younger siblings, friends two to five years younger, friends over five years older, neighborhood friends of the same age, schoolmates of the same age, parents, and special friend. The five pairs of reference groups to whom the amount of influence accorded was similar were:

1. Friends two to five years older and school personnel
2. Media and clergy
3. Media and older relatives
4. Clergy and older relatives
5. Clergy and school personnel

Influence was accorded in similar amounts by women to the following pairs:

1. Friends two to five years older and media
2. Friends over five years older and older relatives
3. Friends over five years older and school personnel
4. Media and school personnel
5. Neighborhood friends and clergy

Seven reference groups were included in these pairs. Five were the same as for the males: friends two to five years older, school personnel, older relatives, media, and clergy. There was no similarity between sexes in which pairs of groups showed the similarity. What the data reveal is a general similarity with specific gender differences.

The most striking finding, however, is that of no attribution of block influence by either sex. Each sample emerged as precise in how they discriminated which reference groups they would seek out to help them in their decision-making. Gender made no difference. Thus, we assume no real difference in level of psychosocial awareness.

THE INFLUENCE OF PARENTS AND OLDER SIBLINGS ON THE GROWING ADOLESCENT

Does the perception of whom to consult change as the adolescent grows and his world becomes larger? The high school years, generally considered to be the middle period of adolescence, continues to be a period of considerable change. We examined the data from each of the grades 9 to 12 in the high schools located in Long Island, New York, to determine if age made a difference in reference group preferences.

T-tests were carried out between grand mean percentages of influence on students in grades 9 and 10, 10 and 11, and 9 and 11. Findings revealed no significant differences between any two grades in amount of influence accorded groups of little influence (younger people, older relatives, and school personnel) and a peer group of considerable influence, schoolmates of the same age. The fewest significant differences were found between grades 10 and 11 (see Table 5.19). We hypothesized incremental movement *away from parents* to other groups with age. Findings displayed in Table 5.20 reveal that students in the 9th grade sought out parental input as a reference group more than students in the 10th, 11th, and 12th grades. No significant differences in parental consultation were found between grades 10 and 11. A significant difference in consultation with parents did occur between grades 11 and 12, with those in the 11th grade seeking them out more. But, interestingly, there were no significant differences between grades 10 and 12. The interruption in the trend of decreasing influence of parents in the 11th grade coincides with the time students begin serious decision-making, pick out job possibilities or colleges to attend, and begin application procedures. Parents are generally involved in these activities. Hence, this finding may represent a temporary reversal of what appears to be a lessening of dependence on parents beginning somewhere around the start of the 10th grade—usually age 15—and leveling off during the high school years.

Findings on use of older siblings (see Table 5.20) reveal no significant difference in the extent of their consultation between grades 9 and 11, 9 and 12, and 10 and 12. However, significant differences are present between grades 9 and 10, with 9th-graders using siblings more; between grades 10 and 11, with 11th-graders using them more; and between 11 and 12, with 11th-graders using them more. The pattern resembles that of parent use. Together the findings point to 10th grade as movement

TABLE 5.19. Significant Differences in Influence
Accorded Reference Groups by Grade.

	9 and 10		10 and 11		9 and 11	
	t	Significance	t	Significance	t	Significance
Older brothers/sisters	3.95	.001	−5.16*	−.001		
Younger brothers/sisters						
Friends 2–5 years younger						
Friends 2–5 years older					−2.00	−.05
Friends + 5 years older	−3.42	−.001			−4.12	−.001
Media	−2.03	−.05				
Clergy			−3.95	−.001	−4.09	−.001
Neighbors same age	−2.49	−.02	−2.11	−.05		
Parents	5.06	.001			3.93	.001
Relatives						
Schoolmates same age						
School personnel						
Special friend	−2.77	−.01			−2.32	−.02

*Minus indicates reference group was less influential on lower grade
N = 70, grade 9
N = 55, grade 10
N = 51, grade 11

away from family, to 11th grade as interruption of the trend of moving out from family members by what well may be external factors, and to 12th grade as resumption of the trend.

Findings from the analysis of significant differences in utilization of the various reference groups revealed an unexpected similarity between grades 9 and 11. In the groups consulted very little (younger individuals, older relatives, and school personnel) and in the second most influential group (schoolmates of the same age), there are no significant differences revealed according to grade. On the other hand, as the adolescent grows older, the special friend is consulted more while parents are consulted less, with what appears a temporary deviation between grades 10 and 11.

COMMENT ON HELPERS IN THE ADOLESCENT PROCESS

These data disclosing the various reference sources the adolescent actively utilizes support theoretical notions that the adolescent commutes between past, present, and future. There are periods of disorganiza-

TABLE 5.20. Significant Differences in Influence Accorded Parents and Older Siblings According to Grade.

	9 and 10		10 and 11		9 and 11		9 and 12		10 and 12		11 and 12	
	t	Significance	t	Significance	t	Significance	t	Significance	t	Significance	t	Significance
Parents	5.06	.001	−1.55*	NS	3.93	.001	5.44	.001	0.84	NS	2.49	.02
Older Siblings	3.95	.001	−5.16	−.001	−0.97	NS	1.88	NS	−1.73	NS	2.94	.01

*Minus indicates reference group was less influential on lower grade

N = 219 (70, grade 9; 55, grade 10; 51, grade 11; 43, grade 12)

tion and of integration. Adolescents' functioning encompasses externally based task completion and internally driven developmental directives, and we often witness the frustration experienced by the adolescent who is trying to explain motivation for behavior, to explain to others what is not cognitively clear to himself. Internally driven developmental imperatives are subliminal, not explicit and identifiable.

The developmental imperative to be close to agemates as much as possible makes it difficult for the adolescent to engage only with generational others. Developmental work needs to be done with agemates. "Who I am" in gender and in work must be hammered out; specific dimensions of personality and identity need to be developed, tried out, and rejected or accepted. For those accepted, the next job is to psychologically cluster specific characteristics with other attributes. Then these new clusters are to be integrated with others to yield a definable self. This takes considerable time. Although the adolescent is eager to leave childhood behind, at times unexpected behaviors may reflect regression to expression of childish needs. Nonetheless, the necessity to cope with the present cannot be escaped, and each day brings subtle changes in physical experiences, intellectual comprehension, and emotional lessons. In the beginning, peers supply most data. After some initial integrations take place and are refined, peer dominance recedes, and we see other reference groups being more aggressively sought out.

The primacy of "today" for adolescents is seen in the findings on discrete peer issues, where there was evidence of little call for the input of generational others. At the same time the data reveal that parents are the top-ranking single reference source and that there are issues where parents are heavily influential. While adolescents are expending enormous energies to carry out daily responsibilities (school, homework, part-time jobs, family membership, chores) and simultaneously meeting the continuous demands of subliminal developmental work (acts of comparison that necessitate spending time with peers in person or on the phone, keeping up with media, etc. and cognitively processing the results of these interactions), parental help in carrying the load of economic and future concerns appears essential. The pragmatic reason is clear; but there is also a dynamic reason.

The dynamic reason proceeds from a condition of "developmental overload." Adolescents deal with overt *and* subliminal functioning *and* effects of their interaction. Thus, adolescents must respond to (1) cognitive directives, intellectually reasoned out, and (2) emotional and physical developmental imperatives. Meanwhile, demands of daily functioning cannot be allocated to others. Information getting on both cognitive and affective bases must proceed. The developmental dynamics of growth can only be met by the adolescent himself; it cannot be "contracted out."

For a time, however, future-oriented needs may be delegable to outsiders. Parents are generally available as willing participants, eager to be involved in their child's planning. Furthermore, since the developmental requisites are in great part clearly informational, the adolescent can tolerate some dependent status. The mature perception of self, which adolescents strive for and resent not having acknowledged publicly, is not as likely to be threatened by future-oriented discussions with parents. Everyday matters necessitate interacting with agemates to assure that behaviors and attributes conform to peer group standards on what to wear; where to go for fun; whether or not to smoke, drink, or take drugs; or how to deal with parents. The data have revealed these matters as discrete peer areas that apparently reinforce the individual's conceptions of independence.

A VULNERABLE TIME

Deliberate attribution of influence to carefully selected reference groups for specific ego purposes lends support to our picture of adolescence as a very sensitive period of life when, despite enormous energies and outward bravado, youths are quite vulnerable. Essentially they exist *in process of* constructing a sense of self, which, once achieved, will afford them a personal anchor in the shifting sands of a complicated society. Stimuli of every variety are subject to interpretation within a developmental perspective; each experience is seen as potentially representing a part of "the real me." During this development period, clearly the individual does not manifest stability. Once true identity has been worked through, the self withstands both intrusive and intriguing stimuli and remains stable. However, before psychosocial maturity is achieved, the individual is very easily influenced; the anchor of identity is not yet formed.

These data afford clear evidence that adolescents seek out opinions and information from reference groups and figures well beyond parents and peers. They reveal discriminating use of reference groups specific to issue, not global preferences for certain groups. Parents, peers, and other groups serve an array of developmental needs. These data support notions that peers are environmental figures of the *present*. Parents take care of present support needs to lighten the load of their offspring's *future* concerns, aiding adolescents in conserving strength for work on the physical, emotional, intellectual, and social realms of development.

The Adolescent Reference Group Index findings strongly support the view that in the course of their development, adolescents do incrementally understand and take in the complex nature of the society they are preparing to enter. Depending on idiosyncratic developmental status, youth of the same age differ in their comprehension of the tasks ahead, the extent of the responsibilities involved, and their preparation. But for all, in some manner, by middle/late adolescence the future encroaches on the present. The assembly of a sufficient number of self elements into a temporary self structure may be gradual or abrupt. Along the way, adolescents utilize the various reference groups flexibly and idiosyncratically to expand their information base as they learn through trial and error to arrive at decisions.

Although the findings of these studies reveal parents to be the single most influential reference group, the influence of peers as a cluster exceeds that of parents. Clearly, adolescents are very interested in one another. The next chapter will provide further details on what it is about agemates that interests other adolescents. These findings will also be connected to the developmental meaning of adolescent preferences and behaviors.

CHAPTER 6

Allure of the Adolescent Peer: Attributes of Relevance

An adolescent society with its own mores and customs is reflected in various forms in the media, in clothing styles, in language, in music, and in choice of recreation (prosocial and antisocial behaviors). We have reviewed the variety of reference groups that make up the influence world of the adolescent. Although parents appear to be the single most influential group, as a cluster adolescent peers emerge as very strong in influence, overtaking parents in a number of areas— and in specific areas even overtaking the family cluster of parents and siblings (see Chapter 5). That adolescents are interested in being together is evident.

As the individual leaves childhood and enters adolescence, he or she begins a dramatic incremental expansion of cognitive, physical, emotional, and social abilities. With maturation, there is a steady decrease in egocentrism. Others coexisting in the world become increasingly significant as does a sense of relative roles. Early adolescents crave the company of others in the same stage. We have emphasized the strong need of adolescents to be in a group, where they can observe the variety of characteristics, opinions, and abilities of others perceived as like themselves.

If a characteristic appears positive, the next step for the adolescent is to test it. Does he or she possess the characteristic or a variant? What is the market value? Adolescents are very pragmatic when it comes to the serious business of developing functional persona. The high degree of pragmatism may appear inconsistent with the outward picture of a casual adolescent. It is compatible, however, with the goal-directed, precision choices disclosed by the reference group data.

This chapter will discuss findings from an empirical study investigating what adolescents look for as they examine their peers.

THE ATTRIBUTE STUDY

The attribute study was part of a larger inquiry into the process of adolescent construction of a sense of identity. The Attribute Interest Form was developed and administered to 1,100 adolescents in various locations to determine how closely adolescents observe one another's characteristics and skills. Our hypothesis that there would be a great deal of interest in one another was based on the theoretical assumption that studying peers is a developmental need. Their examination of one another is carried out in a series of deep-structure, semiconscious comparative acts in which they select and sift traits to be acquired or discarded. Hence, we hypothesized that (1) curiosity is keen and extensive and (2) the atmosphere of peer interaction is one of reciprocal examination of characteristics and abilities.

The 67 attributes selected were a product of pilot-testing adolescents of both sexes of high school age in the greater Philadelphia area. The attributes were listed randomly and covered five categories: physical traits, talents, learned skills, character traits, and family perceptions. Four empty lines were included for the individual to add characteristics not listed on the form.

The total sample was composed of two subsamples of adolescents in grades 9–12 from the Midwest and the East. Included were 338 males and 357 females from public high schools in Canton, Ohio. This student body was 74% white and 24% black; the remainder were of Asian descent. The majority were Christian, primarily Protestant, with a small representation of other major religions. They were from middle- and working-class backgrounds. Also included were 405 males from an all-male Catholic high school in Philadelphia; they were primarily middle-class with business, professional, and working-class backgrounds represented. For the Canton sample, questionnaires were administered in study halls throughout the day. The Philadelphia students filled out the questionnaires in homeroom periods. The subjects were asked to read over the list of 67 attributes and rate each one as to the frequency with which it is noticed in agemates. The range of frequency included "always," "usually," "sometimes," "hardly ever," and "never." The prediction that adolescents would "always" or "usually" notice at least 70% of the 67 attributes was supported.

The findings in the tables to follow were developed from various stages of the research and thus reflect either specific subsamples or the grand total of 1,100 individuals participating (743 males and 357 females). Tables indicating $n = 695$ report findings of the balanced-gender sample from the Canton, Ohio, public schools (338 males, 357 females). Later in the study we collected data on the male students in Philadelphia. The tables noting $n = 405$ show these findings. $n = 357$ represents female-only findings; $n = 743$ represents total male-only findings. Due to unanticipated loss of some data from the Canton male sample, gender comparisons are based on Canton females ($n = 357$) and Philadelphia males ($n = 405$). All studies were carried out between 1983 and 1985.

ATTRIBUTES OF HIGH INTEREST

The Power of the Observable

Findings are displayed according to attribute and frequency. The 10 top-ranked attributes in the "always" category (see Table 6.1) reveal primary interest in appearance and sex appeal. Five of the top 10 ranks reflect a high degree of interest in how agemates look and how they are received by the opposite sex. Implied is a keen awareness of evolving gender roles. The data also reveal the high importance of matters of

TABLE 6.1. Top 10 Attributes "Always" of Interest.

Attribute	Percent of students	Rank
Cleanliness	59.7	1
Loyalty to friends	49.6	2
Clothes	48.4	3
Dependability	42.7	4
Trustworthiness	42.6	5
General physical appearance	42.5	6
Maturity	40.9	7
Popularity with opposite sex	40.8	8
Figure/build/physique	38.6	9
Honesty	37.7	10

$N = 695$

character and a low interest in skills and abilities. Ranks 1 and 2 went to cleanliness (59.7%) and loyalty to friends (49.6%). The power of cleanliness was unexpected. Rank 3 was accorded to clothes (48.4%). Whereas the interest in clothes could be attributed to conformity needs, concern with both clothes and cleanliness may be additional indicators of a keen awareness of a changing body and of the degree of interest adolescents have in the physical attributes of their peers.

Four of the 10 top-ranked characteristics reflect outward appearance. Outward appearance offers information about social class, imaginativeness, individualism, conformity, noncomformity, political philosophy, etc. Furthermore, outward appearance reveals physical maturation and sex appeal. Close appraisal of physical attributes of an "other" indicates the need for a model to either imitate or differ from, a decision influenced by how the group is perceived to value the particular attributes. Adolescents swiftly and intuitively assimilate the impact of an individual's attributes on group members. Also, close observation of outward appearance is important if one is to adopt similar styles. Thus, the degree of attention paid to the "outwardly observable" is not for entertainment or diversion. It is for the identification of the range of possible behaviors functional to meeting two very strong needs—conformity and experimentation.

The Prominence of the Unobservable

The remaining characteristics ranked in the top 10 are not outwardly observable. Loyalty to friends, honesty, dependability, and trustworthiness become apparent over time, as does maturity. Maturity represents the end goal of adolescent development. Adolescents strive to be "older." When maturity is manifested in a peer, it offers comfort and example. Comfort is gained by the recognition that a "fellow traveler" has bridged the gap. The maturity they model is also instructive.

The adolescent world of today is generally different from the world of yesterday because of one's own change or that of another. New understandings and talents obviate conclusions of yesterday or lead to reacceptance of conclusions previously discarded. The cycle of change, rejection of the old, and integration of the new makes adolescence an unstable posture, a "no man's land" (Lewin, 1951). It makes sense that the adolescent looks for *dependability* in agemates. Finding agemates who are dependable (1) tempers psychological uncertainties through demonstration that someone who shares the same status can become stable and (2) offers models to identify with and imitate. There is a third factor that should also be kept in mind. Dependability observed in others offers the adolescent some respite. The adolescent is called upon to adjust not only to his own changes, but to the developmental swings of others. Growth changes in peers can be interpreted as lack of dependability. The individual's own vicissitudes contribute to experiencing changeability in peers as particularly painful.

The data revealed *trustworthiness* as ranking high. It is a corollary interest to dependability. Adolescents' transitional status robs them of their former supports—their parents. Hence, they are attracted to attributes in others that, by association, help fill this gap. Trustworthiness translates into "I will not forsake you or your confidences." Adolescents feel very deeply. They are very much in the present and in the presence of the specific emotion: fear, disappointment, envy, hurt, anger, love, etc. Sharing these feelings and sharing new dreams and aspirations that grow out of newly developed capacities entails considerable interpersonal risk. In later adolescence, trustworthiness continues to be important but has different emphasis. The task changes from maintaining stability of self to risking intimate revelations.

Honesty and *loyalty to friends* also apply to what adolescents seek during this period of transition and relative instability. Adolescents' experimentation with their own changing perspectives is often reflected in inconsistency, which can appear to the agemate as dishonesty. As family ties are incrementally reduced in service of independence seeking, resources for invariable "straight talk" diminish. Hence, because of the status of "changing" they all share, honesty in agemates is vitally needed to fill the gap created by the combination of stage-related conditions: the need to distance oneself from family and the sense of betrayal brought on by inconsistencies interpreted as dishonesty. Accordingly, the premium placed on loyalty in friends once more speaks to the need for solid support from peers.

Stage-Related Traits

The importance of each trait to the adolescent varies according to the point of the adolescent's developmental progression; different characteristics are important at different periods. Conformity needs surface first, to be replaced by traits of a more interpersonal character, leading to intimacy. Adolescents, during the early period particularly, use specified friends as "stand-ins" within their own cognitive self structure to represent a desired characteristic they themselves do not possess. They borrow it, unconsciously, from their friends to try it out. Borrowing also means temporary possession of the characteristics, which brings a good feeling and is stabilizing.

For example, a rather unattractive individual may "borrow" the characteristic of beauty from a beautiful friend. (It is very important to be physically near to this friend in order to feel the presence of the characteristic). This unconscious borrowing helps the individual to handle a sense of insecurity about appearance while she continues to compare with other peers as necessary to assess her own relative position on the characteristic. If this evaluation makes the adolescent more comfortable with her own appearance, some insecurity relative to this attribute is lifted. Then borrowing for temporary stability becomes unnecessary, and maintaining the friendship becomes less crucial. If the outcome is disappointing, the need for this element may be devalued, or the element may be regarded as unattainable. This same dynamic process is utilized by adolescents on a myriad of elements, each with different outcomes. In sum, borrowing an element permits a temporary stability while the adolescent determines whether she is strong or weak on the attribute; afterward she will decide to keep or eliminate it as part of her self-picture.

TABLE 6.2. Top 10 Attributes "Always" of Interest to Adolescent Males.

Attribute	Percent of students	Rank
Athletic ability	45.3	1
Popularity with opposite sex	42.7	2
Maturity	39.6	3
Clothes	38.7	4
General physical appearance	37.8	5
Stubbornness	35.5	6
Father's occupation	34.1	7
Impatience	32.8	8
Figure/build/physique	32.5	9
Dependability	32.4	10

$N = 405$

Elimination of a facsimile self element is deeply felt since it offers a stabilizing force from outside to balance a tenuous stability within.

The Opposite Sex

Data from separate analyses of males and females provide interesting gender differences. Data on "always of interest" disclose that males (Table 6.2) ranked popularity with the opposite sex as surpassed only by athletic ability. Females gave popularity with opposite sex 10th rank. (Table 6.3). Several factors may be contributory, including (1) sex differences in intensity of sexual feelings, (2) an increased interest of male students of a sexually segregated school in the opposite sex over those individuals who interact with the opposite sex every school day, and (3) female concern with interpersonal character and friendship issues.

Always/Usually

In order to determine how combining the high- interest categories affects the power of an attribute, we clustered the "always" and "usually" categories for analysis (Table 6.4) Findings revealed little change. Nine of the top 10 attributes "always of interest" remained in the top 10 (see Tables 6.1 and 6.4). Figure/build/physique was displaced by complexion (at rank 10). Interestingly, the top 10 reflect sharpest attention distributed between biology and behavior. Five were character attributes, four were

TABLE 6.3. Top 10 Attributes "Always" of Interest to Adolescent Females.

Attribute	Percent of students	Rank
Cleanliness	59.4	1
Clothes	53.7	2
Loyalty to friends	52.6	3
General physical appearance	50.1	4
Trustworthiness	46.4	5
Dependability	44.5	6
Figure/build/physique	43.2	7
Maturity	42.7	8
Sensitivity to others' feelings	41.3	9
Popularity with opposite sex	39.4	10

$N = 357$

TABLE 6.4. Top 10 Attributes "Always/Usually" of Interest to Adolescents.

Attribute	Percent of students	Rank
Loyalty to friends	79.0	1
Cleanliness	77.3	2
Clothes	77.1	3
Trustworthiness	73.8	4
General physical appearance	72.9	5
Honesty	71.9	6
Dependability	71.6	7
Maturity	70.9	8
Popularity with opposite sex	70.5	9
Complexion	65.2	10

$N = 695$

outwardly observable physical attributes, and one was a social skill. Interest in abilities did not realize these high ranks.

ATTRIBUTES OF LITTLE INTEREST

At the other end of the continuum are attributes that attracted little interest. Lack of interest in specific attributes of peers tells us as much about norms as does a high degree of interest. Hence, we looked at which characteristics/skills adolescents rarely noticed when they first encounter one another. Attributes in the "never of interest" category were most often acquired abilities. Musical ability topped the list (48.3%). Acting, typing, and mechanical skills ranked 2, 3, and 4, respectively. Femininity ranked 8 (see Table 6.5).

The small amount of interest in femininity may appear in conflict with the high interest in popularity with the opposite sex. The data imply that the two are unrelated. It may be that the strength of popularity with the opposite sex is due to the prominence of this social skill in the adolescent's portraying himself as handling his emerging sexuality comfortably. In early/middle adolescence, interest in popularity with the other sex may be more related to assessment of self-functioning than to interest in another.

Table 6.6 presents data showing that the lowest percentages in the "never of interest" category were for some of the attributes that emerged

TABLE 6.5. Top 10 Attributes "Never" of Interest to Adolescents.

Attribute	Percent of students	Rank
Musical ability (instrument)	48.3	1
Drama/acting	41.7	2
Typing skills	40.9	3
Mechanical ability	36.7	4
Cheapness	36.6	5
Snobbiness	36.5	6
Prejudice	33.3	7
Femininity	32.8	8
Mother's occupation	32.2	9
Father's occupation	29.1	10

$N = 695$

as being of greatest interest. The data reveal just how high interest in one another's attire is. Only 2.9% of students never looked at clothes, which means that 97.1% did with varying frequency. Eight of the remaining attributes in Table 6.6 involve personality and character. The 10th is school work ability.

These data demonstrate that characteristics that are seen as universally relevant were least ignored (e.g., clothes, school work ability). More idiosyncratic attributes (e.g., musical ability, typing skills) were of minor interest. Yet what is stunning is that *no* attribute received zero attention. On the other hand, no attribute escaped never being noticed. Table 6.7 displays the highest and lowest percentages of students for each interest

TABLE 6.6. Lowest 10 Attributes "Never" of Interest.

Attribute	Percent of students	Rank
Clothes	2.9	1
Honesty	3.2	2
Loyalty to friends	3.4	3
School work ability	3.5	4.5
Sense of humor	3.5	4.5
Dependability	3.8	6
Friendliness	4.5	8.5
Maturity	4.5	8.5
Niceness	4.5	8.5
Trustworthiness	4.5	8.5

$N = 695$

TABLE 6.7. Highest and Lowest Percentages of Each Interest Level.

Interest level	Highest	Lowest
Always	59.7 (Cleanliness)	5.1 (Cheapness)
Usually	40.4 (Friendliness)	6.1 (Snobbiness)
Sometimes	41.7 (Impatience)	11.7 (Cleanliness)
Almost Never	26.8 (Selfishness)	3.9 (Honesty)
Never	48.3 (Musical ability—instrument)	2.9 (Clothes)

$N = 695$

level as well as the respective attributes. The findings are consistent with the general psychosocial status of the stage. By the high school years, the adolescent has achieved sufficient cognitive abilities to be discerning and can conceptualize which attributes/skills are valued and which are not.

The data reveal a discriminating adolescent. Interest in which attributes are to be closely observed or ignored is reflexive in character—essentially self-related; how others perform is compared to self-performance. At any one moment, an adolescent may be concentrating on an attribute in a peer to decide whether to try to acquire it, or he may be evaluating the pros/cons of a particular talent or personality attribute already possessed to determine if the quality of the attribute compares favorably with that of a peer.

In sum, these data strongly reinforce the position that peers do provide data for comparative acts. Watching others carefully offers information that can be used as the adolescent sorts through and sifts out identity elements and determines their relevance to the immediate group. The response an "other" with specific attributes receives from agemates is particularly potent material that contributes in major proportion to decision-making regarding which attributes will be respected by the greater age cohort.

MALE-FEMALE DIFFERENCES

For an overall view of gender differences in examining characteristics of agemates, we analyzed data utilizing the total sample of 1,100. Findings revealed that females "always" or "usually" examined more attributes of agemates than did males (see Table 6.8). The data imply that more psychological time and energy are expended by females in

**TABLE 6.8. Percent of Attributes
"Always" and "Usually"
Examined, by Gender.**

	Always	*Usually*
Males	27	32
Females	40	35

N = 1,100
Note—Total Number of Attributes = 67

comparative acts then by males. Differences may be accounted for in part by: (1) more time spent by males in comparing specifics of the attributes of highest interest (e.g., athletic ability, macho behaviors, and risk taking) with less attention devoted to other attributes and (2) more rapid physical and socioemotional development of females, manifested in greater involvement with agemates. The findings revealing greater interest by females than by males in issues of character (see Table 6.9) support this notion. They suggest that female adolescents look to transfer intimacy and trust from parents and other family members and may be attempting to define the attributes involved. Considerable care and thought need to be given since risk is undertaken when peers are used for the emotional supports previously received from family.

We were interested in whether subtle sex differences existed in the level of interest accorded each of the attributes. Table 6.9 displays the findings of a comparison of mean differences between the sexes on combined levels "always" and "usually." The table also indicates the degree of the sex difference on each attribute. What stands out is higher male than female interest in outwardly observable attributes and less male interest in those of a socioemotional nature. Although females accorded a good deal of attention to abilities, they are not abilities of a public nature as are those emphasized by males (e.g., athletics and sportsmanship). On the whole, male interests appear to be objective and task-related and are not so much concerned with character attributes.

Table 6.10 displays specific percentages for the differences of less than 1% and 3%. A striking finding is that differences of less than 1% existed between the sexes on only two attributes—sense of humor and openness to new ideas. They both pertain to style of interpersonal relating. This finding reveals an advancing social sophistication apparently shared by both sexes. Six additional attributes differ by less than

3% between the sexes. Of interest here, and again surprising, is the high amount of interest of both sexes in mother's occupation. Does this finding suggest an impact of the womens' liberation movement on this generation of near-adults?

TABLE 6.9. Gender Differences in "Always"/ "Usually"
Level of Interest (Mean Percentage Differences)

Attribute	Gender showing higher interest
Friendliness	F
Sense of humor	ND
Leadership	M
Artistic talent	F†
Music ability (singing)	F
Music ability (instrument)	M*
Athletic ability	M
General school work ability	F*
Enthusiasm	F
Creative writing ability	F
Drama/acting ability	F*
Mechanical ability	M
Cooking	F
Typing	F
General physical appearance	F
Clothes	F
Figure/build/physique	F
Complexion	F
Popularity with same sex	F
Popularity with opposite sex	M*
Ability to put feelings into words	F
Ability to put thoughts into words	F
Knowledge of current events	M
Good listener	F
Sexiness	F
Sportsmanship	M
Generosity	M†
Masculinity	M
Femininity	F
Wealth (rich/poor)	M
Cleanliness	F
Laziness	F†
Impatience	M
Cattiness	F*
Selfishness	F*

TABLE 6.9. *(Cont.)*

Attribute	Gender showing higher interest
Religiousness	M†
Snobbiness	M
Cheapness	M
Type of family one comes from	M*
Studiousness	F
Cooperativeness	F
Self-confidence	F
Prejudice	M
Adventuresomeness	M
Mother's occupation	M†
Father occupation	M
Morals	M
Sensitivity to others' feelings	F
Car driving	M
Stubborness	M
Religion	M
Meanness	M
Niceness	F
Stick-to-it-iveness	M*
Attitude toward one's family	F*
Competitiveness	M
Maturity	F*
Creativity	F
Honesty	F
Loyalty to friends	F
Dancing ability	F
Determination	F
Trustworthiness	F
Dependability	F*
Patriotism	M†
Openness to new ideas	ND
Cliqueishness	F

ND = no difference (sexes differed by less than 1%)
†1–2.9% difference
*3–4.9% difference
N = 1,100

Interest in 19 of the 67 attributes differ by less than 5% between the two sexes. The higher differentials in the remaining 48 raise questions about the influence of socialization practices—and also about the impact of biology. Can it be that, notwithstanding the increasing opportunities

TABLE 6.10. Mean Percent of Interest According to Gender for Differences Less than 1% and 3%.

	< 1%		< 3%	
Attribute	Male	Female	Male	Female
Sense of humor	56.2	56.9		
Openness to new ideas	51.6	51.9		
Artistic talent			27.8	29.5
Generosity			59.5	58.0
Laziness			23.1	25.6
Religiousness			25.3	22.9
Mother's occupation			32.0	31.0
Patriotism			36.3	33.7

$N = 1,100$

and changing aspirational levels for women, there are universal sexual differences that remain stable over time?

DEVELOPMENTAL PERSPECTIVE

The question arises of whether degree of interest in the attributes of others rose or decreased with age. At this point in the study, we were able to analyze data collected from 1,100 students from grades 9–12 according to grade (67.5% male, 32.5% female). Values assigned to the various categories for purposes of analysis were: 1 = always, 2 = usually, 3 = sometimes, 4 = hardly ever, 5 = never. The median interest level for each of the 67 attributes was calculated by class, and the numbers of attributes are specified according to this median value. For example, the numbers under the median ranges 1–1.49 and 1.50–1.99 in Table 6.11 reflect the number of characteristics "always to usually" looked at by at least half of the students in the specific grade.

A review of Table 6.11 reveals that active "looking" continues through all grades. The "always," "usually," and upper-level "sometimes" categories received most attention (224 listings), and the lower-level "sometimes," and the "hardly ever" and "never" categories yielded 44 listings. The most utilized category across all grades was "usually," indicating that *by ninth grade* adolescents are very interested in one another's attributes.

TABLE 6.11. Number of Attributes Noticed According to Grade and Interest Level Median

Grade	Always		Usually		Sometimes		Hardly Ever		Never		Total number
	1–1.49	1.50–1.99	2–2.49	2.50–2.99	3–3.49	3.50–3.99	4–4.49	4.50–4.99	5–5.49	5.50–5.99	of attributes
9	0	4	14	20	13	11	3	2	0	0	67
		(4)**		(34)		(24)		(5)			
10	0	7	21	15	18	3	3	0	0	0	67
		(7)		(36)		(21)		(3)			
11	1	11	16	16	12	9	2	0	0	0	67
		(12)		(32)		(21)		(2)			
12	2	9	18	16	11	9	1	1	0	0	67
		(11)		(34)		(20)		(2)			
Sum	(3	31)	(69	67)	(54	32)	(9	3)	0	0	
	(	34)	(	136)	(	86)	(	12)			

**Sum for entire interest category

Grade 9: n = 207
Grade 10: n = 431
Grade 11: n = 200
Grade 12: n = 262

Median interest values on each attribute according to grade can be found in Table 6.12. Seven attributes are revealed to be of less interest to 12th-graders than to 9th-graders (based on a minimum 0.4 median increase): athletic ability, snobbiness, cheapness, prejudice, mother's

TABLE 6.12. Median Amount of Interest According to Grade.

	Grade			
Characteristic	9	10	11	12
1. Friendliness	2.29	2.21	2.09	2.28
2. Sense of humor	2.29	2.36	2.22	2.15
3. Leadership	2.66	2.79	2.84	2.83
4. Artistic talent	3.42	3.52	3.33	3.50
5. Musical ability (singing)	3.95	3.91	3.69	3.52
6. Musical ability (instrument)	4.54	4.38	4.39	4.60
7. Atheletic ability	1.65	2.01	2.09	2.62
8. General school work ability	2.16	2.24	2.13	2.08
9. Enthusiasm	2.69	2.41	2.42	2.63
10. Creative writing ability	3.40	3.35	3.02	3.24
11. Drama/acting ability	4.21	4.18	3.96	4.32
12. Mechanical ability	3.63	3.42	3.38	3.82
13. Cooking	3.45	3.01	2.76	3.06
14. Typing skills	4.12	4.32	4.11	3.82
15. General physical appearance	2.04	1.75	1.69	1.66
16. Clothes	1.94	1.70	1.60	1.38
17. Figure/build/physique	2.08	2.10	1.82	1.66
18. Complexion	2.49	2.27	1.99	1.75
19. Popularity with same sex	2.45	2.41	2.40	2.18
20. Popularity with opposite sex	1.88	1.79	1.67	1.75
21. Ability to put feelings into words	2.99	2.65	2.29	2.41
22. Ability to put thoughts into words	2.91	2.51	2.19	2.35
23. Knowledge of current events	2.77	2.72	2.74	2.82
24. Good listener	4.01	3.04	2.40	2.52
25. Sexiness	3.64	3.17	2.64	2.70
26. Sportsmanship	2.63	2.22	2.02	2.25
27. Generosity	2.74	2.14	2.03	2.23
28. Masculinity	3.11	3.22	2.89	2.42
29. Femininity	3.27	3.18	3.04	3.02
30. Wealth (rich/poor)	2.40	2.55	2.79	2.75
31. Cleanliness	2.06	1.60	1.33	1.40
32. Laziness	3.41	3.35	3.27	3.16
33. Impatience	2.42	2.63	2.98	2.81
34. Cattiness	3.69	3.39	3.64	3.42
35. Selfishness	3.63	3.78	3.57	3.51

TABLE 6.12. *(Cont.)*

Characteristic	9	10	11	12
		Grade		
36. Religiousness	3.59	3.41	3.64	3.35
37. Snobbiness	3.04	3.42	3.93	3.64
38. Cheapness	2.90	2.24	3.85	3.60
39. Type of family one comes from	3.57	2.69	3.13	2.74
40. Studiousness	3.54	3.03	3.06	2.84
41. Cooperativeness	3.55	2.76	2.49	2.33
42. Self-confidence	3.18	2.76	2.23	2.29
43. Prejudice	2.76	3.06	3.51	3.24
44. Adventurousness	2.71	2.63	2.57	2.59
45. Mother's occupation	3.11	3.22	3.50	3.62
46. Father's occupaton	2.34	2.42	3.02	3.22
47. Morals	2.20	2.30	2.54	2.24
48. Sensitivity to others' feelings	2.68	2.20	2.03	2.02
49. Car driving	2.56	2.39	2.12	2.36
50. Stubbornness	2.27	2.62	2.84	2.84
51. Religion	3.45	3.42	2.45	3.17
52. Meanness	2.72	3.00	3.14	2.96
53. Niceness	2.49	2.25	3.27	2.33
54. Stick-to-it-iveness	2.70	2.42	2.61	2.58
55. Attitude toward one's family	4.64	3.41	2.93	3.02
56. Competitiveness	2.90	2.62	2.53	2.57
57. Maturity	1.93	1.80	1.68	1.74
58. Creativity	3.04	2.67	2.64	2.64
59. Honesty	2.77	2.41	1.98	2.01
60. Loyalty to friends	3.20	2.22	1.54	1.82
61. Dancing	3.64	3.40	3.13	3.50
62. Determination	2.49	2.28	1.90	2.30
63. Trustworthiness	2.15	1.92	1.62	1.77
64. Dependability	2.18	1.83	1.75	1.77
65. Patriotism	3.48	2.91	2.78	3.07
66. Openness to new ideas	2.67	2.33	2.28	2.40
67. Cliqueishness	3.36	2.95	3.11	1.62

N = 1,100 (grade 9, 207; grade 10, 431; grade 11, 200; grade 12, 262)
1 = always; 2 = usually; 3 = sometimes; 4 = hardly ever; 5 = never

occupation, father's occupation, and stubbornness. Twenty-three were revealed to hold increased interest for 12th-graders than for 9th-graders (based on a minimum 0.4 median decrease): musical ability (singing), clothes, figure/build/physique, complexion, ability to put feelings into words, ability to put thoughts into words, good listener, sexiness, generosity, masculinity, cleanliness, type of family one comes from, studiousness, cooperativeness, self-confidence, sensitivity to others' feelings, attitude about one's family, creativity, honesty, loyalty to friends, dependability, patriotism, and cliqueishness. The change in older teens reflects an increased interest in the attributes of others in general and, specifically, a greater involvement with attributes of character, interpersonal skills, and outward appearance.

Continuity and Change

Attributes of key interest to ninth-graders ("always") maintained continuity over time. Examination of Table 6.13 discloses that interest level was retained over the four grades in three of the four attributes of keen interest: clothes, popularity with the opposite sex, and maturity. Athletic ability was the exception; keen interest stopped with passage from the ninth grade.

Clothes, popularity with opposite sex, and maturity occupied central interest over time. General physical appearance, cleanliness, trustwor-

TABLE 6.13. Attributes Always Noticed According to Grade.

	Grade			
Attribute	*9*	*10*	*11*	*12*
Athletic ability	*			
General physical appearance		*	*	*
Clothes	*	*	*	*
Figure/build/physique			*	*
Complexion			*	*
Popularity with opposite sex	*	*	*	*
Cleanliness		*	*	*
Maturity	*	*	*	*
Honesty			*	
Loyalty to friends			*	*
Determination			*	
Trustworthiness		*	*	*
Dependability		*	*	*
Cliqueishness				*

Grade 9: $n = 207$
Grade 10: $n = 431$
Grade 11: $n = 200$
Grade 12: $n = 262$

thiness, and dependability increased in interest in the 10th-grade and maintained adolescent interest thereafter. The strength of the last two character attributes at 10th-grade level is compatible with data of reference group choices reported earlier, which revealed significantly less influence attributed to parents in the 10th grade than in the 9th and significantly more influence accorded to schoolmates. The striking finding that athletic ability was of keen interest to at least half the subjects in the 9th grade but decreased in the later grades points to the adolescent's increased social interests with age.

In 11th grade high interest is revealed for the first time in appearance qualities of figure/physique/build and complexion, and character attributes of honesty, loyalty to friends, and determination. The former qualities may reflect sexual maturation and heterosexual attractions. As for the latter group, whether a peer is loyal and honest is a matter of greater concern because of the increasing desire to emotionally distance oneself from parents; character qualities in others, who take the place of parents, must be closely examined. Honesty and determination are of keen interest only in 11th grade, not before or after. It may be that since this is the grade where students begin to make serious career and college commitments (PSAT, SAT tests, college and job information sessions by school counselors, etc.), these two qualities are extremely relevant. However, after the tests and applications, the immediate impact of the future recedes, and these qualities may lose their urgency. While the adolescent is very much involved in future planning, it is vital to always bear in mind how responsive he or she is to the impact of immediate matters.

The data reveal that cliqueishness finds prominence in the 12th grade for the first time, even though adolescents may have been members of cliques for many years. *Cliques* are associations of individuals who generally have a lot in common and enjoy being together. An initial reason for joining a clique grows out of the instability and insecurity that accompanies becoming an adolescent. Hence, adolescents desire to affiliate with others and draw social strength from the affiliation. Furthermore, this close association affords opportunities for examining personality traits, skills, attributes, and vocational/career choices of peers.

A different set of circumstances exists by 12th grade. By this time most adolescents possess a strong sense of who is a "similar other" based on a six-to-seven-year period of looking, listening, assessing, comparing, and measuring—of trying on and trying out. By about the senior year in high school, the task is completed. The adolescent has incrementally constructed a temporary self structure. Then the task turns to comparing and evaluating elements of this temporary structure with those of others who appear similar. Now small groups of similar others, or cliques, offer the context for more precise comparison, evaluation, and refinement of self elements to complete the process of development. Twelfth grade, or the end of 11th grade, is generally the period when this small group is sought out (Seltzer, 1982). Thus, the data that reveal interest in cliques appearing for the first time in the 12th grade are in keeping with the notion that smaller, more intimate groups satisfy advanced developmental demands.

However, not all adolescents proceed through the stage smoothly. Some seek cliques for maladaptive reasons. The adolescent who enters the stage with a sound socioemotional history will busily engage the developmental dynamics and will closely observe the range of behaviors. But if an adolescent avoids the psychological arena and restricts social-izing to a few known others, he or she will miss the exercise of its growth dynamics, and smooth maturation will not follow. The individ-ual will not enter adulthood with a fully developed personality. Some adolescents are very uncertain and fearful, perhaps because of physical and/or emotional trauma in childhood. Others find the present experi-

**TABLE 6.14. Attributes of Increased
Level of Interest between 9th and 12th Grades.**

	Median interest level		
Attribute	Grade 9	Grade 12	Net median increase
Good listener	4.01	2.52	2.49
Cliqueishness	3.36	1.62	1.74
Attitude toward family	4.64	3.02	1.62
Loyalty to friends	3.20	1.82	1.38
Cooperativeness	3.55	2.33	1.22

N = 1,100
1 = always;
2 = usually;
3 = sometimes;
4 = hardly ever;
5 = never

ences taxing; biological, emotional, and cognitive changes experienced from within are overwhelming. Anxiety can be present in such proportions that energies that should be devoted to growth tasks are depleted. Defensive maneuvers may be used to protect oneself from new stimuli. A clique of others, many of whom may also be unready to enter the arena, can serve as an escape. Unfortunately, maladaptive, antisocial functioning may be a product of joining. (See Chapter 10 for a more detailed analysis.)

Findings presented in Table 6.14 reveal an increase of interest of more than one full level in five attributes, including cliqueishness, between the 9th and the 12th grades. The table displays an absence of increased interest in physical skills. The attributes showing increase of interest over time involve relationships between persons. What these data also seem to show is evidence of socioemotional maturation.

In the preceding sections, we have presented empirical findings on the high degree of interest adolescents show in one another's attributes. Now we turn to a regard of how they put their observations to functional use.

HOW ADOLESCENTS UTILIZE THE INFORMATION THEY GAIN ABOUT PEERS

The sharp awareness that comes with age is different from the more global awareness of agemates manifested in younger years. Who and what others are as well as the range of their interests becomes more important. The more one looks at a myriad of characteristics, the more raw material is gathered. Scrutiny goes beyond comparing self and other to observing the group response to particular attributes of others. If it is considered desirable, the next step is for the adolescent to try the attribute out himself and observe closely both how he experiences it and how the group reacts. The adolescent then decides either to discard the characteristic, to keep it, or perhaps to combine it with another and try out the blend. This process is a subliminal one, not deliberate. It is of a deep-structure nature and is motivated by internal psychological growth needs. It is as natural and spontaneous as breathing. It is available to consciousness only when probed for.

It is extremely important to keep in mind is that this process is not an isolated event, occurring occasionally. The dynamics are active for *many* attributes *every* day. They occur simultaneously. This process by which attributes are discovered, tested out, and accepted or discarded goes on for *years*. We generally see resolution of the first stage at the end of the high school years, when the myriad of dynamic comparative acts are worked through sufficiently to ascertain which characteristics are experienced as part of "self." Then they are integrated with others of a related character to form "clusters of self elements." Clusters must be syntonic with one another to blend into a harmonious cognitive self structure. This resolution and possession of a temporary self structure marks the end of this first important stage of growth—the primary peer arena period. Clusters are assembled of elements that feel valid for present functioning and appear to hold potential to serve future goals.

The adolescent then moves on to the next stage, the secondary peer arena period, for more critical examination of attributes and clusters selected in the first stage. Since the array of attributes attributed to self have now been delineated, the dynamics of the secondary peer arena period focus on a small proportion of the attributes considered during the first stage. Now only others who appear similar to one's own current picture of self are used for comparison.

Possible Vicissitudes

The most intensive dynamic comparative activity generally is held to occur during early-middle and middle adolescence (generally occurring between the 7th and 11th grades). Satiation of the need to compare signals the first-stage resolution and construction of the temporary self structure. This generally occurs near the end of high school. Some adolescents who reach first-stage resolution at the end of high school do experience some regression in the early college or job experience. Most do not. Although all adolescents experience some need to reassess certain aspects of self with new people, most first-stage conceptions of self are firm enough to withstand the temporary disorientation. Others, however, are less substantially integrated and need more psychosocial work.

REGRESSIONS. The regressions experienced occur because the newly acquired temporary self structure is sent into turmoil by interaction with a large, *new* group of agemates. These youngsters experience temporary but distinctly uncomfortable regression to a former state of decreased equilibrium and heightened uncertainty regarding self-attributes. The personal turmoil, often reported and referred to as "freshman adjustment," represents more than acclimatization to a new room, roommate, classes, and professors. The reality of a picture of "who I am" radically different from "who I thought I was" can stimulate considerable tension, anxiety, and fear.

Furthermore, it may be that the adolescent who suffers such a setback is also coping with loss. The loss is psychological, not physical. The temporary self-picture that the adolescent framed under prior environmental conditions may be seriously altered or injured, and sometimes even completely shattered.

An illustration is the often quoted tale of psychological distress of the "small town's brightest student" who confronts an altered status in relation to new college peers at a national university such as Harvard or Yale. For most students the new information requires some readjustment of the self-picture, but it is generally not seriously contradicted. Those youth who do experience dissociation with prior conceptions of self-worth need assistance.

The path to reassembling a sound sense of self, congruent with the picture the youth brought to the college campus at the outset, involves repeating the same set of growth dynamics felt to have been resolved at the end of high school. Once again, new, strange peers must be examined closely and compared with. The consensus about self arrived at in high school may have been accurate, but the new college milieu has challenged its validity. In order to arrive at a comprehensive and appropriate assessment, current evaluations must be integrated with prior conclusions arrived at before coming to the new environment. At the same time, concurrent expectations for fulfilling academic responsibilities, self-maintenance needs, and other tasks, and assuming a feigned social ease do not abate. It is period of heightened stress in which a high degree of energy is called forth. Generally, the distress stimulated by this situation is experienced emotionally and is not intellectually understood. The reconciliation of "altered" pictures of self proceeds without cognitive awareness.

Situational Factors

Undoubtedly, situational factors also affect psychological equilibrium. The case of a very bright student from a blue-collar family (we will call her Ann) who was awarded a scholarship to an Ivy League school will illustrate. The scholarship award reinforced feelings of intellectual ability and the notion that hard work reaps rewards. Ann felt confident and optimistic notwithstanding some social and economic concerns. Although fellow students come from differing social and economic backgrounds, the college environment provides enough of a mix for the student to find similar others. Two general outcomes may ensue: (1) Ann may be successful in establishing a social milieu for herself not too different from the one she comes from. Little dissonance between past and present will be experienced, and the temporary first-stage self structure will not be threatened. Ann can proceed to finalize a "self" by engaging secondary-stage peer arena dynamics. On the other hand, (2) Ann may find through comparisons that she is not as bright as she believed and/or that working hard does not necessarily result in the same rewards as it did in prior times. She now sees lifestyles that were not part of prior experiences. New aspirations, previously unknown, may assert themselves. Accomplishment of these aspirations may be threatened by conditions of family background. A mixture of feelings may arise that can result in crippling conflict. For example, conflict may occur between (a) increased motivation for acquisition of new talents and attributes that comparison and evaluation processes have determined as being essential to meet aforementioned goals and (b) increasing feelings of guilt over a sense of distance and emotional separation from past environmental customs and nurturing figures. It is possible that this psychosocial crisis can be managed with little problem. It is also possible that considerable anxiety may manifest itself in an inability to carry the academic and/or social load, or that escape from anxiety may be sought in substance abuse, semidelinquent behaviors, etc. For some, it can represent the end of a dream.

Cases such as this are real. Two factors and their interaction effects are crucial: (1) the strength and flexibility of the incoming temporary self structure, and (2) the degree of dissonance between the prior environment and the college/job milieu.

Such experiences need to be clearly identified as *developmental* crises, not "adjustment" issues. Ironically, it is well accepted that college is the time to expand mind and self. Yet this openness to expansion is possible precisely because the self is *not yet set*. The psychosocial task to be completed during the post–high school years is final identification, consolidation, and integration of the elements that make up the self.

The findings presented in this discussion indicate that in the high school years, the dynamic comparative act processes have indeed begun. With this understanding of adolescent development, the "helping professions" can zero in on the true, not the apparent, conflict. Professionals who are alert to the dynamics of the stage—and to the feeling of tenuousness adolescents experience despite outward bravado—can support the strength and the integrations already accomplished, despite temporary floundering. However, if the professional does not understand that in the adolescent years who and what peers do is paramount and central to actions, erroneous and nonproductive diagnoses and treatment plans may be set forth. Therapy and counseling may proceed with outdated or misguided directives.

CHAPTER 7

Socialization Practices: Public Postures and Private Contradictions

The ongoing private psychosocial activity that accompanies public socialization, in school or in leisure activities, can best be understood in light of adolescent psychosocial interactions with the most relevant reference group—peers. Clearly, adolescents live *actively* with peers. The data to be discussed in this chapter also reveal a major private world where processing of the physical and psychological interactions takes place. The data reveal needs for expansive social contact and limited intimacy. Comparison data offer evidence of conscious psychological processing of peer interactions. These reflective processing activities constitute the dynamics of psychosocial growth, eventuating in self-knowledge, self-direction, informal goal setting, and a "sense of identity."

THE CONCEPT OF "FIRST CALL"

The adolescent's transitional status is one of individuation, marked by attempts to shed dependence on parental figures. Relationships formerly occupied by parents and family are now vacated; hence, there exists an emotional emptiness. But, other teens in a similar state cannot fill this need. Energies cannot yet be released on behalf of others because the system is still utilizing these energies internally. Self needs at this stage of development have first call.

The concept of "first call" is crucial in adolescence. Since first call goes to self, intimacy in adolescence is unachievable. In true intimacy, "first call" *can* go to others. Achieving selfhood is not jeopardized by the release of energies to serve the other. The pull of forces to develop and complete the self structure constitutes the unifying primary dynamic of adolescent behavior. To the outside world it appears to be "a self-serving orientation" of the adolescent. Over time, as adolescent egocentricity reduces, self-development is less threatened by time and energies devoted to the other. Progressive strides in development of cognitive and emotional understandings bring (1) a decreased need to focus on self, thus increasing abilities to see others as discrete—not filtered through a lens of "me" and (2) a corresponding readiness to give up energies to serve needs of others. When at last psychosocial maturity is reached, conflict involved in serving self-development needs diminishes, and energy for serving others is available. It is then "natural" to think of the other first.

In early adolescence friendships are generally of three types: (1) with similar others, for continued support and feelings of being "OK"; (2) with very different others, who serve as positive or negative comparison figures; and (3) with persons who represent a desired element or elements of personality to be psychologically borrowed for tryout. Since adolescence is not adulthood, reciprocity of relationship takes on a very different definition: being mutually available to offer support and to be borrowed from.

SOCIALIZATION

The data of this section examine adolescent friendship. Findings bring into question whether adolescent friendship involves true exchange. The adolescent is by definition egocentric; only on the onset of adulthood do we witness the disappearance of egocentricity. "Peership" represents the functional relationship adolescents have with one another—functional for individual ends via parallel paths, namely, resolution of the questions "who am I?" and "where can I go with what I am?"

In adolescence, selfhood is not yet achieved; it is "in process." Thus, adolescent cohort relationships are different from relationships at other stages of life. Although teens need to be in proximity with one another, individual deep-structure developmental need dominates the course and quality of relationships. Agemates serve as developmental models. Earlier chapters discussed how they supply the raw materials of personality by modeling various qualities, characteristics, talents, deficiencies, etc. They use one another and are available to be used by one another.

They relate, they talk, they discuss—but in their discussions the comparative and evaluational process proceeds consistently and inexorably. It does not abate until the end of adolescence, when the adolescent has completed his or her developmental inquiries and experimentation to arrive at a completed set of self elements, which together constitute the "sense of self" marking closure on the identity formation process.

PREFERRED NUMBERS: AN EMPIRICAL STUDY

Adolescents need large numbers of others to people arenas for interaction. They have an automatic arena by day in school. They are surrounded by many agemates, but they have no choice of who or how many. However, they have some choice during their leisure time. Since the literature to date tells little about teen preference in numbers of others they associate with for leisure activities, we elected to ask groups of teens about their preferences. We developed an instrument to ascertain how many others they seek out for company. Our assumption was that the developmental stage would influence the numbers. Since our subjects were early-middle adolescents, we predicted they still needed many others to compare themselves with and evaluate themselves against.

The sample of 1,105 students combined five subsamples. Three were male samples from three Philadelphia Catholic schools, with n values of 253, 157, and 383. The fourth comprised 37 males and 57 females from public schools in suburban Philadelphia; and the fifth included 104 males and 114 females from public schools in Long Island, New York. The total sex distribution was 934 males and 171 females. Of the total 1,105, 312 were public school students (171 females and 141 males). Those in the fifth group were primarily white, middle- or working-class. All races and religions were represented. Over 30% were Jewish. Questionnaires were completed in homeroom classes. The n values reported in tables to follow vary somewhat from the sample number of 1,105 due to nonresponse.

Students were asked seven questions about their socialization practices (see Table 7.1). The first question was factual: How many kids were at the last party you attended? The mean of 63.8 tells us that students participated in socializing with a large number of others. The second question tapped their wishes: How many would you choose to invite to

TABLE 7.1. Socialization and Friends.

Question	Mean
1. How many kids were at the last party you attended?	63.83
2. If you could throw a party in the school gym and money was no object, how many kids would you invite?	160.06
3. How many kids do you say "hello" to when you see them?	107.24
4. How many kids do you feel understand you?	24.47
5. If you had an important decision to make, how many kids' advice would you seek?	6.55
6. How many different kids do you speak to on the phone each week?	9.58
7. How many kids do you consider to be your good friends?	9.12

$N = 1,105$

a party if price were no object? The numbers were considerably higher. The mean rose almost 100 points, to 160.06.

The dynamic functional interaction (DFI) model of development, which establishes the adolescent peer as a crucial developmental figure (see Chapter 4), connects the desire to interact with many, many others to a deep-structure developmental need. This expressed preference for large numbers is the surface-structure reflection of the "adolescent imperative" to be in the company of many similar others during early and middle adolescence. A variety of developmental needs are met in this way, for example:

1. Accessing the arena for tryout and evaluation
2. Feeling the emotional comfort of being near others going through a similar period in a like condition
3. Accessing a peer-structured set of behavioral norms to replace the prior structures set down by parents and family
4. Access to the raw materials agemates model in various attributes to borrow and try out
5. Measuring self-behavior to ensure that it is congruent with that of others

Question 3 asked a simple question to provide a measure of sociability: How many kids do you say "hello" to? The data reveal a median of 34.9. (The large disparity between the median and the mean of 107 reveals some individuals to be extremely social.) Of interest here is that the self-report reality-based questions ("How many were at the last party?" and "How many do you say hello to?") elicited means lower than the wish-level response to "If you could invite as many as you wanted. . . ."

The data for question 4—"How many kids do you feel understand you?"—indicates much about the private world of the adolescent. The median was 5.1, and the mode was 5.0. These small numbers give quite a different picture of private reflection on social relationships from the image revealed by the data on socializing wishes and practices. These data become even more cogent when we consider the findings on question 5: "If you had an important decision to make, how many kids' advice would you seek?" Here the median was 3.36 and the mode 3. Even the mean (which better reflects the input of respondents in the sample who are highly social) is extremely low (6.55) in comparison to the reported mean of 160.06 for "How many kids would you invite to a party?" Socialization is actively sought—in reality, and even more in fantasy; lagging far behind in priority is feeling understood and engaging in intimate exchange.

The findings for question 5 may be explained by two components of adolescent psychological posturing. The first is a *hesitancy to reveal too much about self* lest it be considered a deviation from the norm— "weird." Adolescent transition means unsettledness and insecurity about attributes, quasi-attributes, borrowed attributes, etc. It appears to be manifested in needs to carefully guard "the current me." The second current is a function of *decreasing egocentricity*, by virtue of increased social awareness that others in the same stage share similar uncertainty and urgency about self and have few energies to devote to genuine concern about others. It is a stage-specific state. Adolescents seem to know intuitively that sharing concerns with agemates yields a short period of attention, after which follows a predictable transition to topical, non–emotionally taxing matters. Skipping from topic to topic, "keeping it light," keeps emotional concerns in check and out of public sight. But "one who understands" must be ready to set aside his or her own concerns for true exchange with another. Most middle adolescents cannot engage in this exchange for very long. In addition, energies must be kept available to complete daily tasks. These data imply that adolescents are cognitively in touch with these dimensions of peer interaction. They can seek company for functional growth needs but not for intimate exchange.

Chapter 5, on reference groups, disclosed adolescents' adeptness at seeking out information. Parents are sought out for future-oriented areas of influence and for issues of character and philosophy. Information about appearance and leisure are more easily asked of peers, as are issues of interpeer morality, such as cheating and marijuana. Very interesting questions arise from comparing the reference group and socialization data. Table 5.1 reveals that adolescents do seek information from peers. Data of Table 7.1 reveal a minimal number of peers sought out for intimate advice. Does the adolescent define *advice* as different from asking for input from others to help make up his or her own mind (as phrased in ARGI)? In the latter instance, respondents freely acknowledged that they sought out the input of their peers. In the data reported in this chapter, they were far more hesitant. The discrepancies may be in part related to the choice of reference groups offered. Perhaps what we see is a third "state-related" characteristic, to be added to their (1) self-protective needs and (2) lack of energies available to give to others. As we consider the tentative, transitional condition of the adolescent, it makes sense that he or she prefers to assume an independent stance, resulting in a minimum amount of close consultation with peers.

Thus, rather than reflecting a condition of emotional aloneness, these data may indicate a need to effect maturity. They may also indicate a strong need to maintain a "mask" with agemates, implying the ever-present pressure of "self presentation." Both Redl's (1974) "group under the couch" phenomenon and Elkind's (1967) "imaginary audience" speak to a constant awareness by the adolescent of being critiqued by others, peers in particular.

Alternating Needs

The vastly different numbers revealed by the data provide a graphic picture of alternating and quite divergent sets of adolescent needs. This may be better understood through consideration of adolescent growth dynamics. Comparative act dynamics that occur when adolescents are together need time to be processed. "Do I possess these attributes? If not, should I try to acquire them? Is such acquisition feasible or unfeasible? How did the group respond? Would the same characteristic be perceived differently if exhibited in a status figure as opposed to a non–status figure? Will this characteristic be of value in the present? Will it be of value in the future? How does it blend with other characteristics?"

It appears that what we see here is a functional aloneness. In contrast to participation in the large arena of agemates, which requires physical presence but not necessarily active interaction, intimate exchange does call for involvement. Questions 4–7 of the instrument deal with intimate interactional experiences. The popular impression that teens are "always on the telephone" is contrary to findings of question 6, which reveal that at least half of the subjects speak with 5 or fewer others on the phone per week (median = 5.39). Even the mean, which includes responses of some very social members, is only 9.58. Perhaps the last question— "How many kids do you consider to be your good friends?"—offers the most dramatic contrast to question 2. Here the mode was 3, as compared to 100 for question 2. In sum, these data reveal a strong desire to *be around* many, many other peers, which lends support to the theoretical premise that an adolescent imperative to be together defines the dynamics. Intimate association with many others is *not* the norm, according to the data. At this age, wanting to be together appears more related to casual exchange and viewing than to intimate knowledge. Half the sample of 1,105 considered less than five others (median = 4.93) to be *good* friends.

These findings disclose behaviors reflecting alternative development needs of socializing with many peers, for information getting and exchange, and nonintimacy with peers, in order to conserve energies for reflective thought, consolidation, and integration. These findings lend themselves to a different interpretation for adolescents than they would for other age groups. They appear to represent developmental aloneness, *not* loneliness. This is not a trait, but reflects a state-related intensified concentration on self and self processes needed to complete the transition from the less complicated formative ego of a child to the complex ego structure of an adult.

Age-Related Differences

The extent to which age makes a difference in how the adolescents responded to the seven questions was examined next. Since we also were interested in whether situational factors made a difference, we chose to analyze findings from both the evenly balanced gender sample (104 males and 114 females) and the sample from an all-male school (*n* = 383) (see Table 7.2). Chi-square analyses revealed a greater number of significant differences between grades in the all-male sample than in the balanced-gender sample, with the numbers of friends sought out increasing with age. The questions on decision-making and on how many kids were said "hello" to per week (questions 3 and 5) were treated similarly by the two samples.

The data suggest that a socializing pattern moves into place earlier in a mixed-sex school. It may be that the students in the all-male school are not encouraged to be social or are not socially stimulated as early as students in the mixed-sex school. Hence, we see a more gradual pattern of increasing desire for socialization. The findings imply a situational impact on the desire for expanded socialization.

Gender Factors

We were also interested in finding what differences exist between the sexes. Since a chi-square analysis on the small balanced-gender sample of 104 males and 114 females disclosed no significant differences between the sexes on any of the seven questions, we carried out the same analysis on the larger sample of 1,075 with unequal sex proportions. A chi-square analysis revealed significant differences in five of the seven questions (see Table 7.3). Females responded with significantly higher numbers to questions 1, 2, 3, 5, and 6. No significant differences were found between the sexes on matters of more intimate functioning—how many kids understand you and how many are considered to be good friends.

TABLE 7.2. Significance of Differences in Socialization Practices Between Grades.

	Significance	
Question	All males*	Mixed gender**
1	NS	.003
2	.03	NS
3	.001	.001
4	.02	NS
5	NS	NS
6	.001	NS
7	.01	NS

* n = 383 (males)
** n = 218 (104 males, 114 females)

**TABLE 7.3. Significant
Differences in Socialization
Practices According to Gender.**

Question	Significance
1	.005*
2	.001*
3	.001*
4	NS
5	.01*
6	.02*
7	NS

N = 1,075 (907 males, 168 females)
*Females sought out more others than did males.

These data imply that females sought more exposure and input and suggest they may socialize more due to a greater need to examine attributes of peers. Males may not need to sift through as many attributes to arrive at conclusions. This would support findings of Chapter 6, which revealed females were "always" or "usually" interested in examining more attributes in others than were males.

It is particularly fascinating that no significant differences were revealed between sexes in the number of perceived good friends or in how many friends respondents felt understood them. We see that, regardless of sex, the adolescent is not seeking out close relationships. These findings support our model of development, which holds that during early and middle adolescence, all youngsters are engaged in a similar set of dynamic processes and developmental stages. First they need many others to serve as raw material and jointly provide an arena for trial and error. After building a temporary self structure, they are satisfied with fewer in the crowd. Only when they have constructed a "self" are they able to engage in intimate relations.

Recapitulation

Like the attribute data, these data imply that males engage in fewer comparative acts than females. When the sexes are in proximity, more comparisons are stimulated; they are probably related to heterosexual issues. The data also clearly reveal that close relationships are no more the province of females during this period than they are of males. Intimacy and closeness do not appear to be the goal for either sex. Looking and being looked at, evaluating attributes of others and making one's own attributes available to be evaluated represents the exchange level. Target interests may vary; the dynamics are the same. There is functional reciprocity but not socioemotional reciprocity. Surface activities cover the subliminal dynamics of development. Adolescents must finish the dynamics of the primary peer arena period (where socialization with many others is essential) before they move to the secondary peer arena period, where smaller numbers suffice. Once the secondary peer arena developmental tasks of self-refinement and identity resolution near completion, they may seek intimacy and closeness.

COMPARISON DATA

Clearly, high school students are very interested in being in one another's company. Peers functionally become comparison objects in the process of hammering out the elements of self structure. A lot of energy and time is taken up by comparative acts. Furthermore, mood swings can be attributed to the result of comparisons. To understand the adolescent, this developmental activity must be regarded as the core of his or her functioning.

Findings discussed in Chapter 6 disclose the impressive number of attributes adolescents are alert to in one another. Our theoretical position argues that this alertness is the first step of the comparative act of evaluating self elements, measuring them against characteristics of others, considering whether to adopt elements observed in others, deciding which self elements to retain and which to discard, and refining retained elements into clusters for integration into the self structure. We were interested in the degree to which adolescents are aware that they compare and if they understand what motivates their comparison. We hypothesized that adolescents would show cognitive awareness of these processes. We developed and administered the 12-question Adolescent Comparison Probe (Figure 7.1). Our findings disclosed that they engage in a considerable amount of comparing.

As shown in Table 7.4, adolescents expressed a need to compare with agemates to achieve greater certainty of mind. The range of intensity

1. When you are with another person (in a group or alone) or more than one other for the first time, how many of their characteristics are you aware of?
   (1) all, (2) almost all, (3) some, (4) a few, (5) none

2. If you think you may be talented at something, how many kids do you compare yourself with on this characteristic to determine the extent of the talent?
   (1) everyone I see, (2) most people I see, (3) a few people I see, (4) no one I see

3. If you think you are not too good at something (e.g., dancing, math), how many kids do you compare yourself with?
   (1) everyone I see, (2) most people I see, (3) a few people I see, (4) no one I see

4. If you could compare with only a few kids, how certain would you be about that deficiency?
   (1) very certain, (2) not so certain, (3) not at all certain

5. How many kids would you need to be sufficiently certain?
   (1) everyone I could find, (2) a lot, (3) a few

6. Would they be members of one group of kids?
   (1) yes, (2) no

7. Would they be members of every group of kids you came into contact with?
   (1) yes, (2) no

8. If you think you are good at something and you want to determine how good, how many kids would you compare your talent with?
   (1) everyone I see, (2) most people I see, (3) a few people I see, (4) no one I see

9. If you could compare with only a few kids, how certain would you be about that talent/characteristic?
   (1) very certain, (2) not so certain, (3) not at all certain

10. How many kids would you need to be sufficiently certain?
    (1) everyone I could find, (2) a lot, (3) a few

11. Would they be members of one group of kids?
    (1) yes, (2) no

12. Would they be members of every group of kids you came into contact with?
    (1) yes, (2) no

Figure 7.1. The Adolescent Comparison Probe.

(choices) is shown to the right of the mean. The findings reveal that although the adolescents are not so certain about an attribute when comparing with only a few others, and that a lot of kids are necessary for them to be sufficiently certain (questions 4 and 5), they are quite discriminating and have put into place which individuals are relevant (questions 6 and 7). The data imply that people in their social environment have already been differentiated into which others are relevant and which are not. (Findings on questions 10, 11, and 12 are similar to findings on questions 5, 6, 7.)

No matter whether adolescents are comparing on negative or positive traits, the large numbers of others necessary for certainty are not restricted to one group. However, certain groups appear to be excluded.

TABLE 7.4. Extent of Comparison Behaviors.

Question	Number in sample	Mean	Choice range
1	1,094	2.71	1–5*
2	1,100	2.49	1–4*
3	1,096	2.70	1–4*
4	1,095	1.70	1–3
5	1,089	2.29	1–3*
6	1,043	1.54	1–2
7	980	1.58	1–2*
8	824	2.30	1–4*
9	824	1.67	1–3
10	822	2.25	1–3*
11	776	1.56	1–2
12	734	1.55	1–2*

*Lower number in range refers to higher extent of comparison.

Thus, the data point to a *multigroup orientation* of these subjects, but one in which groups of others that are relevant are discerned from those that are not. These data are congruent with the developmental period of middle and early-late adolescence, by which time comparative acts have theoretically been engaged in for 3–6 years. Sufficient comparisons have already been made for the subjects to have some notion of which others are relevant and for what purposes.

Can the data help us understand when the need to compare subsides? Here data of question 2 are helpful. They lend support to a dynamic functional interaction (DFI) premise that when the adolescent feels sufficiently certain of the value of a self-attribute, the need to compare further becomes satiated. The question deals with discerning the extent of a talent. Findings were closer to "a few people" (median = 2.6) than to "everyone I see." This suggests that identification of an attribute as a talent is the result of positive reinforcement from self-observation and/or relevant others. It has already been well scrutinized and evaluated. Many additional comparisons, even for refinement purposes, may be unnecessary. This may be interpreted as the empirical counterpart of satiation. Satiation of the need to compare occurs when enough comparison has been engaged in to bring a resolution as to the quality of an attribute (Seltzer, 1982). The adolescent has completed the testing and evaluation process. He or she needs no further outside input to decide on its value and whether or not to incorporate it as part of the concept of "self." These data reveal only a few people to be necessary to confirm an attribute that has already been identified as a talent.

Behavioral Impressions

Findings on questions 3 and 8, which are obverse in nature—comparison on positive and on negative attributes— shed light on another aspect. The data reveal a need to compare with fewer others on an attribute one is unsure of than on one the adolescent is more comfortable with. The data of questions 7 and 12 also reveal that members of certain groups would not be relevant and thus are not automatically included. Therefore, it is important to bear in mind that both positive and negative strokes appear to be pungent only when they are from groups that are valued for specific purposes. Not only negative response but positive reinforcement may fail to be integrated if it is from irrelevant individuals.

The table discloses that more people are necessary for comparison to verify a perception of a positive trait than a negative trait. Interestingly, although adolescents responded they need to compare with only a few persons on negatively perceived traits, they also responded that to adequately assess the attribute, it must be compared with a number of others; they would be "not so certain" about it if only a few others were compared with. We may be seeing in these findings that the need for greater certainty to claim a trait as "good" may be related to its potential to be incorporated as an aspect of self.

A good deal of certainty is also required for the adolescent to verify a trait as negative. Comparison with only a few may be less painful as it allows continuation of the uncertainty. The adolescent thus avoids risking verification. Furthermore, comparison with fewer others maintains the adolescent's freedom to question the validity of the judgment as it may be considered less dependable.

The risk that many comparisons will verify negatively perceived attributes and result in a very low self-image may explain "escape" behaviors of the adolescent into excessive leisure preoccupations, serious alcohol consumption, or drug usage. These escapes, or withdrawals, have a developmental cost. When adolescents withdraw into themselves, the result is developmental deprivation. They miss participating in informal and educational settings where raw materials of personality traits and attributes are available for observation, comparison, and evaluation. Adolescents who allow themselves to experience *unanticipated* emotional highs or lows (dependent on results of the comparisons and the evaluations) engage the developmental dynamics of growth. Those who have found this too difficult and utilize "escapes" lose out on the interaction that is functional to yielding necessary information about self in relation to others.

Gender Comparisons

We were again interested in the impact of gender. Did sex differences exist in how males and females experience comparison needs? Since for the smaller, balanced-gender sample of 104 males and 114 females a chi-square analysis revealed a significant difference in only 1 of the 12 responses, we carried out the same analysis on the large, unbalanced-gender sample. As shown in Table 7.5, three significant differences were observed. That females are found to observe more attributes of others than males (question 1) complements findings of the attributes study (Chapter 6), which reported that females are interested in a greater variety of attributes than are males. That they made a greater number of comparisons than males to verify a trait they perceived themselves as "not good at" (questions 3 and 4) is particularly interesting and suggests that boys may be either (1) more accepting of deficiencies or (2) more ill at ease about negatively perceived characteristics and choose to avoid additional information about self. Implications are raised that social messages influence females to be more concerned with self-other

TABLE 7.5. Significant Differences in
Comparison Behavior by Sex.

Question	Significance
1	.0001*
2	NS
3	.0001*
4	.005*
5–12	NS

*Girls need to compare more.
N = 1,075 (907 males, 168 females)

contrasts and different social messages to males stress demonstration of expertise and nonacknowledgment of weakness.

Developmental Differences

Whether or not age makes a difference in how adolescents compare with one another was also examined. The balanced-gender public school data were analyzed by grade. A chi- square analysis disclosed no significant differences in patterns of comparison according to grade.

We carried out a second chi-square analysis on 383 males. They were from the same four grades but attended a private, all-male Catholic school. Findings again revealed no significant differences between the grades in how adolescents compare. The two sets of data lead us to conclude that there is a social pattern of comparison behaviors that begins early and remains stable throughout the high school years.

Recapitulation

The findings have revealed adolescents to be very aware of one another and to utilize one another to assure themselves of the validity of their own attributes. There appear to be some sex differences but little age-level differences in the type and manner of comparison. We have also seen that generally both male and female adolescents are drawn to be with many, many others but relate closely with only a few. Friendships serve different functions and take on a different character in adolescence. Also, comparison in adolescence serves different functions from those served at any other period of life. The following discussion may place into a broader context the findings discussed in this chapter.

ADOLESCENTS AND SOCIAL COMPARISON

Leon Festinger first framed the notion of comparison behavior in his theory of social comparison (1954) as he pondered issues of how people come to judgments and evaluations where there are no objective measurement criteria— in other words, where the differences may be more qualitative than quantitative. It followed from his theory of informal social communication (1950), in which he sets forth the premise that in a situation where there is no objective measure, people communicate to arrive at consensus. This agreement becomes the informal measure against which behaviors and attitudes are measured. When it comes to talents, abilities, or attributes, for which there may be no formal measure, Festinger holds that one arrives at a consensus as to their value by comparing them with those of others. However, one's own assessment after such comparison is insufficient; attitudes of the group one strives to be in are central. Thus, in evaluating an attribute/ability, it is necessary to ascertain where the group stands. Through the private act of comparison and the consideration of group norms, which legislate the status accorded the ability/attribute, the individual arrives at a decision regarding the worth of the attribute under consideration.

Adolescence is an excellent example of a condition where there is no framework for standardization and appraisal. The adolescent is an individual in transition. To invoke childhood valuations is regressive; to apply adult valuations is inappropriate to the stage. Agemate standards are relevant. To access both models and measures, the teen must utilize the peer groups of the collective peer arena.

Comparisons go on constantly with all relevant others in the various peer arena groups. The school offers one of the largest, most easily accessible groups and, hence, is a very important arena. It is from schools that we drew samples for our empirical studies.

A conglomerate of data is yielded from psychosocial interactions in the various school groups. Here the adolescent compares and contrasts his or her own abilities and attributes with those of others. The healthy adolescent develops attributes that seem strong and comes to terms with those that seem weaker or less complimentary. This range of attributes is the foundation for the first-stage temporary self structure. The permanent self structure evolves later, following a period in which comparative acts are more precisely focused, directed at specific attributes selected from the first-stage self structure. These selected attributes are refined and redefined. Eventually, as the adolescent nears the end of the developmental stage, flexible clusters of congruent elements are framed. These clusters are developed out of past and present experience. They are seen both to be functional to the present and to serve directions and goals of the future. Together the integrated clusters of self elements form the final self structure. Acquisition of this "self" marks the end of the psychosocial period known as adolescence.

Being alert to the sociocultural environment, its consistencies, and its areas of change is essential to active participation in the culture. Adding new talents or changing perspectives when necessary is essential for survival in a rapidly changing society. Indeed, social comparison goes on in later life stages, but it is different from that of adolescence. It is aimed at isolated characteristics and has various purposes: adjusting to new and different situations where conformity is desired, growing and developing new tastes, activities, knowledge, etc. The social comparison process for adults is used to evaluate self in relation to the needs and values of a changing culture, to learn by watching others, and to develop necessary knowledge and behaviors.

The period of adolescence is quite different from the individual's subsequent stages, when he or she is alert to changing technologies and mores and attempts to adjust. The period of adolescence is not a period of adjusting and updating personality elements. It is a period of *establishment* of personality elements. Adolescence is a developmental stage devoted to preparation for adult functioning. Many different alternatives must be experimented with on a myriad of dimensions. It is a period of enormous energy output and continues for roughly a decade, until the operative personality anchor is formed. Updating the personality is a continuing process of adult functioning. Adolescence is a time for construction of the anchor. Insufficient construction of this anchor has serious ramifications for the quality of the remaining course of life.

Because the comparative acts of adolescence are different from the social comparisons of adults, the character of the relationships between adolescents is also different. Findings reported earlier in this chapter revealed adolescents' acute awareness of one another, their strong desires to be in one another's company, and, paradoxically, the paucity of closeness.

The Functional Meaning of Agemates

We introduced the concept of "peership" as the adolescent corollary to friendship. According to basic premises of the theory of dynamic functional interaction, the "adolescent imperative" functions like a magnet to draw the adolescent to be with as many peers as is possible. The early adolescent in particular, newly emerged from customary dependence on parents and family, seeks familiar others. They offer a sense of stability and normality, especially if they are of the same age and appear similar in a number of respects. A few familiar others do not meet developmental needs of this stage, but represent a support system for entering the larger peer settings. Because of the high degree of egocentricity of early adolescence, even "close friends" do not relate in true exchange. They serve as mutual social supports in the large arena where, with many other adolescents like and unlike themselves, the developmental work of comparative acts begins.

Thus, our model suggests two different sets of needs, which are reflected in two types of adolescent relationships. One is closer to "peer-ship" and characterizes the majority of adolescent relationships. It is reflected in the adolescent's searches for large groups of other agemates. The second approximates the reciprocal relationships of true adulthood. These relationships are much fewer and generally last longer. They reflect the need for continuing safe relations as a substitute for the stability previously yielded almost exclusively from parents and family. The quest is for an "other" or a few others who manifest real interest and support.

Often we hear teens talk of friendships that are short in duration. When friendships are short and there is no emotional sense of loss following their termination, we can with considerable certainty assume they are "peerships." The interaction is based on developmentally pertinent parameters. The initial need to be physically near the new acquaintance reflects a desire to identify with or try out a characteristic the other represents. The action is reciprocal.

In sum, adolescent agemate relationships are based on the need for support during the transitional period and on the need to determine a sense of self. These two currents are manifested in a few long-lasting relationships, but many more are short-term.

CHAPTER 8

How Adolescents Meet:
Contacts and Contexts

We have referred to the peer arena as the "psychosocial aggregate of any and all interactions in any and all peer groups." Implied is that the adolescent is not restricted to one membership group consisting of favorite friends, but that he or she interacts physically and psychologically in a number of different groupings that range in size. Some are small enough for considerable exchange; others are activity groups; others are groups where participants act more as audience than actor. Yet there is little information available about which groups they choose most of their friends from. Five days a week, nine months of the year, adolescents are in contact with each other in school classes and activities, and on the way to and from school. Where else do they get to know each other? How do they meet? Which settings are the sources for friendships? Which associations go beyond first meetings? What groups do they continue to spend time with?

PREFERRED GROUPS

To gain more information on adolescent socialization practices and preferences, we administered a simple questionnaire to 24 males and 49 females from the 12th grade in a Canton, Ohio, public school. They were three fourths white, middle- or working-class and of predominantly Christian faith. Almost one fourth were black. Other races and religions were represented to a minor degree. The questionnaire, completed in study hall, listed 16 groups. The respondents were asked to place a check next to any group they spent time with. There was also space

TABLE 8.1. Sources of Teen Socialization by Gender, Number, Percent, and Preference Rank.

	Number			Percent			Preference Rank		
	M	F	Total	M	F	Total	M	F	Total
Close friends	24	49	73	100	100	100	1	1	1
General acquaintances	14	39	53	58	80	73	2.5	2	2
Other (#1)*	8	21	29	33	43	40	5	3.5	3
Teammates (#1)	14	14	28	58	29	38	2.5	7.5	4
Kids in church/synagogue	7	20	27	29	41	37	6.5	5	5
Kids you work with	5	21	26	21	43	36	8.5	3.5	6.5
Kids in neighborhood	10	16	26	42	33	36	4	6	6.5
Club of own choice (#1)	7	14	21	29	29	29	6.5	7.5	8
Band	4	8	12	17	16	16	10	11	9
Choir	3	8	11	13	16	15	11.5	11	11
Newspaper staff	3	8	11	13	16	15	11.5	11	11
Other (#2)	0	11	11	0	22	15	18.5	9	11
Club of own choice (#2)	2	7	9	8	14	12	13	13.5	13.5
Teammates (#2)	5	4	9	21	8	12	8.5	17	13.5
Summer camp	1	7	8	4	14	11	15	13.5	15
Club of own choice (#3)	1	4	5	4	8	7	15	17	17
Drama group	1	4	5	4	8	7	15	17	17
Yearbook staff	0	5	5	0	10	7	18.5	15	17
Other (#3)	0	2	2	0	4	3	18.5	19	19
Other (#4)	0	0	0	0	0	0	18.5	20	20

*The first "Other" category refers to special friends of the opposite sex.

N = 73 (24 males, 49 females)

provided for the respondent to list 4 additional groups. Table 8.1 reports findings from the total group of 73 adolescents, as well as from a second analysis that looked at gender-related differences.

All 73 teens indicated that they spent time with close friends. Second in rank was general acquaintances. The third most popular category was "other," which generally referred to a friend of the opposite sex. Teammates and "kids in church/synagogue" ranked fourth and fifth, respectively.

Subtle sex differences were revealed. Both sexes ranked close friends as number 1, but differences appeared in rank 2. Females accorded rank 2 to acquaintances; for males, two categories shared rank 2.5: general acquaintances and the primary group of teammates. The next category for males, rank 4, was "kids in the neighborhood," which might partially reflect time spent in sports. Thus, the data imply the prominence of athletics in adolescent male contact.*

"Kids in the neighborhood" ranked 6 with females. By contrast, rank 3.5 for females was shared by "kids you work with" and "other"—in this case, a friend of the opposite sex.* What is most striking in the male-female analyses is the rank difference between the two teammate categories. Teammates occupy ranks 7.5 and 17 for females and ranks 2.5 and 8.5 for males. Athletics do not seem to be as central to the female experience.

An interesting commonality between males and females is that "kids in the neighborhood" and "kids met in church/synagogue" are sought out more than teens who are part of school activity groups. Clearly, it is the informal, not the formal, arenas that attract adolescents. They appear to prefer those that are self-selected rather than those structured for them.

---

*These data are consistent with the data of the attribute study, which revealed a high interest by males in athletic ability of others (see Table 6.2).

*These data for females are consistent with findings from a different sample on primary sources of influence (Chapter 5), where the females ranked "special friend" very high. These same data on males revealed that boys utilized neighborhood agemates as sources of influence more than girls did, consistent with findings in this analysis on time spent (see Table 5.18).

GROUP NUMBERS

The second portion of this study was designed to determine how many individuals participated in the various groups—how many were considered "close friends," "general acquaintances," etc. Thus, after subjects checked the groups they spent time with, the instrument asked that they go back over the list and write down the approximate number of kids in each of the groups. Table 8.2 presents findings.

The table reveals a clustering of socialization preferences under the two smaller groups (1 to 9 and 10 to 24). Nevertheless, there is an impressive amount of socializing in groups of between 25 and 49. Findings on close friends are particularly interesting compared with the findings from the much larger sample reported in the preceding chapter (Table 7.1). Here the mean number for the sample of 1,105 was 9.12 in response to the question "How many people do you consider to be your good friends?" Notwithstanding the much smaller number of students in this sample and the slightly different phrasing of the questions, striking similarities are revealed. We found that 83.3% of the males and 73.5% of the females responded that nine or fewer others composed their groups of close friends. Data of these two studies disclose that adolescents do not identify many others as close friends. Groups of general acquaintances are more expansive.

Gender Differences

Findings on gender differences revealed similarities in the numbers considered "close friends." For both sexes, the upper limit was the 10–24 category. For general acquaintances, the male spread was broader than that of the female: 42.8% of males selected groups ranging from 25 to over 100, as compared with 25.8% of females. More females selected the 10–24 category. This finding, which reflects a gender difference in the developmental need to stretch familiar boundaries, representing an outward manifestation of cognitive and emotional growth, may in part be influenced by males' larger build, physical strength, and ability to adequately defend themselves if necessary. Preferences between the sexes were similar for neighborhood friends just as they were for close friends. Here socialization takes place in smaller groups.

TABLE 8.2. Percent of Participation, by Sex, in Socialization Groups of Selected Sizes.

	1–9		10–24		25–49		50–74		75–99		100+	
	M	F	M	F	M	F	M	F	M	F	M	F
Close friends	83.3	73.5	16.7	26.5								
General acquaintances	35.7	30.8	21.4	43.6	21.4	10.3	7.1	2.6		2.6	14.3	10.3
Other (#1)	75.0	42.9	12.5	33.3	12.5	9.5				4.8		9.5
Teammates (#1)	42.9	14.3	42.9	64.3	14.3	21.4						
Kids you work with	40.0	57.1	60.0	33.3				4.8				4.8
Kids in church/synagogue	42.9	30.0	28.6	25.0	14.3	45.0	14.3					
Kids in neighborhood	60.0	62.5	30.0	31.3	10.0	6.3						
Club (#1)		7.1	28.6	35.7	42.9	21.4		21.4	14.3	7.1	14.3	7.1
Band	25.0			37.5				12.5			7.50	50.0
Choir						25.0		25.0	100.0	50.0		
Newspaper staff		12.5	33.3	62.5		25.0	66.7					
Other (#2)		63.6		9.1		9.1		9.1				9.1
Club (#2)		14.3	50.0	28.6		42.9	50.0					14.3
Teammates (#2)	60.0		40.0	100.0								
Summer camp				14.2	100.0					14.2		57.4
Club (#3)			100.0	50.0		25.0						25.0
Drama group		25.0	100.0	25.0		50.0						
Yearbook staff		40.0		20.0		20.0		20.0				
Other (#3)				100.0		20.0						

N = 73 (24 males, 49 females)

145

Findings are different in relation to heterosexual socializing. The first "other" category (responses referred to friends of the opposite sex exclusively) ranked 5 with males and 3.5 with females. Table 8.2 discloses that 75% of males select a group of 9 or under, and the same proportion of females distribute their preferences between two groups: 9 or fewer and 10–24. It appears that males prefer to socialize with fewer individuals of the opposite sex at a time. Girls spend more time with larger numbers.

Table 8.1 reveals a higher amount of male socialization with teammates. A higher proportion of males participated in two teams of nine or fewer. Females participated in only one team of nine or fewer, and the percent that participated was considerably lower. The findings reveal that males generally prefer to interrelate in smaller numbers than females in both sports and other types of socialization.

It is not improbable that more defined adult sex roles for males result in a need to discover a narrower range of potential skills than for females. More defined roles lessen the breadth of comparative acts males need engage. Furthermore, for males the athletic field/court offers an accessible natural arena where a number of the attributes of interest to them are open to view: sportsmanship, physical build, abilities, etc. Sportsmanship well represents the "intertwined" levels of present functioning and future potential unique to adolescence. Level of present functioning hints of the potential for future success. The competitive arena of sports serves as a natural and fruitful setting for comparative acts. Teammates and the athletic field for males may be the counterpart of the more extensive special-interest groups of females.

GROUP AND SELF-PERCEPTION

In prior chapters we suggested that adolescent socializing is only partially for fun. Being together with peers stimulates dynamic processes of psychological development—comparative acts. Part of accurate self-evaluation is assessing how one manages as part of a group. It is necessary to know how one is judged by others. Thus, self-assessment must be couched in a framework of others' regard on the particular attributes. Questions such as what qualities are respected and admired and which are held in low esteem need to be considered.

We structured a questionnaire to explore how these psychosocial assessments are perceived. Subjects were asked to select 12 self-attributes from a list of 65 that feel most pertinent when they are with the *close* friends they referred to in the first part of the instrument. They were directed to circle the 12 attributes and to rate themselves from 0 to 10 on each of the characteristics, 10 being the high score. Finally, they were instructed to indicate what rating they thought the group of close friends would give them on each of the 12 attributes.[*]

Our analysis calculated the difference for each individual between the self-rating and the perceived group rating on each attribute. We then summed and averaged the differentials over all individuals. A plus (+) indicated the individual's self-estimate to be higher than what the individual believed the group thought of him; a minus (−) indicated that the individual believed the group gave a higher rating than he gave himself. Findings revealed that no difference between self-appraisal and perceived group appraisal exceeded + 3 or − 3.

We then examined whether differences in the direction of self versus group perceptions existed between the sexes. Table 8.3 displays findings. An interesting difference between sexes is revealed. Almost one third of the females felt that they were underestimated by their group, as compared to almost two thirds of the males. Far more females than males felt their group of close friends rated them higher than they would rate themselves. For both groups, matching self- and group ratings were a small minority, especially so with males.

The data imply that females are less certain about themselves than males are with close friends. A number of conditions may contribute. Males may base their conclusions on a more intense comparison of fewer monitored characteristics. A further argument could be advanced that since males are more concerned with athletics and athletic ability than are females, some of their higher self- than perceived group assessment may be traced to a perception that there is little opportunity to display their true abilities because of the structure of competitive team sports. In sum, the data reveal that both sexes' self-estimates deviated from perceived "close friend" group estimates.

---

[*]The instrument utilized varied slightly from that reported in Chapter 6. "General physical appearance" and "musical ability—instrument" were inadvertently not included.

TABLE 8.3. Comparison of Self-ratings and Perceived
Group Ratings on 65 Attributes, by Sex.

Perception	Percent of Males	Percent of Females
Self-rating higher than close peer group rating	63.7	31.9
Close peer group rating higher than self-rating	35.4	59.5
Self-rating same as close peer group rating	0.9	8.6

N = 73 (24 males, 49 females)

Attributes of Primary Interest

A separate analysis revealed interesting male-female similarities and differences on the self-attributes they selected as most pertinent when they
interacted with their group of close friends (Table 8.4). Both sexes
were most aware of two personality attributes: sense of humor and
friendliness. Next in importance to females were interpersonal relationship qualities; males were alert to their observable social and athletic
skills. Overall, both sexes were more conscious of their personality
attributes and showed far less concern with learned competencies. These
findings are especially fascinating when we return to the findings involving larger samples reported in Chapter 6, on attributes of greatest interest in *others*. For example, only a 0.7% difference in interest existed
between the sexes in grades 9–12 for sense of humor (Table 6.10).
Furthermore, the top interest of males went to athletic ability and popularity with the opposite sex ranked second (Table 6.2). With females,
loyalty to friends achieved rank 3 (Table 6.3). The reader will note other
similarities when comparing results in Table 8.4 with those presented in
Table 6.12 for 12th-graders, particularly with learned competencies.

Number of Hours Spent with Close Friends

Respondents from both groups were also asked to estimate how many
hours every week they spent with the individuals identified as close
friends. Findings in Table 8.5 disclose that although the range for each
group was large, at least half of the females indicated they spent more
hours per week with close friends than did the majority of males.

The findings reported in this chapter offer some insight into adolescent preferences in terms of the manner in which they choose to

**TABLE 8.4. Ranks and percentages of Characteristics
Selected for Self-Rating According to Gender.**

	Male		Female	
Attribute	*Rank*	*Percent*	*Rank*	*Percent*
Friendliness	2	76	2	74
Sense of humor	1	94	1	76
Leadership	22.5	23	25.5	17
Artistic talent	60	0	46.5	6
Music ability (singing)	29.5	17	33	12
Athletic ability	5	58	25.5	17
General school work ability	9	35	18	23
Enthusiasm	15	29	25.5	17
Creative writing ability	49.5	5	50.5	4
Drama/acting ability	60	0	50.5	4
Mechanical ability	49.5	5	62.5	0
Cooking	39	11	42.5	8
Typing	60	0	56.5	2
Sexiness	22.5	23	21.5	19
Clothes	29.5	17	8.5	42
Figure/build/physique	15	29	7	44
Complexion	49.5	5	25.5	17
Popularity with opposite sex	3	70	6	51
Popularity with same sex	4	64	29	14
Ability to put feelings into words	9	35	13	34
Ability to put thoughts into words	15	29	21.5	19
Knowledge of current events	22.5	23	56.5	2
Good listener	15	29	4	70
Sportsmanship	7	41	50.5	4
Generosity	15	29	16	29
Masculinity	29.5	17	62.5	0
Femininity	60	0	33	12
Wealth (rich/poor)	22.5	23	33	12
Cleanliness	29.5	17	19.5	21
Laziness	60	0	42.5	8
Impatience	49.5	5	42.5	8
Cattiness	60	0	62.5	0
Selfishness	49.5	5	42.5	8
Religiousness	29.5	17	42.5	8
Snobbiness	49.5	5	38	10
Cheapness	29.5	17	62.5	0
Type of family one comes from	49.5	5	25.5	17

TABLE 8.4. *(Cont.)*

	Male		Female	
Attribute	*Rank*	*Percent*	*Rank*	*Percent*
Studiousness	49.5	5	50.5	4
Cooperativeness	29.5	17	33	12
Self-confidence	22.5	23	11	38
Prejudice	39	11	56.5	2
Adventurousness	49.5	5	33	12
Mother's occupation	60	0	56.5	2
Father's occupation	60	0	62.5	0
Morals	29.5	17	15	31
Sensitivity to others' feelings	15	29	10	40
Car driving	9	35	19.5	21
Stubbornness	49.5	5	42.5	8
Religion	39	11	50.5	4
Meanness	39	11	50.5	4
Niceness	39	11	17	25
Stick-to-it-iveness	39	11	56.5	2
Attitude toward one's family	60	0	25.5	17
Competitiveness	60	0	33	12
Maturity	39	11	8.5	42
Creativity	22.5	23	62.5	0
Honesty	60	0	5	61
Loyalty to friends	15	29	3	72
Dancing ability	6	47	38	10
Determination	39	11	33	12
Trustworthiness	39	11	13	34
Dependability	15	29	13	34
Patriotism	15	29	56.5	2
Openness to new ideas	39	11	38	10
Cliqueishness	39	11	46.5	6

n = 49 females
n = 24 males

TABLE 8.5. Estimated Hours Per
Week Spent With Close
Friends, According to Gender.

	Median	Range
Males (n = 24)	21–25	2–60
Females (n = 49)	26–30	4–75 +

gather. Generally the findings reveal adolescents to be sociable but discriminating. There is a clear distinction in numbers between acquaintances and close friends. Some interesting gender differences were also revealed. Although these may be interpreted as reinforcing notions of the female as more gregarious than the male, the variations are best considered within a framework that questions whether they are state- or trait-related.

CHAPTER 9

Synopsis of Findings: Snapshots of Social Interactional Life

This section has presented findings on the adolescent world of contacts and interactions. Revealed is the enormous capacity of these youth to attend to both present and future matters while in a period of enormous change in the four domains of growth. The many similar others to whom they flock in order to ease the insecurities they have about themselves supply this comfort but also add dissonant notes.

Data imply that adolescents share a subliminal awareness of the parallel processes at work in their transitional states and that they may intuitively understand each other. Adolescents are involved in large-group interactions but also are "alone" in retreat and reflection, reassessment, and evaluation.

Proper interpretation of the chameleonlike friendship and social participation patterns of this adolescent period demands understanding the deep-structure imperatives and dynamics of their functional interactions. Thus, our discussion of social interactional life examined a variety of behaviors with peers, focusing on how adolescents interrelate with a variety of peers and other generational members, attributes of agemates that adolescents find particularly intriguing, and structural components of their social functioning.

PERSONS OF INFLUENCE

Chapter 5, on reference groups, dealt with how the adolescent conceptually organizes and utilizes sources of counsel and advice. With increased discriminatory abilities, the adolescent intellectually sorts out the most relevant sources. The data disclose the high school student to be a discerning individual who does not accord influence globally. The studies reveal a reference world differentiated into individuals or groups distinctly identified as expert on specific categories of issues. These data strongly support notions that parents are used as consultants for future-oriented serious matters; peers are used for leisure and for issues that are almost exclusive to generational counterparts. Decision-making and action on several "peer" matters are embedded in peer group norms. Interestingly, older siblings crossed generational lines. They were utilized for both present and future concerns.

Parents are a strong reference group. Parents achieved rank 1 of the 13 discrete reference groups for both sexes. Even when we clustered five discrete groups of peers, who together constituted the top influence source on the majority of issues, parents followed very closely. Furthermore, trend data spanning the 10-year period of the ARGI study disclosed that parents had gained more in influence than the peer group cluster. The data were similar for both sexes, with some indication of earlier movement for girls than for boys away from parents to special friend.

The trend over the 10-year period was stability more than change. These findings can reassure parents, who may fear being "displaced" or even "replaced." They are seen as figures who represent experience and wisdom and who are consulted about both philosophical and future-related issues. Other authority figures, such as school personnel, are consulted on objective or factual issues limited to future education and job concerns.

Across the 10-year period, the influence distribution remained the same among parents, peers, siblings, and authority groups. In both the earlier and later samples, the second most potent influence group was schoolmates of the same age. It was stronger for females than males. The transitional role of the older sibling as a swing figure between generations stood firm. When influence of siblings was added to that of parents, this family cluster displaced the five-group cluster of peers as first-rank influence source on a number of issues. Conversely, when influence of siblings was added to the peer cluster, parents were often displaced as first rank. Since a sibling can be conceptualized as either a generation mate or a family mate, they are seen as understanding both worlds. Thus, they offer strong influence to either strengthen a resolve or reduce an ambivalence.

ATTRIBUTES OF INTEREST

Findings from Chapter 6, examining attributes of particular interest to adolescents about one another, lend support to popular impressions and also reveal some surprising facts. Males emerged as more interested than females in outwardly observable characteristics. Females were more interested in attributes of character, such as loyalty to friends and sensitivity. In the 10 attributes of greatest interest, little difference between the sexes was found.

Important insights are afforded by these data on concerns connected with interpersonal relationships with peers. For example, concern about loyalty to friends on the part of females implies that they feel "at risk" when they share information. In transition away from the support of parental and older-generational figures, they seem to need dependable new allegiances. These data indicate that girls may be more careful than boys. In corollary fashion, the greater interest revealed by boys in outward appearances implies that these youngsters are already worrying about present and future image. It makes for speculation that the need for observable success may be more burdensome to males than to females. The interest both sexes share in clothes is interpreted here as a conformity issue.

Notwithstanding the strength of the need to conform (the adolescent must closely keep track of what "is in" or "is expected" and what will make a good surface impression), the close attention adolescents pay to one another also serves deep-structure developmental needs. The degree of interest in attributes of the other is a function of the adolescent's important task of resolving which personality and character elements "belong to me" and how they fit together to provide a structure of self. Preoccupations such as staring, lack of attention, and other disconcerting overt behaviors may be better understood in the context of two types of simultaneous growth: (1) the overtly observable, or surface-structure, behavior and (2) the hidden, or deep-structure, psychosocial development. Complex and confusing behaviors often reflect deep-structure growth work—the secret arena.

A TIME TO BE ALONE

Among the fascinating revelations disclosed in the data on socialization practices is that teens, although participating in huge parties, do not have very many close friends whose advice they will risk asking. In other words, *the intimacy level is very low while the activity level is very high.* As discussed in earlier chapters, this condition is due to three factors. First, there is a strong need to be alone in order to have the time to process the outcomes of the large gathering, to reevaluate for better understanding or interpreting the comparative act that motivated the attendance, etc. The deep-structure developmental basis for elation or disappointment experienced may not be cognitively clear to the adolescent. Second, the adolescent is still in a state of self formation. True intimacy is not achievable until the individual possesses a sense of self with which to truly engage the other. While a self is in process of formation, new material and perspectives are utilized "self-reflectively": How does it affect me? What would I do in such a situation? Would I like that opportunity? Am I like that? How would it influence my future? Until these answers have been worked out and the qualities involved are either rejected or attributed to self, there is interference to intimacy with an "other."

Third, intimacy also involves time commitment. Lack of real intimacy conserves energies the adolescent must still devote to: (1) task completion (school work, duties), (2) family responsibilities, (3) peer group dynamics, which include vast energies invested in comparative acts, (4) meeting conformity requirements so that he or she is not denied access to the arena for development—peers and peer groups, and (5) personal physical health and body presentation needs. Time away from stimulation and demand is essential to keep up with the energy drain of the period; the system must spend some time integrating and resting. *Thus, the aloneness one sees in adolescents is generally not loneliness. It is a necessary and healthy aloneness.* It is a functional necessity of the period.

We have referred to "locking oneself in one's room," or lack of communicativeness with family (when there appears plenty of time for conversation with friends), as a possible manifestation of the need to conserve energies. Aloneness may be misinterpreted as hostility or excessive isolation. Without the knowledge that both intense socialization and aloneness are normative and appropriate, overt manifestations of the need to withdraw temporarily can be misdiagnosed as antisocial and even neurotic. Unless it is carried to obviously extreme degrees, it is a normative process and not cause for concern. That it is appropriate is supported by the model presented in this book.

PEER ARENA, NOT GROUP

Adolescents interact in a number of different groups, not only one or two major groups. These many groups make up their "peer arena," in which they contact many types of agemates. Some are compatible in many areas, and close relationships ensue; others may be valued for a specific talent. They may also be valued because they do not have a talent, which allows the other individual to feel more competent by comparison. These combinations of agemates drawn from various groups afford the developing adolescent the variety of raw materials to learn from, to compare to, and to identify or reject as elements of self. The concept of a "peer arena" replaces that of "peer group." The latter refers to a favorite group selected from the various groups that compose the psychological peer arena. The data offer insight on adolescent interactional life as a conglomerate of multi-group participation.

With the exception of "close friends," socialization groups often number from 10 to 24 members or more. The data reinforce notions that adolescence is *not* a period of intimate relations. "Intimate" conversations overheard between agemates are repeated with any number of other agemates. Adolescents are in a developmental posture where talk is a *means to garner information about others*. Words are primarily invitations for further exchange, not serious deliberation. Adolescents provide one another with opportunities to gain information and to test out how their own responses are received. *Adolescent conversation is not geared to content but to the reciprocal process*. Each concentrating on self, not on other.

In essence, adolescents are in a tryout mode. It is essential to understand this experimental orientation lest the thoughts expressed be mistaken for a well-considered position. It is important to pay close attention to the adolescent at the moment of communication, but it is also essential to anticipate that a contrary position may be adopted the next time the topic is broached. Movement from group to group, engaging comparative acts while interacting within the various groups, and the subsequent private reflection and integration capture the multidimensional world of adolescents. They experience emotional responses of varying intensity from activities engaged in the large groups, but they have few confidants. While each is available to the other for developmental fodder, they are not yet available to one another for the true exchange that comes with possession of a sense of self.

A SECRET ARENA

The notion of a "secret arena" of adolescent growth where the peer is prominent may be unfamiliar to many readers. Interpretations of adolescent behaviors that trace determinants solely to the early years and to problems in parent-child or family relationships may be misleading. These conceptions are not broad enough in their theoretical framework to accommodate the influence by sheer volume of the young people since the postwar baby boom. The change in the size and power of the younger generation relative to the older met with platitudes about adolescent development that fed outdated theories and notions of rebellion, generation gap, etc. What has been generally overlooked is that peers (by force of numbers alone) in this period became the primary developmental environmental other. The analyses here are based in this current reality.

The book seeks to explain adolescents' complicated behavior not within restrictions of conscious and unconscious, but through premises drawn from a blend of developmental theory, observations of behavior, and empirical exploration.

The adolescent imperative for growth demands that functional psychosocial interaction be accomplished with others who are and will continue to be in the same stage of life. Large numbers of others are necessary to provide sufficient raw materials for comparison for the adolescent to arrive at ideas of relative merit. Not going to a party is more than a disappointment. It is experienced subliminally as deprivation of a developmental imperative to access others for developmentally essential comparison purposes.

Deep-structure dynamics of the adolescent dialectic move the youth away from attractions and securities of childhood to engage the call of adulthood, its responsibilities, and the crucial necessity to accomplish self-knowledge and self-direction. The adolescent dialectic stimulates each young person to search out others in the same condition. Their developmental work is done very individually but in parallel motion— in the same arenas, using identical dynamics to reach parallel goals of individual identity construction.

Before the adolescent period, relationships between children do not extend beyond the activity of the moment. Parents and family define the relevant world. Friends are truly playmates. But in adolescence relationships are serious, notwithstanding outward frivolousness. Preparing for the future is a concern these contemporaries share. Each has left a protected period of life and now possesses an ever-increasing awareness that adulthood and responsibility will soon follow. For this reason, not only must the contours of the greater society become more familiar, but the individual also must know the silhouettes of those others who will be traveling alongside.

Toward these ends, the adolescent selects individuals and groups of individuals for information. This information is gained nonverbally through use of the senses—looking, listening, touching, smelling, and tasting—and by verbal communication. Biological, cognitive, and emotional growth stimulate a continual "changing" during the period. Extensive periods of relative disorganization may occur as new abilities upset the equilibrium of prior functioning. Once these new levels of growth are consolidated, we see some outward equilibrium only to be again interrupted by uneven growth spurts until new integrations take place. New thinking and questioning are continuously stimulated. Questions are framed that were inaccessible to thought in younger years. Growth during the adolescent period differs from the growth of childhood. New cognitive and physical abilities encompass longer distances and afford leaps of independence. To some extent, there is an awareness of the responsibilities that accompany these new freedoms.

PART FOUR

Deviance and its Misinterpretations

This section examines three categories of deviation: those of psychosocial origin, those of a physical basis, and those due to geographic circumstances. Chapter 10 deals with adolescents who demonstrate maladaptive behaviors. These behaviors include social problem activity such as drug and alcohol abuse and cults. Maladaptive behaviors that may in part be a result of peer deprivation are also described. Other behaviors that may appear quite suitable but actually depict premature development are introduced. They represent "aborted adolescence." Their impact on attainment of maturity is described.

Chapter 11 first discusses issues connected with physical problems that afflict adolescents temporarily or permanently. Conflicting concerns of adolescents, who nonetheless must simultaneously cope with adolescence and prepare for the future as adults, are examined. The latter portion of the chapter addresses the serious potential for psychological growth deprivation in situations where adolescent youth are culturally distant or geographically isolated from easy access to socialization opportunities. Intervention strategies are offered for professionals in societal institutions, and recommendations are made for participation by parents and relevant environmental figures.

CHAPTER 10

Maladaptations in Smooth Progression: Adolescents in Trouble

A sense of self-esteem is beneficial at all times but is a particularly valuable asset in a period of stress. Self-confidence is lost and found often during the period of adolescent growth. Loss of esteem is heavily pronounced in adolescence because at no other growth period is the individual so attuned to and involved with discovery and integration of elements of self. Thus, at no other period is there such a volume of comparative acts. The adolescent continually deals with the results of these automatically occurring psychosocial dynamics. At future stages in the life cycle, a central sense of "self" exists and remains stable in spite of moments when specific characteristics are viewed as inadequate or lacking. The whole house of cards does not come down with some misplays. In the adolescent period however, the house of cards is still being built. Hence, a wrong play may be all that is needed to bring down an already shaky structure.

Adolescents, like all others, want to feel good about themselves. It is hard to see oneself as inferior to anyone, particularly to relevant others. One means of defending against ego assault is to join in or identify with a group that one feels more comfortable with. Such movement can refurbish energies and build new strengths. Alternatively, it can serve as a "hideout" from dealing with the physical and psychological interactions required for developmental growth, facing the conclusions drawn, and consequently adjusting aspirations upward or downward. To know one's relative status among peers in a number of groups is functional to preparing for life. Defensively hiding within the contours of one very well known milieu is not.

ADOLESCENT PROBLEM BEHAVIORS AS FLIGHT FROM PEERS AND DEVELOPMENTAL HARDSHIPS

To define psychosocial identity requires that the adolescent engage in continuing comparison with others, particularly peers, and in subsequent evaluations of attributes and characteristics of self in relation to those peers. Results of comparisons may be very disappointing or even debilitating to the ego. At times, the experiences may be so painful that the adolescent may seek to leave the physical or psychological arena of peers. Adolescent evaluation does not just affect present performance; present performance carries implications for performance in future life. Hence, it is serious business. Escape allows a respite from being the subject and object of the continuing comparison and assessment of adolescence. This escape can be accomplished through a variety of routes. Youngsters who come into adolescence with emotional strength and who do not encounter serious trauma during the period can generally manage the affective ups and downs that result from comparisons. Those whose experience is otherwise may have a difficult time and can elect a defensive form of flight to escape the pain of disappointing outcomes. In this chapter we will look at various types of adolescent problem behaviors from the perspective of a flight response to unbearable pain encountered in the psychosocial transactions characteristic of and essential to the developmental stage. Although freeing oneself from the emotional assaults of peer comparisons is not the exclusive reason for defensive responses, it must be considered paramount.

Defensive flight can be masked and not recognized as escape from peer arena developmental activity. When masked, it is often misdiagnosed. Some examples of masked flight follow.

The Pseudoadult

Some children appear to be more comfortable with adults than with others of their own age. In most cases, history taking reveals that a greater number of positive reinforcements for their behaviors come from adults than from their peers. Hence, they choose to be in the company of adults rather than agemates. This situation becomes more serious when the child becomes adolescent, since contact with other adolescents is the setting where most psychosocial growth occurs. Access to the arena for psychosocial growth (the peer groups that make up the peer arena) is necessary for access to the raw materials of growth that agemates model. Through the processes of comparison, assessment, and evaluation of self in relation to peers, the adolescent forges her own identity. The process is long and arduous. Positively reinforcing moments are far less frequent than difficult times. Some adolescents find they cannot exchange the self-confidence and emotional stability provided by adult reinforcements for uncertainty. Joining the company of peers presents a psychological risk. Seltzer (1982) suggests that these adolescents may often retreat to defensive flight that is outwardly masked. Their direction is decidedly maladaptive. One such maladaptation is the *pseudoadult*; another is the *settled adolescent*. Both of these defensive postures appear to be prosocial and normative. In actuality full development is at best postponed and in some cases not experienced at all (Seltzer, 1982).

The pseudoadult never constructs a personal set of self elements since psychologically he does not really enter the peer arena and thus does not engage its dynamics. It is too risky. He stays away from peers as much as possible, and when he is in their company, he does not psychologically engage the developmental dynamics of the period. He shuts them out. He thus remains in an immature stance. He continues to borrow elements of self from parents and elders just as he did when he was a child. This provides a facsimile self and a sense of stability. The primary difference from the facsimile self of childhood is that the cognitive advance of the pseudoadult allows him to pick out the self elements he wishes to *copy*. Unlike the child, he no longer copies wholesale. But he does copy; he does not construct a set of elements particular to himself. Thus, he never is in possession of a self-constructed structure signifying psychosocial maturity, completion of the identity search, and readiness for adult functioning. His outward behaviors, including decision-making, are based on an identity that is not his. To the outside world, the pseudoadult appears adult even through the rigorous times of adolescence. "Kidlike" dimensions of adolescent behavior are not evident. His maturity is not truly his own; it is copied and borrowed.

This individual goes through life exerting extreme care. He is not a risk taker; risks frighten him since he has not engaged in psychological risk taking and thus has not developed the self elements to deal with it. Flexibility is not his hallmark. It is necessary that he design his life within the closely structured boundaries of *what he has seen before*. Hence, he is a candidate for high anxiety or even an inability to cope if he confronts the unforeseen. An adolescent who adopts this type of defense enters adulthood without developing and exercising coping mechanisms for dealing with the ups and downs of life. Instead, we see a restricted adolescent who appears adult.

Paradoxically, this type of adolescent is often held up by adults as a model for the adolescent who does actively participate in the vicissitudes of the period and does display emotional ups and downs. The pseudoadult generally shows early resolution of vocational choice and thus personifies a youth with direction, not one who is floundering and experimenting. The former generally brings a false comfort to parents, who are not expected to be familiar with the formal developmental process. Parents relax when they feel their children have sensible goals. Prior reinforcements from adults for pseudoadult behaviors are strengthened by current reinforcements from parents and other adults. The pseudoadult receives few, if any, signals from outside sources that his defensive cover has dangerous implications for full and positive functioning.

The Settled Adolescent

The maladaptive psychological defense of the settled adolescent is similar. The settled adolescent is different form the pseudoadult in that elements of the self structure are not borrowed; they are constructed. However, the models are adults, not agemates. This type of adolescent did try out the peer arena and adolescent psychosocial comparison dynamics, but too much psychological distress was experienced to remain engaged. Thus, she physically and/or psychologically left the developmental arena and made adults her models.

Rather than being a painful process, this type of flight allows a generally positive experience. If some comparison finds the adolescent lacking, she can rationalize it due to age differences. If a comparison shows her to be superior, it can be ego-enhancing. Since this adolescent is psychologically withdrawn from peers, interactions are less stressful since they lack the emotional dimensions.

However, this avoidance of risk taking, which foreshortens the developmental process, does not fulfill the adolescent task of forging true identity. Knowing who one is is integrally related to the social context and the others who do and will continue to people it—one's generation. Other factors also negatively affect the validity of the settled adolescent's notions about the "self" she constructs. As discussed earlier, sufficient numbers of others are necessary for adequate amounts of raw material and valid feedback. Although the settled adolescent has substituted adults for peers, large numbers to provide a range of choices are still essential. However, accessibility to many large groups of adults is generally limited, as is the opportunity to interact closely with members of these groups. For example, these adolescents do not have the counterpart of school in which to meet adults. Quantities of raw materials so necessary to first-stage, primary peer arena comparisons and evaluations are extremely limited. Thus, the type and quality of self elements that can be fashioned are severely affected.

Both the pseudoadult and the settled adolescent experience these deprivations, but the pseudoadult strategy of defensive flight is far less dependent on numbers since the pseudoadult does not engage in the process at all. He borrows an adult structure *as is*. The settled adolescent tries to hammer it out, albeit with age-inappropriate models. Thus, the settled adolescent suffers because of both inappropriate age group *and* insufficient numbers.

Since the settled adolescent tries out and borrows mature characteristics, she, like the pseudoadult, appears "regular" and adultlike at quite a young age. The eccentricities and extremes of adolescent behaviors, which are overt manifestations of the trial-and-error process, generally do not appear in the repertoire of the settled adolescent. Although the defensive structure of the settled adolescent is not as rigid as that of the pseudoadult, since the former did engage somewhat in comparative acts with peers, neither enters adulthood fully developed. The settled adolescent projects a more tenuous stance than the pseudoadult's since she has not borrowed wholesale. But the number and range of adult models available do not allow full trial and error experimentation and eventual resolution of her own self elements. The settled adolescent also has defensively limited possible exposure to vulnerability and pain by psychologically leaving the peer arena. This type of adult is more susceptible to psychological distress than the normatively developing individual and, like the pseudoadult, will fare better with a well-structured life that does not undergo much variation and change. Stressful and open-ended situations may lead to unbearable stress, or even breakdown.

Ironically, the settled adolescent also may be an individual to whom adults point as a model for their children. They manifest a steady calm and reasonable goals. However, these goals are formulated through comparative and evaluative exercises with an older though currently comfortable age group that does not and will not represent their age cohort now or in future years. Hence, the congruity that settled adolescents experience as they work out a self structure runs a severe danger of being short-lived—unless, perhaps, they can manage to psychologically remain a generation older.

Addictions

We are deeply concerned today about the increasing number of adolescents who abuse alcohol and drugs. In considering the factors that may be contributory, it is important to bear in mind that adolescence is a period of frameworklessness and instability—a critical period when adolescents find it necessary to seek acceptance by others they perceive to be like themselves. Uncertain adolescents who need relationships are easy prey. Conformity to popular behaviors assures acceptance.

Earlier it was suggested that adolescents must have continuing access to a group to satisfy their deep-structure need to be in contact with the models offering raw materials for development. Although adolescents experience frameworklessness (in contrast to their protected younger years), the need to continue distancing themselves from parents and elders to serve demands of individuation is strong. Thus, they require substitute supports. Other adolescents, because of their similar condition, are most attractive. Being with peers stimulates adolescent developmental dynamics of comparison, assessment, and evaluation, which remain active whether the outcomes are pleasant or painful. Pain due to intolerable disappointments in self may reach crisis level. Temporary reduction of pain may be sought in addictive behaviors. They offer many advantages. The adolescent can continue to appear associated with a group and to be accepted as a member. At the same time, the addictive behaviors can produce "self-anesthesia," sparing the youth from experiencing the results of comparison dynamics.

It is important to bear in mind that the ability of the individual to cope may have been worn away. Too many psychological assaults may have been endured. The peer arena comparative act process may have been too difficult. Alcohol consumption protects adolescents from further experiencing disappointing results of comparisons. It is paradoxical that a powerful reason for alcohol and drug abuse is to escape the group and its conformity pressures at a time when being with similar others is experienced with near-drive intensity. Such consumption offers flight from the developmental dynamics that being with the peer group stimulates into activity.

The escape is psychological, not physical; thus, public appearances continue to be served. The adolescent appears to be participating with others fully; in truth, he is not in an interactive posture. Drug and alcohol use afford opportunities for deadening the impact of developmental work while one overtly retains "membership in good standing." Public compliance requirements and private defensive actions are served. Thus, alcohol and drug consumption provide an acceptable "cover," not only to others but to oneself. Actions can be attributed to effects of the drug or alcohol. Use of drugs and alcohol provide both opportunity and rationale to retreat from the continuing scrutiny of "self and other" that characterizes the psychosocial activity of peer arena interaction.

Professionals who adopt this theoretical framework are able to understand how addictive habits operate to protect. It sheds some light on why adolescents seek out drugs over and over again in spite of clear medical information, tragic models, and parental discouragements. We suggest that drug and/or alcohol abuse can be both the ticket to membership in a group (particularly one where the *only* criterion for membership is participation in drugs or alcohol) *and* the means to dull or even eliminate the impact of the group's interactive developmental dynamics. Tragically, the end result is a moratorium from development and lost years. The development process can be aborted or seriously hindered.

The Cause-Committed Adolescent

Another often unrecognized defense against stressful anxiety stimulated by adolescent developmental activity is illustrated in the *cause-committed* adolescent. He channels the need for defensive flight from the dynamics of interaction in the peer arena into a more socially accepted avenue than does the drug-alcohol abuser. Psychodynamically, however, he is a close cousin. This adolescent spends *inordinate* amounts of time and energies working on a cause or a project. It is another self-destructive pattern since energies are diverted away from essential psychosocial growth work. The motivation is the same as for the categories mentioned in preceding sections: escape from the pain of dissonant responses to comparative acts. This form of flight can be effected through socially accepted outlets—political activity, health-related projects, etc. Its cover of social acceptability makes it more difficult to identify. The maladaptation is recognizable by the exaggerated *degree* of involvement. The adolescent spends the majority of available time on this cause. There is little evidence of other interests. Thus, there remains little time to seek out social opportunities with peers. Two or three peers may be engaged together in such activity. Conceivably, it represents a defense for all, depending on each individual's degree of involvement.

The Person-Committed Adolescent

A variation on the cause-committed individual is one who displays overinvolvement in another person—the *person-committed* adolescent. Adolescents may be "best friends" with each other or may be involved in romantic infatuations to experiment with close interpersonal relating. But if these relationships become *all-consuming* timewise, with little or no time for anything or anyone else, we must be on the alert to the possibility of defensive flight. Again, it is the duration and the intensity that identify the behavior as a defense. The other person may be older, younger, or the same age. The maladaptation is most clearly observable when the overcommittment is with a younger person, less apparent when it is with an older person such as a teacher or mentor, and difficult to detect when it is with a same-age peer.

CHAPTER 11

Adolescents Out of the Mainstream: Psychosocial Dimensions and Dangers

Prior chapters have detailed how adolescents need other adolescents as a source of the raw materials of psychosocial development. They study and assess the characteristics observed in peers, and sometimes they borrow characteristics for trial. Eventually, the characteristics are resolved into one's own self elements or rejected as foreign. Prior chapters have also discussed the groups adolescents are attracted to and which attributes of others they are especially interested in. Findings support a picture of adolescents terribly interested in one another and choosing to spend a lot of time together.

There are, however, adolescents who do not have easy access to one another: (1) those who live in rural settings quite far from the regional schools where after-school or weekend activities take place, (2) those who suffer from physical handicaps or illnesses, (3) those who are either homebound or in health care facilities, and (4) those who recently arrived in this country and who cannot psychologically handle peer group dynamics of a new culture in addition to their own. They may defensively withdraw from peer group activity and isolate themselves.

Small numbers of peers limit choices for tryout. Youngsters who fall within the aforementioned categories are denied the opportunity for physical and psychological interaction with the numbers of peers essential for full exercise of the dynamics of the adolescent dialectic. They are kept from the rich "supermarket" of attributes, qualities, and skills a large group of agemates offers. Although these dynamics will be engaged with those peers that are available, limited models may lead to a premature closure on elements of both the temporary and the permanent self structure.

THE ADOLESCENT WITHOUT A GROUP

Adolescents seek stabilization and support during periods of frame-worklessness, when it has become inappropriate to borrow identity and when prior guides are seen as irrelevant and even as a threat to the task of achieving independence. Having enough similar others reinforces a sense of "I'm OK." Although sufficient difference must be provided for leaps of fantasy and aspiration, there must be enough similarity to allow a basic sense of comfort. Those individuals whose situation keeps them from natural access to the necessary age cohorts need help.

First and foremost it is essential for the professional and for significant others to recognize that these children are subject to a developmental deprivation: denial of the developmental aliment consisting of opportunities to look at, listen to, and interact with their age cohort.

Where insufficient involvement is due to geographic limitations, it would be advantageous for administrators of regional schools, which combine small districts, to strongly encourage parents to arrange for adolescents to attend as many school activities as possible. Furthermore, parents should be encouraged to vacation in populated settings and to have their adolescents attend summer camps and weekend activities sponsored by religious or community groups, which will expose the young people to large numbers of agemates. A nontraditional avenue for bringing isolated adolescents in contact with peers is the media. Movies, TV, and books provide all types of models, often in considerable detail. The VCR offers the opportunity to present carefully selected movies about teenagers and teenage issues. Time spent by adolescents in any of these activities will help counteract the deprivations brought by insufficient peer interaction.

For other groups of adolescents, the problems are not geographic but physical.

THE DIFFERENT ADOLESCENT

The different adolescent represents a category of youth that is best thought of not as disfigured adolescents, but as disfigured *and* adolescent. We do these individuals a disservice if we allow their physical appearance to cloud their developmental stage and behaviors. Some moods are reflective of the adolescent condition, not the disfigurement. Different adolescents are as subject to mood swings and behavioral oddities as their normative counterparts.

On the other hand, for these individuals the adolescent condition is exacerbated by unusual physical appearance. In early and middle adolescence there are periods when physical, cognitive, and emotional changes experienced from within can be outwardly evident. Similarity in outward appearances is reassuring and sought after. Seeing others who look like oneself neutralizes the uncertainties related to internally experienced changes. To be perceived as "different" is extremely painful and particularly difficult during the adolescent period.

Pressures to conform stem from two sources: (1) from within—the individual wishes to appear as similar to the rest of the group as possible, and (2) from without—pressures from the group are put on the individual to maintain similarity. The latter may take the form of ridicule, rudeness, exclusion, or indifference. Such social tactics are exerted to redirect deviators from the group toward conformity and concordant behaviors.

Not all adolescents can appear similar. Some adolescents may wish to conform, but certain outward features cannot be adjusted into concordance, no matter how strong the motivation. These physically imperfect children suffer frustration and shame, and they risk isolation and ridicule. They may resist going to school and participating in school-related or other social gatherings, and psychosomatic responses may result.

Adolescents who suffer from physical disfigurement deal not only with the deformity. They must still manage the age-appropriate physical and psychosocial growth imperatives. Some of these adolescents must also deal with the constant awareness of projected short life or a life of continuous medical care.

What these young people do share with healthy adolescents is the experience of pubertal changes. They undergo subliminal psychological changes, experience new needs, and share the adolescent imperative to separate from parents and begin the path to adulthood. But their physical condition brings complications. For example, they may be dependent on parents for physical or medical assistance or emotional support. Thus, it is difficult for them to be independent or even to assume independent postures, to express the belligerence that offers a necessary sense of psychological distancing. Adolescents uncertain about the impact of the disfigurement on their opportunities in life deal with confusion in relation to preparation for adult functioning. Complicating matters further, there are few similar others to offer some reassurance of one's "normality." Earlier we discussed the reassurance normal adolescents experience when they are able to access a number of similar others. Disfigured adolescents experience the disorientations of developmental changes and feel the inappropriateness of continuing dependency on parents but are frustrated in identifying with similar others.

Not only are disfigured adolescents denied the reassurance that access to many similar agemates brings, but they also experience limited access to normative peer models who offer a range of characteristics and skills for comparison, assessment, evaluation, and experimentation. Regardless of their appearance, they must interact and live with other individuals. Restricted access to large groups of agemates who are not disfigured inhibits preparation for normal adult life. Although television does provide an opportunity for some comparisons with normal adolescents, as do books and other literature, these youths need living others they can touch and be with. The right to smooth psychological movement into adulthood must be supported by the numbers enabling the variety of comparisons essential to such development. If not, we risk adding psychological infirmity to the physical problem.

ADOLESCENTS WITH DISABILITIES

Those youngsters who suffer physical handicaps or illnesses also endure restricted access to peers. Within these groups are adolescents who can expect a normal life span and others who are aware that their illness or incapacity will shorten their lives. Members of these two groups have some conditions in common and others that are quite different. All are denied the numbers of peers necessary for them to fully engage the developmental dynamics required for completion of the psychosocial adolescent task. They must all develop compensatory outlets and strategies as they attempt to manage the deprivation. Parents and professionals need to recognize that it is not just social life that suffers. Developmental progression can be seriously affected if the psychosocial setting for the exercise of developmental tasks is not accessible.

Adolescents inhibited in access to enough similar peers due to physical disability or illness can be divided into two general categories. One group must prepare for life with an acknowledged "difference" from age cohorts; the second must prepare both for this different kind of life *and* for death. For the former category, some elements to be compared and evaluated correspond to those of their nonhandicapped peers, and other elements are not at all cogent. For example, a crippled boy does not compare an athletic ability just as normal teens do not observe the ability to get around in a wheelchair.

Those elements of common interest to the normal and the afflicted nevertheless differ in relative importance. For example, a normal girl's rating of her skill in math as compared to that of others may not matter as much as the same rating for a crippled girl. The normal girl has the choice of comparing many more elements involving nonacademic talents, including physical skills. Thus, disabled youngsters must devise a method for carrying on two different sets of comparative processes — one with the normative group against, for, and with whom they will be transacting life's business to certain, specified points; and another with a second group, who share the experience of going through life afflicted. Such a youngster must perform the double duty of arriving at a self-picture in relation to each type — and both! It is crucial for this adolescent to observe how *each* group manages *and* to move back and forth in the comparative act process *and* to engage the adolescent dialectic dynamics with groups that are highly similar in one area and highly different in others. Identity resolution for these youngsters is based on a flexible set of self elements that incorporates similarities but also recognizes differences between the two camps of adolescent others. The set of interrelated personality elements must also reflect congruence and fit attainable life goals.

This complex task must be carried out in the context of limited access to similar others. Professionals working with adolescents who are ill and/or incapacitated need to be aware of the developmental costs of restricted opportunity, in the early stage of adolescence, for contact with the necessary large numbers of peers and, in the second and last stages of adolescence, for a sufficient number of peers who feel similar. Lack of sufficient agemates works against the innate imperative to complete identity resolution. An educated parent group can be an important aid to appropriate strategies for increasing access of disabled adolescents to other adolescents. Efforts will be greatly facilitated by a group of parents alert to the special problems related to peer interaction: (1) The peer is not just social company but provides developmental raw materials. (2) Peers for these children are hard to come by. Hence, some of the tension manifested with agemates arises from the awareness that they must not alienate and thus lose access to these scarce peers. (3) Mood fluctuations are in part attributable to peer relations and peer assessments, which result in pride or disappointment in self. (4) Part of the pain of the illness or handicap is related to the stage of life, when it is developmentally natural and essential to engage in almost constant comparison and evaluation of self in relation to peer. Professionals must stress to parents that these youngsters need to be in steady contact with healthy adolescents notwithstanding the pain associated with the comparisons. They need to engage in comparative acts with teens who correspond to the healthy side of themselves.

Parents of afflicted adolescents need to be assisted to understand that their child experiences a special type of conflict. They experience the adolescent imperative and the normal, necessary preoccupation with being with peers. On the other hand, an afflicted adolescent may strongly resist being with agemates to escape the pain of making comparisons. He or she may also resist treatment of the physical condition and/or wearing therapeutic devices in an effort to avoid being different. Although the need to conform is high in all adolescents, it is much more so for the different adolescent. Medical treatment may involve wearing an apparatus or leaving class at a certain time to take medicine or food. Since the adolescent is subject to what Elkind (1967) calls the "imaginary audience," which is in attendance at all times, any deviation from the norm is experienced by the adolescent as a glaring difference. If the experience of difference is too painful, he or she will try to find reasons to stay away from peers. Physical pain may actually be experienced, but it could also be exaggerated or fantasized. Professionals must be alert to such possibilities.

At the same time, it is necessary not to automatically attribute mood fluctuation to the illness or disabling condition. Self-reflective assessment as a response to peer arena comparisons may stimulate the mood change. Comparisons with others that lead to feelings of painful reality may raise present, future-related, or status-oriented concerns, which may or may not be related to the disability. They may be related to the activity of normative developmental dynamics.

Because this stage of development requires such a volume and intensity of self-examination and comparison, it is futile for the professional to encourage the afflicted adolescent to forget his disability. However, it is essential for professionals to regard the disabled adolescent primarily as *like*, not *unlike*, other adolescents. Thus, they should first assume mood changes or mood states to represent the adolescent's affective responses to the operative comparative act dynamics. The task of the period to forge an identity includes afflicted adolescents, too.

The more the professional can help the adolescent acknowledge both his positive and his painful circumstances, the more the adolescent feels understood as *not just* a sick adolescent. To encourage a "turn the other cheek" attitude and focus only on the positives is experienced as frustrating and is destructive. The proper therapeutic approach with *any* teen is to encourage engagement of the psychosocial processes and then be available to assist the teen to appropriately handle his or her individualized responses. It helps for the afflicted adolescent to know that "normals" also have problems and weaknesses. At all times, clients need help to live with, not ignore or disguise, the realities of their condition. To cooperate in shielding the disabled teen from full participation in and experience of adolescent dynamics and their impact would constitute *denial of adolescence*.

Future Orientation

A major factor that differentiates adolescence from childhood is that for the adolescent, the future intrudes regularly on the present. A present-future stance essentially defines the adolescent condition. A sick or handicapped individual is not immune, nor does he cease to experience the ups and downs that accompany this posture. In the second and last stage of adolescent identity formation, when final decisions are made on which are the "real" elements of one's self, heavy emphasis is placed by the adolescent on what attributes will serve future goals. Again, this is as true for disabled/sick adolescents as for any others. Professionals need to remind parents that the future is very much in the minds of their adolescents, notwithstanding their concern over present needs and the circumstances of the infirmity (including hospitalization). The professional must discuss the present handicap with the exceptional child and parent regardless of the pain it may cause. Moreover, to address its impact on the future but not include the present experience of engaging in peer comparisons would be a serious disservice.

Assistance in bringing the peer group to the adolescent may become necessary. Here, the media may be of help. They offer any number of opportunities for exposure to the peer group: television, VCR movies, radio, newspapers, magazines, books, etc. Professionals may choose to bring small groups of exceptional children together for media-presented stories dealing with character studies or situations relevant to an afflicted adolescent. The picture of how others dealt with the issues and what necessary attributes were present or absent may challenge the adolescent to examine her own potential and versatility. With skilled professional help in bringing present condition and future functioning together, the objective experiences viewed can be relived and expanded upon with reference to personal circumstances.

ADOLESCENTS WITH TERMINAL ILLNESS

Different conditions exist for the child with terminal illness, who must prepare for life and for death concurrently. As is the case for peers, the stress of acting "appropriately" and conforming is crucial. When the going gets rough, however, this adolescent may be tempted to retreat into the attitude of "it's not worth it anyway since I will die soon." Again, the professional must be alert to the inner conflicts. This retreat may reflect serious depression over the illness, but it may also be a response to normative adolescent pain.

More times than not, the professional focuses on what the foreshortened life prognosis means to the patient and how best to help the patient deal with her short life. What is usually not dealt with but must be is how an uncertain future affects her work on constructing a picture of who she is *now*—her identity in the present and who she will be in the short-term future. Clearly, the adolescent's own anger ("why me?") in addition to a nebulous future exacerbates a tendency toward isolation and depression. To support the adolescent's denial of the anticipated early death is destructive. The most productive focus is to determine whether the prospect of early death has made the hard work of adolescence seem futile.

The challenge to the professional is to elicit adolescent strengths and will power to energize the youngster to live fully and at the proper developmental pace *as long as he or she does live*. To be fully adolescent is to be fully engaged in the tasks of the period—to face the question of "who will I be in love and in work for the rest of my life," however long that is. Identity discovery is subject to unpredictable bodily and environmental experiences. By definition, adolescence is an unstable period. For the terminally ill, too, living fully means experiencing the pain of uncertainties. The therapeutic experience should be geared to full experience of the current life stage including its psychosocial tasks, regardless of emotional vicissitudes. The subject should be encouraged to assume normality and deal with a healthy adolescent's developmental tasks *in spite of terminal illness*. Even at an advanced level of the disease, efforts need to be expended to expose this individual to as many agemates as possible, in person or through the media, so that the adolescent imperative remains stimulated and the normative process of psychosocial growth is thus continued.

The ill adolescent needs encouragement and support of the right to explore the same matters as do healthy adolescents. Who influences him? What attributes in agemates is he most interested in? How many friends would he like to have? How many does he have? In which ways are they alike or different? How are they better or worse? What are his own aspirations? What are his friends' aspirations? How does he compare strengths and weaknesses? A framework for normality is possible when the professional recognizes that the adolescent with a foreshortened future has a right to arrive at a sense of identity. The appropriateness of the quest should not only be strongly supported, but the professional should focus part of the intervention plan on helping the adolescent develop strategies to get to peers and to fully engage. However, this stance must realistically coexist with and complement preparation for the inevitability (barring a miracle) of early death. Both these dimensions lay a substantive base for a foundation of meaningful treatment. It is a complex therapeutic plan and difficult emotionally.

THE IMMIGRANTS

Children of immigrants have left their home countries at varying points along the continuum of adolescent development. For all, the process of identity formation was put on hold while they were in transit. Now, in a new and strange environment, the growth process must be engaged. Not only must they carry on normative adolescent tasks, but such work must be completed in a context where they (1) lack knowledge of the new culture and its relative values, (2) do not have the language skills with which to accurately communicate in order to effect appropriate self-presentation, (3) must integrate a fantasy of America with the realities they see, and (4) complete daily tasks. They use great energy to deal with acculturation needs. Yet they must also manage normative adolescent growth tasks. Denied familiar others with whom to compare and contrast, their task is twofold: (1) to physically and psychologically find their bearings and, at the same time, (2) to adjust to a changing body, mind, and set of emotions.

The immigrant adolescent resembles the exceptional adolescent in that each is denied large numbers of peers in a truly similar condition, and for each the informal peer group is hard to access. Some "immigrant" adolescents are a part of ethnic ghetto populations. This situation is again similar to that of the exceptional adolescent in that two groups of models must be closely scrutinized: groups of Americans, of which he is not a part but which he may aspire to join, and groups of nationals from his region of origin, who represent what he may or may not wish to be. Two cultures coexist physically and psychologically.

Within the same person, two very different varieties of adolescent, each with varying possibilities, engage the adolescent dialectic. In the possible blending of the two, additional stress can be stimulated. Complications do arise; what is appropriate in "culture 1" may not be appropriate in "culture 2." Agemates of their native culture, a group similarly aspiring to assimilation into a new land, are highly relevant objects of comparison and are subject to intense scrutiny. New aspirations may collide with the value system of their native culture. Rejection and anger of elders may be risked. On the other hand, there is great concern about what yields acceptance or rejection by agemates of the new culture. The depth and volume of inner tensions that arise from such comparative acts are generally not known to teachers or even to elders. Teachers may not be aware of the dynamics of the psychosocial task. Elders are aware of the problems of being "new" but may not be as attuned to the need for relevant others. Thus, there is a great opportunity for mental health professionals to bring the understanding discussed in preceding sections of this chapter to this group of exceptional adolescents, too.

PART FIVE

Peer-Oriented Clinical Instruments: The Peer Progression Battery

This section introduces as clinical tools the instruments utilized in the research investigations reported in Part Three. The reader may already have a fair grasp of the instruments from what has been presented in Chapters 5–8. Nevertheless, they are presented here in their entirety to be available for use by the clinical or educator. They have been reworked and assembled into two separate batteries specified for use with adolescents and, in some cases, pertinent environmental figures. Together they constitute the Peer Progression Battery, whose data offer a rather extensive look at adolescent social interactional life. Chapter 12 presents the Socialization Battery, which examines the adolescent's contact with the larger social world as well as social habits and psychological interactions with the most relevant environmental figure of the period—the peer. This battery elicits information on public and private socialization practices as well as public preferences and personal reflections. Chapter 13 introduces the Peer Arena Battery designed specifically to pinpoint the degree of adolescent development within the context of the peer group progression schedule of the peer arena model. Additional clinical tools are introduced for eliciting information not only from adolescents, but from parents, teachers, and others considered pertinent in the social world. Since these instruments are "peer-centered," the discussion connects them to the underlying principle of this book. To understand adolescence, comprehending the contours of participation in the peer arena is crucial.

CHAPTER 12

The Socialization Battery

Prior chapters on the psychosocial world of the adolescent discussed findings from a number of studies. The instruments utilized for this research and reported in those chapters are also very useful clinically. The information they produce sketch a picture of the relationship of the adolescent to his social reference world and provide a measure of his comfort in it. This chapter is devoted to a discussion of the instruments in the Socialization Battery and how they can be utilized clinically. We will discuss what information can be elicited and how it can be utilized in working with the adolescent. The instruments can be utilized individually, in combination, or as follow-up to the Peer Arena Battery.

In this section the Peer Progression Battery (PPB), composed of two major parts—the Socialization Battery and the Peer Arena Battery—is introduced. The PPB examines the overall social progress of the respondent, the scope of the social reference field with special attention paid to the ratio of peer/parent influence, relationships with peers, and perceptions of one's own social value. Specific instruments included in the Socialization Battery are: the Adolescent Reference Group Index (ARGI), the Attribute Interest Form and the form profile, the Comparative Characteristic Inventory, the Group Socialization Inventory, and the Socialization Preference Inventory. The second battery, the Peer Arena Battery (discussed in Chapter 13), includes four discrete Peer Arena Progression Profiles (PAPPs)—two for adolescents and one each for parent and major environmental other (e.g., teacher). The instruments are generally used for diagnostic purposes. They yield a broad base of information from which to formulate clinical hypotheses for direct follow-up with the client and/or with which to stimulate the adolescent to offer information that might not otherwise be volunteered.

BACKGROUND

The theoretical approach our instruments draw on is that the developmentally crucial interactions in adolescence are those that take place between peers. Although family relationships remain vital, they no longer carry their prior impact. Individual and family history should be closely reviewed for cues to current functioning. Family patterns may support or sabotage growth. But the most potent interaction is between peers. Peer relations also constitute the primary locus of adolescent problem behavior. "What the group thinks of me" feels prototypic of what the world will think of me. Negative evaluations and rejections from others do not remain psychologically confined to the single experience but are more often globalized to the entire self-picture. Since the adolescent, particularly the early and middle adolescent, experiences the impact of the present strongly, these negative self-assessments are not recognized by the adolescent as merely "in process" traits that will continue to undergo change. They *feel* permanent. Future, and a perspective of present in relation to future, does not emerge fully until late in the stage, when cognitive and emotional growth are essentially complete and integrated. Thus, it is very important to remember how intense the experience of "today" is for the adolescent.

The crucial time period is the present; the past has become irrelevant, and the future is too abstract. Those similar in status hold primary psychological relevance. The DFI model of adolescent psychosocial development, the theoretical base for the batteries, firmly establishes peers as the "hub of the adolescent wheel" (Seltzer, 1982), affecting most adolescent behaviors. Our instruments provide practical data identifying peer influences on the adolescent growth process and attendant social functioning.

COMPONENTS OF THE SOCIALIZATION BATTERY

Adolescent Reference Group Index

The Adolescent Reference Group Index (ARGI) (see Figure 12.1) is a paper-and-pencil instrument that presents the adolescent with questions on 10 issues (plus an 11th, summary question) and a list of 13 reference

Directions:

We all know something about England, though few of us have ever been there. In general, we learn to use information and opinions of others in developing our own opinions and making our own decisions. Depending on what the question is, we pay attention to different sources of information. For example, if we were to plan a trip to England, we might give more weight to information we get from a visitor who lives in England than to an acquaintance who has taken a two-week tour of England. Similarly, in regard to what course (subject) to take, a person might weigh information and opinions of older friends more heavily than those of a younger brother or sister.

Following are questions on some issues and a list of different sources of information. For each issue, please select whose information and/or opinions you would most probably seek out to help you make up your own mind. Use as few or many as you like. In fact, on different questions, you may pick different sources and divide them up in different proportions. It is not necessary to use all the sources. Once your selections are made, divide up the amount of attention (%), you would pay to each source. Make sure they add up to 100%.

The questions are:

1. Should murderers who planned the murder in advance be given capital punishment (death)?
2. Should I get my hair cut?
3. Is taking a year off between high school and starting a serious job/college a good idea?
4. I am on the honor system. I see a close friend cheating on a test. Shall I report him?
5. Where is a good place to shop for a jacket?
6. Should marijuana (or any soft drugs) be legalized?
7. Should people live together before deciding whether to marry or not?
8. What qualities are important to look for in other people and to develop in myself?
9. What should I do with a day off from school next week?
10. What job/college should I try to get into, and why is it important?
11. On most matters, whom would you consult?

Select from the following list of reference groups. For example, for the question: "What movie shall I see tonight?" you might elect to ask the five reference groups indicated below, dividing the amount of influence accorded each group as shown. (Remember that the percentages must total 100%.)

1. Brothers and sisters, older	_____
2. Brothers and sisters, younger	40
3. Friends two to five years younger	_____
4. Friends two to five years older	_____
5. Friends over five years older	_____
6. Media (literature, magazines, TV, etc)	_____
7. Minister, priest, or rabbi	_____
8. Neighborhood friends of the same age	_____
9. Parents	15
10. Relatives, older	_____
11. School friends of the same age	35
12. School personnel	5
13. Special friend (please specify—e.g., girlfriend)	5

Figure 12.1. The Adolescent Reference Group Index.

groups he or she may choose to consult for advice or information. The subject is asked to indicate which reference sources would be utilized for each issue.* Each question is listed at the top of a separate page with the list of 13 reference groups beneath it. It provides information as to how the adolescent orders both his own and other generations; it identifies the figures and groups that are prominent. It also provides information with which to assess cognitive and social development. Findings from the ARGI reveal whether or not the adolescent can cognitively distinguish the essence of issues—can he or she cluster issues appropriately? Analysis also offers data on the manner and extent of the subject's ability to determine which social reference sources are appropriate to each issue.

For example, the adolescent is asked how he would act on the issue of marijuana. Media is one of the reference groups offered. Does the respondent accord influence to the media, or does he ignore this source of information? The data may reveal a balanced, broad array of sources. On the other hand, an overabundance of influence may be accorded one reference source—for example, parents or "special friend." The results can be used to help the professional frame various questions. Does the overall profile show an overdependence on family? On peers?

Findings from the ARGI are never conclusive, but inappropriate responses can provide initial hypotheses for the professional to bear in mind as the rest of the protocol is examined and as clinical diagnoses are developed. The age of the adolescent makes a differences. For example, the profile of a 13-year-old adolescent would be expected to show less use of the media as an influence source than would that of a 19- or 20-year-old. Findings should be considered along with data from other instruments in the battery as well as interview data.

Variations in How the ARGI Can be Utilized

Depending upon the information sought, the ARGI can be utilized diagnostically in a number of ways—for example, to gain information to support or reject specific early clinical hypotheses. A professional may

---

*Chapter 5 discusses findings on 798 adolescents with whom the ARGI was utilized as a research instrument. These findings can serve as a comparative group for the professional to assess findings on an individual adolescent.

suspect a parent-child separation problem. Thus, it may be of interest to assess how the adolescent utilizes parents as a reference group in contrast to her use of other groups. Data on a large group of adolescents offer an objective perspective by which to assess a specific adolescent's distribution of influence.

The average amount of influence accorded to parents relative to that accorded other reference groups over a number of issues is easily computed. If the individual's protocol shows a sizable deviation from the normative figure, the protocol can be examined as to the nature of the spread. For example, if parents received markedly less attention as an influence source, who was the influence accorded to? On the other hand, if influence accorded parents was much higher than the norm, it would be important to find which influence sources were ignored.*

A profile from a sample of adolescents in Washington, D.C., to whom the basic ARGI instrument plus two questions of special topical interest was administered, offers a case in point. Jeremy accorded from 5% to 50% influence to parents on 9 issues. On the 10th, whether to use marijuana or not, they were accorded no influence at all. The distribution of accorded influence on marijuana was as follows: younger brothers and sisters, 10%; minister/priest/rabbi, 10%; school friends of the same age, 10%; and the media, 70%.

Interestingly, a different picture is presented by his response to the question "Should I drink alcoholic beverages?" Once again, this youngster depended heavily on the media but far less so than in the case of marijuana. Thus, other categories were accorded more influence. Media was accorded only 30% influence. School friends were the major influence source, accorded 40%—30% more than on marijuana. Minister/priest/rabbi was accorded 15%, 5% more than on marijuana. This time parents were included and were accorded 15%.

Response to another question helps to round out the picture of this adolescent. On the question "Should I start smoking?" younger siblings were accorded 5% influence. Parents were accorded 20% influence— 5% more than on alcohol. A changed picture appears with schoolmates and the media. Schoolmates were accorded 5% less influence than on

---

*The reader will recall that the influence accorded to parents by the sample group of 732 (reported in Chapter 5) was 29%.

marijuana and 35% less than on alcohol. As with marijuana, the influence was attributed primarily to media, which was accorded 70% influence. For this youth certain issues seem to be *nondiscussable* with parents; this protocol reveals drugs to be one. Unlike marijuana, alcohol and smoking were discussed with parents in spite of the very strong influence accorded media.

Continuing examination of the profile provides more insight. How this adolescent accorded influence to the minister/priest/rabbi category adds a very interesting dimension. Religious authority figures were accorded influence on 3 of the 10 issues: legalization of marijuana, use of alcohol, and the acceptability of capital punishment. They were influence sources for no other issue. It appears that upon reflection Jeremy grasped the commonalities in the issues and clustered them as moral issues. This is an example of how the examiner can be apprised of more than who the social influences are. It is apparent from the responses that the final stage of cognitive development has been reached. The adolescent is abstracting and categorizing.

The findings reveal a second cognitive distinction. Smoking does not appear to be considered by this youth as a moral issue, but rather as a health issue. He accords 70% influence on the smoking issue to media, does not include clergy, and feels the topic neutral enough to seek out parental influence (20%). The responses portray an adolescent who can conceptualize a field of potential advisors. He categorizes the issues and approaches different reference groups according to the categorization.

Turning now to how Jeremy's profile reflects his relationships with agemates, we note issues where peer input is very important. Alcohol is one of them. The strong influence attributed to media on smoking and marijuana is not expressed for alcohol; influence is reduced to 30%. Parents and minister are accorded 15% each, but schoolmates of the same age were accorded a lot of influence—40%. In sum, this profile reveals a youngster who has cognitively advanced to a point where: (1) he classifies issues, (2) he identifies the groups appropriate to each issue category and utilizes them accordingly, and (3) he has begun to emotionally separate from parents to peers, and identifies issues where he feels parents are no longer relevant.*

The last question on the instrument is structured to allow comparison between the respondent's affective perception of general allotment of influence and the actual attributions reported for the first 10 questions.

Findings reveal how the emotional can exist in a logic-tight compartment beside the cognitive. The question is "On most matters, whom would you consult?" Here Jeremy leaves media out completely, whereas he accorded it 70%influence on marijuana and smoking. Apparently, it was used by him as an information-specific source, but it left no emotional residue. He accords younger siblings (he is the oldest child) 10%, friends two to five years older 10%, and the ministry 8%. School personnel, at 2%, appear to be a second group regarded as information-specific but not emotionally encountered. (He accorded them 40% influence on the issue of what college to go to.) The greatest amount of influence on the "most matters" question went to two reference groups actually used heavily by the youngster: schoolmates of the same age and parents. Each was accorded 35%.

The socioemotional picture this analysis provides is of some movement away from parents to peers. The results do support the premise that Jeremy has begun the separation and individuation process emotionally and intellectually. They also reveal that Jeremy is not yet involved in close one-to-one relationships. He has achieved definite conceptions of adults in his world and their respective areas of expertise. He has defined issues as peer-specific, parent-specific, and role-specific. We can assess Jeremy's developmental progress to be within a normative range. Yet it is important to stress that a definite conclusion is out of order without a review of findings from other instrumentation and interview sessions.

Social Relational World

The ARGI can be very profitably used as a communication strategy in the interview session. The instrument generally yields information within 20 minutes. As the adolescent fills in the answers or discusses the responses, access is gained to his social relational world. For example, we have already seen how the questions tap the adolescent's progress from rigidity to flexibility as he considers various reference groups and decides which is relevant to each issue. Assessment can also be made

---

*Two issues on which schoolmates were attributed 60% influence were "Which attributes should I look for in others and try to develop in myself?" and "Where should I go to shop for a jacket?"

of how many diverse paths to a projected end the adolescent negotiates and how many combinations and permutations he wrestles with. Clearly, while the stated goal is to tap the social dimension, we also uncover the level of cognitive development underlying the social organization.

This dimension of the ARGI is very appropriate for work with teens where problems of underachievement are being investigated. If responses reveal that the adolescent demonstrates flexibility of mind when dealing with issues not ordinarily connected with scholarship or academic productivity, the underachievement problem may be situationally or emotionally, and *not* cognitively, based. The data may suggest the need for innovative strategies to investigate school or home environment problems that contribute exacerbating factors such as inhibition of effort and fear of failure. Other potential causes can be investigated: Are there environmental realities that inhibit access to information and direct interaction with an enlarged social world? Might this be a situation of parental overprotectiveness? Does the analysis point to neglect? Is lack of parenting skills indicated? The child may not have been supported in incremental forays away from home, and perhaps even discouraged (e.g., the possibility of overprotectiveness or infantalization can be explored). These problems may be fostered by needs on the part of either parent or child or both to keep the child a child; often the child's and parent's neurotic needs interact.

Clues for Remediation

Clues to adolescent patterns of socialization may be revealed by a quick review of how many reference groups are interacted with, what particular groups are heavily utilized, and which ones are barely or never consulted. This type of ARGI review offers hints as to which groups are "comfortable" and which are regarded as quite the opposite. Sometimes the smallest bit of additional information elicited from the adolescent in the discussion of reference group selections yields valuable openings to sensitive areas. Of course, it is best to proceed slowly and delicately. It may benefit a reluctant or frightened adolescent to rehearse strategies for approaching peers and nonpeers. "Practice" with the counselor is a means of providing both skills *and* support. Identification with the helper might bolster a weakened adolescent resolve when the feared situation is actually encountered.

An ARGI profile indicating heavy use of family-based reference groups and few outsiders may mean that a long period of intervention is necessary; it is also very possible that what is needed is training in concrete social skills. It is often surprising how "basic" such help can be. For example, the anxiety level of an adolescent who finds it hard to talk to others may be reduced substantially by giving concrete information on how one negotiates a library information desk, on when the best time is to approach a busy teacher, or on how to become part of a group of peers engaging in some activity. Social paralysis stimulated by abstract fears may be pierced by specific learned strategies.

Of course, in reviewing an ARGI profile that shows a restricted social influence field, the other side of the "causative coin" also must be kept in mind. Fear of new others does not necessarily represent fear of the new but may be grounded in a fear of letting go of what one already has. The familiar is comfortable—even if it begins to feel outgrown. At times, the individual himself generates the fear that immobilizes; at other times, others hold him back. A paucity of reference groups revealed in the profile may be a sign of some type of separation problem. In the healthiest of parent-child relationships, some need to "hang on" remains for all parties. The issue is usually not the presence or absence of this restraining force, but *how strong* it is and how to effectively deal with it.

Restriction of reference groups revealed in an ARGI profile may also point to a separation difficulty for the parent. Some can handle the emotional demands of watching a child mature toward adulthood and independent functioning. For others, resistance to the changing relationship with the adolescent may be manifested in discouragement of a more expansive social sphere or even deliberate roadblocks. By the same token, an ARGI profile that reveals overinvolvement with peers and near exclusion of family members may be a different manifestation of the same type of underlying separation difficulty. Such a profile should alert the helper to a range of potential acting-out behaviors due to possible conformity pressures as well as to family history issues.

Thus, the ARGI approach can offer initial clues to areas needing remediation in the relationships between adolescents, their parents, their peers, and environmental others. On the other hand, profiles that do not appear age-appropriate in terms of the balance between older- and same-generational others may suggest something beyond social difficulties. Rigidity and restriction of use of social influence figures may be related to organic difficulties; such a possibility should be investigated further.

THE ATTRIBUTE INTEREST FORM

The Attribute Interest Form (AIF), a second instrument in the Socialization Battery, offers a means by which to assess what is relevant to the individual adolescent in the personality makeup of his or her peers.

In the adolescent period, when the individual is in a period of try-out, interests flourish and recede. The degree of interest expressed in a specific characteristic may remain stable over time, or it may change. The Attribute Interest Form provides information on what is of importance to the adolescent *today*; it is state-related more than trait-related. The adolescent inclination to modify behavior to conform to "today's" values is normative adaptive behavior for this stage of life. Thus, data yielded from adolescents is time-specific and changeable. Accordingly, findings from the AIF are not considered indicative of "traits" but rather are an index to the immediate value system. The AIF can be profitably readministered at biannual intervals to update changing values relative to advancing psychosocial development.

The AIF lists 67 characteristics and attributes (see Figure 12.2). The adolescent is asked to respond if she "always," "usually," "sometimes," "hardly ever," or "never" notices each characteristic/attribute in other adolescents when she comes into contact with them. Thus, the AIF provides information on three dimensions: (1) whether or not the adolescent is involved in psychological comparative acts, (2) the depth of interest in the characteristics/attributes of peers, and (3) identification of characteristics that are of most and least interest. A "personal interest profile" disclosed by the findings can be drawn to place the individual on a continuum ranging from an extremely social orientation to social isolation.

Relation of Adolescent Growth to AIF

There is a difference in the extent of interest in specific characteristics/abilities of other adolescents according to the age of the adolescent. In the beginning of adolescence, there is less interest. It grows as the child experiences biological and intellectual changes that unseat previous psychoemotional anchors, such as parents and family. Forces stimulate desires to move toward more independence and lead the individual to

Please fill out the following information. *Do not* write your name.

Age_____

Grade in school_____

Sex: Male_____ Female_____

Religion_____

Mother's occupation_____

Father's occupation_____

Number of brothers_____

Number of sisters_____

What order are you in the family? (Check one)

Oldest _____ 2nd _____ 3rd _____ 4th _____ 5th _____

6th _____ 7th _____ Other _____

Parents' marital status: Married _____ Separated _____

Divorced _____ Widow _____ Widower _____

One way we get to know ourselves better is to look around at others. When we are with others, either a few or many, it is very common to compare ourselves on various characteristics, skills, and abilities.

Directions

Following are some numbers and a list of characteristics. The numbers correspond to the frequency with which you compare on the particular characteristics. Please go down the list of characteristics. Next to each characteristic, place the number that corresponds to the frequency with which you compare on that characteristic. For example, if you *usually* compare how friendly you feel you are with how friendly others seem to be, place a 2 next to "friendliness." If you feel you are *always* comparing your sense of humor to the sense of humor of others, place a *1* next to "sense of humor." Go down the list in this way.

At the end of the list there is space to add some characteristics or skills which we have not included. We would appreciate your adding them. Please remember to place a number next to your own addition, too.

Numbers: 1 = Always
            2 = Usually
            3 = Sometimes
            4 = Hardly Ever
            5 = Never

_____ friendliness   _____ knowledge of current events

_____ sense of humor   _____ good listener

_____ leadership   _____ sexiness

_____ artistic talent   _____ sportsmanship

_____ musical ability (instrument)   _____ generosity

_____ musical ability (singing)   _____ femininity

_____ athletic ability   _____ masculinity

_____ general school work ability   _____ wealth (rich/poor)

Figure 12.2. Attribute Interest Form.

_____ enthusiasm	_____ competitiveness
_____ creative writing ability	_____ cleanliness
_____ drama/acting ability	_____ laziness
_____ mechanical ability	_____ impatience
_____ cooking	_____ cattiness
_____ typing skills	_____ selfishness
_____ general physical appearance	_____ religiousness
_____ clothes	_____ snobbiness
_____ figure/build/physique	_____ cheapness
_____ complexion	_____ type of family one comes from
_____ popularity with same sex	_____ studiousness
_____ popularity with opposite sex	_____ cooperativeness
_____ ability to put feelings into words	_____ self-confidence
_____ ability to put thoughts into words	_____ prejudice
_____ mother's occupation	_____ adventurousness
_____ father's occupation	_____ maturity
_____ morals	_____ creativity
_____ sensitivity to others' feelings	_____ honesty
_____ car driving	_____ loyalty to friends
_____ stubbornness	_____ dancing
_____ religion	_____ determination
_____ meanness	_____ trustworthiness
_____ niceness	_____ dependability
_____ stick-to-it-iveness	_____ patriotism
_____ attitude toward one's family	_____ openness to new ideas
_____ other	_____ cliqueishness
_____ other	_____ other

Figure 12.2. (*Cont.*)

identify peers as the most pertinent environmental objects from which to learn. These new growth imperatives stimulate the comparison dynamics of the adolescent dialectic, which yield material for self-other evaluation.

To understand the role one can play in the present and forthcoming peer society, estimation of the relative strengths and weaknesses of one's "self" is necessary. This constitutes the first set of necessary knowledges. Identifying self elements and knowing their merit relative to those of fellow travelers through life is important. This process involves utilization of mental operations we have termed comparative acts, including the individual components of assessment, relative assessment, evaluation, and relative evaluation of one's characteristics/abilities against those of peers. These developmental dynamics are engaged again and again as necessary until resolution of the relative value of the self-attribute(s) under consideration is arrived at.

Responses to the AIF inform the professional as to the dynamics operating and the areas of the comparative focus. These dynamics are intensely active during junior high years and most of high school. As discussed earlier, for most youth the comparative process reduces in scope and intensity at the conclusion of the first of the two peer arena periods, when a temporary self structure is formed (four to six years into adolescence). In-depth scrutiny follows on a subset of self elements selected as valid components of one's emerging self. There are individual differences in the tempo and course of development, but over time all adolescents who fully engage the dynamics of the dialectic achieve psychosocial maturity.

For correct interpretation of findings from AIF, the chronological age of the adolescent must be considered. The number and range of characteristics of interest increase through the junior and early senior high school years. They decrease in the later high school years and continue to decrease in years of college (or first serious job for the non–college student). For those individuals who mature more slowly, the decrease may not be apparent until the initial college/job years. If during the early years of adolescence AIF data reveal little interest in others, there is cause for concern and further investigation. Conversely, if interests do not become more circumscribed in later years, this is also worthy of concern. Adolescents who experience considerable stress in filling out the form or who generally respond using the "never" or "hardly ever" categories are probably experiencing difficulties, and further examination is indicated. Comparing the responses of the target individual to normative findings should offer cues about the appropriateness of the adolescent's socialization.

Attribute Interest Form Profile

Interests listed in the Attribute Interest Form fall within six clusters (see Table 12.1):

1. Physically observable
2. Public impression
3. Character traits

4. Family

5. Interpersonal

6. Talents

On the data sheet (see Figure 12.3), the number of choices in each cluster offers a graphic profile of the concentration or spread of the adolescent's interests.

The clustering pattern can be considered adapative if the profile reveals a relative balance among categories. On the other hand, imbalances should not always be treated as serious. They may serve as benign indicators of the necessity to intervene and encourage transfer of adolescent energies away from "safe" interests toward comparisons that are more challenging or even threatening. Of course, imbalances may indeed signal serious disorders that need further investigation—for example, if "always" and "usually" are attributed to the "physically observable" cluster alone or in conjunction with the "public impression" cluster, with an absence of focus on character traits, imbalance is suspect.

The profile also reflects areas of least interest about others. A balanced profile will disclose a minimum of "never noticed" attributes. If the profile reveals the majority of characteristics to draw the "hardly ever" or "never" response, the professional should be alerted to the possibility of a serious withdrawal. Further close examination of the adolescent should be arranged. However, initial questions should be raised from alternative points of view. For example, is the lack of interest in certain attributes due to a developmentally appropriate narrowing of interest areas or to a defensive closing out indicative of psychosocial flight?

Final diagnostic decisions as to which AIF profile is adaptive and which is maladaptive are best arrived at in conjunction with other data, for example, factors of history, findings from other social battery information or other tests, and interview findings.

Information yielded from the AIF is also functional to a variety of normative counseling objectives: vocational or academic planning, future goal setting in accord with interests and aspirational levels, adjusting interests to be in line with projected future goals, and insights into relative strengths and weaknesses in self-perceptions, which may be revealed by an unbalanced profile. The data can also provide necessary information for treatment/planning decisions—for example, retaining the youngster

TABLE 12.1. Clusters of the Attribute Interest Form.

I. Character traits

adventurousness	maturity
cattiness	meanness
cheapness	morals
competitiveness	niceness
cooperativeness	openness to new ideas
creativity	patriotism
dependability	prejudice
determination	religiousness
enthusiasm	selfishness
generosity	sportsmanship
honesty	stubbornness
impatience	studiousness
laziness	trustworthiness
loyalty to friends	stick-to-it-iveness

II. Family

attitude toward one's family	mother's occupation
father's occupation	type of family one comes from
	religion

III. Interpersonal

cliqueishness	popularity with same sex
·friendliness	sense of humor
good listener	sensitivity to others' feelings
popularity with opposite sex	snobbiness

IV. Physically observable

cleanliness	general physical appearance
clothes	masculinity
complexion	sexiness
femininity	wealth
figure/build/physique	

V. Public impression

ability to put feelings into words	knowledge of current events
ability to put thoughts into words	leadership
car driving	self-confidence

VI. Talents

artistic ability	general school work ability
athletic ability	mechanical ability
cooking	musical ability (instrument)
creative writing ability	musical ability (singing)
dancing	typing skills
drama/acting ability	

199

	Number of occurences				
Cluster	A	U	S	HE	N
I. Character traits					
II. Family					
III. Interpersonal					
IV. Physical observable					
V. Public impression					
VI. Talents					

Figure 12.3. AIF Data Sheet Profile

in a specific social setting and setting treatment goals for adjustment to the group versus transferring the adolescent to a setting where group interests will be more similar. The treatment of choice is not always adjustment; transfer to a more compatible group may be preferable.

THE GROUP SOCIALIZATION INVENTORY

That adolescents participate in a number of groups is common knowledge. The literature is rich with discussion of adolescent socialization with peers. The Group Socialization Inventory (GSI), the third instrument in the Socialization Battery, is shown in Figure 12.4. It is very valuable for use as a clinical instrument as well as a research tool.*

The inventory asks the adolescent to indicate the groups generally socialized with, what the activities are, how many other agemates participate in each of the groups, and how many hours of the week are generally spent with each group. The data offer a bird's-eye view of socialization habits. With clinical utilization of the GSI, we may ascertain where and when a specific adolescent accesses other teens, what the activities are, and how much time is spent with them. This information provides valuable data that help to: (1) assess if and how problem behaviors correspond to a socializing pattern and (2) generate initial hypotheses and treatment probes and plans. Patterns may range from socialization that appears to encompass integrated interests of adequate balance, to the other extreme of sharp discontinuities, excesses, or withdrawals. The

---

*Chapter 8 provided some interesting findings, yielded by use of the GSI as a research tool, as to how many different groups adolescents participate in, how many other agemates take part in each of the groups, and how much time is spent in each of the groups.

Below you will find a list of various settings in which you may be meeting with your friends. Please look at the list and complete the following information next to each of the categories. Leave them blank if they do not apply at all.

1. Please rank the groups according to how often you meet with them.
2. How many others usually participate in these groups?
3. What are the activities you engage in together?
4. How many hours a week are you generally with these friends in these group activities?

Group	Rank	Number of others	Activities	Number of hours
Close friends				
General acquaintances				
Kids in neighborhood				
Kids in church/synagogue				
Club				
Club				
Club				
Teammates				
Teammates				
Band				
Choir				
Summer camp				
Kids you work with				
Newspaper staff				
Yearbook staff				
Drama group				
Other				
Other				
Other				
Other				

Figure 12.4. Group Socialization Inventory.

professional can examine the profile to identify extremes of oversocialization or isolation, or adaptive behaviors. Generally, a profile of integrated activities implies that the adolescent is beyond the "tryout" period. However, it is essential to bear in mind that it could also mean "fear of the new." Knowing the age of the adolescent helps here. Tryout generally occurs earlier; integration is more appropriate to the late-middle adolescent. Thus, the GSI also offers information with which to assess point of developmental progression.

Discussion of the findings with the adolescent opens the door for the professional to understand:

1. The rationale for selection of each group.

2. The ease or difficulty the adolescent has in accessing preferred groups.
3. The general level of comfort/discomfort the adolescent feels within the selected groups.
4. Whether he/she is a leader or a follower.
5. Frustration or satisfaction with the social sphere in which the adolescent moves.
6. Which groups he/she prefers to belong to and why.

THE COMPARATIVE CHARACTERISTIC INVENTORY

A fourth instrument in the Socialization Battery can serve as an index to the state of the adolescent's security and self-confidence in relation to the others in a group. The Comparative Characteristic Inventory (Figure 12.5) can be used as a valuable clinical aid as well as for research. It adds data to the profile by comparing the adolescent's self-ranking on specific attributes to his perception of how the group rates him or her on the same characteristic.

This profile provides two measures: a self-concept measure and a group-related self-concept measure. The difference between the two measures is an index of their degree of congruence, implying the level of comfort the subject feels with the group regarding the quality in question. A ratio where self-assessment is higher than group assessment may indicate, for example:

1. The group is unappreciative.
2. The group ignores or does not understand "the real me."
3. The group has a set of values that are quite different.
4. Unfair or hostile treatment exist.
5. The target is unable to function freely when with the group.

On the other hand, a greater group than self-perception could be based on factors such as:

1. The target is engaging in unnatural behaviors when with the group and is not being "himself" (e.g., plays the comic or the intellectual).

Below are listed 67 characteristics. Please select 12 of the 67 which you would generally take note of in others when you are at a gathering with friends. Under column 1, list the score (from 1 to 10) you feel the group would give you on each of the 12 you have selected. Under column 2, list the score (from 1 to 10) you would give yourself. In both cases, the number 1 represents the lowest score; the number 10 represents the highest score. You may use either extreme or a number in between.

Characteristic	Group rating	Self rating
Friendliness		
Sense of humor		
Leadership		
Artistic talent		
Music ability—singing		
Music ability—instrument		
Athletic ability		
General school work ability		
Enthusiasm		
Creative writing ability		
Drama/acting ability		
Mechanical ability		
Cooking		
Typing skills		
General physical appearance		
Clothes		
Figure/build/physique		
Complexion		
Popularity with same sex		
Popularity with opposite sex		
Ability to put feelings into words		
Ability to thoughts into words		
Knowledge of current events		
Good listener		
Sexiness		
Sportsmanship		
Generosity		
Masculinity		
Femininity		
Wealth (rich/poor)		
Cleanliness		
Laziness		
Impatience		
Cattiness		
Selfishness		
Religiousness		
Snobbiness		
Cheapness		
Type of family one comes from		
Studiousness		

Figure 12.5. Comparative Characteristic Inventory.

Characteristic	Group rating	Self rating
Cooperativeness		
Self-confidence		
Prejudice		
Adventurousness		
Mother's occupation		
Father's occupation		
Morals		
Sensitivity to others' feelings		
Car driving		
Stubbornness		
Religion		
Meanness		
Niceness		
Stick-to-it-iveness		
Attitude toward one's family		
Competitiveness		
Maturity		
Creativity		
Honesty		
Loyalty to friends		
Dancing ability		
Determination		
Trustworthiness		
Dependability		
Patriotism		
Openness to new ideas		
Cliqueishness		
Other		
Other		
Other		
Other		

Figure 12.5. *(Cont.)*

2. A difference exists between standards set by group and by the individual, with the group having lower standards.
3. Feelings of artificiality accompany group participation for the target.
4. The subject has personality characteristics of self-derogation.
5. The subject practices heavy use of energies when with the group to excel or conform.

In evaluating the differentials indicating either overvaluation or undervaluation of self, the professional must bear in mind the impact on self-image of attitudes expressed by family members about the adolescent or members of the specific group.

The information elicited by this instrument presents avenues for the professional to delve further into adolescent perceptions about the groups participated in. In which groups does the target feel comfort or discomfort? Does the target feel he will function differently in a different group? If so, why, which group, and how? A creative therapist may choose to work with persistent themes through fantasy and role play before recommending actual group membership change. Therapeutic plans may include having adolescents select characteristics they feel best or worst about in themselves, playing out group perceptions and responses, varying the attributes or groups considered, etc. Therapeutic tryouts suggesting changed self-perception with different group memberships can be checked against real-life results after a stated period.

THE SOCIALIZATION PREFERENCE INVENTORY

The fifth instrument included in the Socialization Battery explores the continuum of public to private social choices of adolescents.* The Socialization Preference Inventory (SPI) (Figure 12.6) provides basic information with which to assess customary social habits. It also sheds light on the level of devleopment of the adolescent. The data provide bases to assess whether the individual profile represents the beginning, middle, or ending period of adolescence. In the primary peer arena stage (first stage), it is developmentally necessary to seek the company of many agemates. The normative pattern is for the younger adolescent to be more interested in wide circles of interactions than the older adolescent. As the youth matures, we look for transition to fewer groups composed of individuals more similar to self, with evidence of beginning intimacies. The socialization preference for intimacy reflects deep-structure advance in emotional separation from dependencies on significant rearing figures, increasing individuation, and progress in transfer of libido to age cohorts. The older adolescent is able to move between

*Findings from adolescents who were administered this instrument were discussed in Chapter 7. These findings can serve as a comparative group for the professional to assess findings on an individual adolescent.

casual contact with a large outer network of acquaintances and more involved relations with a small inner network of others seen as real friends.

Findings from the SPI provide the professional with information contrasting public socialization patterns and private experiences of a reciprocal nature. The data can be used to open avenues of communication with the adolescent about both public and private needs and public and private personas. Depending on the developmental age of the adolescent, intimacies with other peers may or may not be desired. At times distance is necessary; at other times lack of intimacy can be most painful. This instrument provides pathways for the professional to determine whether or not the pattern of friendship numbers and choices is satisfactory, painful, compensatory, or developmentally appropriate.

The following seven questions ask you to think about how many of your peers you socialize with and how. Please try to give as accurate a response as possible. Thank you.

	Number of Peers
Question	

1. How many kids were at the last party you attended?
2. If you could throw a party in the school gym and money was no object, how many kids would you invite?
3. How many kids do you say "hello" to when you see them?
4. How many kids do you feel understand you?
5. If you had an important decision to make, how many kids' advice would you seek?
6. How many different kids do you speak to on the phone each week?
7. How many kids do you consider to be your good friends?

Figure 12.6. Socialization Preference Inventory.

CHAPTER 13

The Peer Arena Battery

The instruments that make up the second of the two batteries of the overall Peer Progression Battery—the Peer Arena Battery (PAB)—can be utilized individually, in connection with one another, or as follow-up to hypotheses generated by the Socialization Battery. The Socialization Battery generates information about overt manifestations of cognitive, physical, and emotional advance as evidenced in the nature and quality of social functioning. The PAB yields information on the psychoemotional impact of developmental dynamics on the adolescent. These affective responses are overtly manifested in confusing behaviors and changing moods. The batteries are also used to gain information on activities and responses of primary environmental figures.

THE PEER ARENA PROGRESSION PROFILE

Two complementary forms of the Peer Arena Progression Profile (PAPP) were developed: one for adolescents (PAPP—A) and one for the secondary field (PAPP—SF) for pertinent other individuals (e.g., parents and teachers). A corresponding, separate version of the PAPP—SF was developed for administration to adolescents when comparison of replies is necessary (PAPP—SFA).

The PAPPs are designed to encourage flexible use by the professional. They use a structured interview format to present some stimulus items. Although the format should be generally followed, the design allows for additional, idiosyncratic questions to complement the basic information yielded by the format. For the experienced professional, they offer a set of general guidelines.

The PAPPs derive theoretically from basic premises of the theory of dynamic functional interaction, which holds that adolescents automatically engage in a series of "comparative acts" involving attributes and skills of others from the various peer groups comprised by the adolescent peer arena. The theory further maintains that these self-assessments and self-evaluations are essential for purposes of psychosocial growth and decision-making, but that the findings are often quite painful psychologically (Seltzer, 1982). Most adolescents carry on. For some, however, the outcomes of the processes are painful enough to interfere with their ability to continue to engage their peers for these developmental purposes. They psychologically or even physically withdraw. The adolescent who has withdrawn defensively will not progress smoothly through the period. To develop psychosocially, the adolescent *must* interact with attributes and skills of a sufficient number of agemates over a sufficient period of time to bring closure on the "self" he or she wishes to be. The PAPPs are designed to assess the progress and to detect setbacks.

The reader will recall that successful completion of the first stage of development is marked by psychological construction of a temporary self structure. Although final identity is not completed until the end of the second stage, the adolescent at the end of stage 1 (middle adolescence) is in stark contrast to the adolescents in the early stage, the primary peer arena period, who offer limited and rather diffuse self-descriptions with little detail and little organization. The second and last stage of adolescent psychosocial development, the secondary peer arena period, is when the temporary self structure is refined, polished and completed. Psychosocial progression into this stage is manifested in verbal ability to broadly sketch "who I am" and coordinate it with general plans for direction of life. An observable indicator that the adolescent is ready to move into the second stage of the two-stage peer arena developmental period is a reduction in the need for a large number of friendships.* The PAPPs elicit this information with questions about numbers of peers adolescents wanted to be with in the past, the number they try to be with in the present, the types of peers they actually interact with, and whether they prefer to spend the majority of time with family or with agemates.

---

*Empirical data reported in Chapter 5 revealed a reduction in utilization of parents as an influence source from 9th to 12th grades, with a corresponding increase in utilization of schoolmates of the same age. These empirical data support the DFI theory on which the PAPPs are based.

The early stage of adolescence demands that they have available to them large numbers of others to provide diverse characteristics, attributes, talents, and abilities to look at and to compare with. Thus, at this point in development, the youngster should be engaging with many, many others. Where there is expressed lack of desire to be with many agemates, the professional should be alert to the possibility of a delay in beginning the necessary peer arena developmental activity. Lack of this involvement, if continued, will seriously delay growth. If responses to the profile questions reveal that a junior high student has little or no desire to be with large groups of others, further examination is in order.

Questions are framed to pinpoint the time and circumstances of defensive flight from the rigors of peer interaction. Was the group left because the adolescent chose to? If so, why?

Responses to the PAPPs may expose separation problems or a problem based in any one or more of the following causes:

1. Lack of social skills with which to successfully transact with peers.
2. Feelings of inferiority based on *internal*, neurotic factors.
3. Factors of *environment*, such as poverty or adverse family conditions.
4. *Physical* features that stimulate rejection behaviors in others.
5. Lack of ability to access groups of peers because of distance, transportation problems, etc.
6. Serious emotional and/or physical problems.

The possibility of defensive flight from interactions in the social arena of peers should be a focus for continuing investigation and treatment. The practitioner should be alert to the potential contribution of transitory factors such as minor illness or test anxiety.

For the older adolescent, DFI holds that normal progression is reflected in an interest in surrounding oneself with fewer friends than would the junior high student. Each period requires psychosocial interactions with different numbers for different purposes. The older adolescent turns more to special friends and outside reference groups.*

---

*For empirical findings that support this position, see Chapter 5.

PAPP—Adolescent (PAPP—A)

The PAPP—A (Fig. 13.1) is designed to determine how far the adolescent has progressed toward completing the psychosocial task of identity resolution. Information gathered from this profile will provide the data to determine whether the adolescent is in the first stage of adolescent development (the primary peer arena period) or has progressed to the second and last stage (the secondary peer arena period). The former is characterized by participation in events where large groups of adolescents are present. The desire to be with many others is strong. The latter period is characterized by the preference to be with smaller, more intimate groups. However, this is quite different from the adolescent who cannot be comfortable with larger groups and thus seeks out a few friends by default.* The findings offer a developmental impression to compare with the adolescent's age and grade in school. It inquires about the specific nature of comparison and evaluation of self characteristics with peers. It focuses on the affective experience with peers to identify if defensive escape (in any of its various forms) from the rigors of peer arena comparative acts may have taken place.

PAPP—Secondary Field (PAPP—SF)

The PAPP—SF profile is designed for use with or by individuals other than the adolescent (secondary-field persons), the most common of whom are parents, other family members, and teachers. Two separate PAPP-SF versions have been developed—one for use with parents and one for use by school personnel, usually teacher or counselor. Information from a major person who is a nonpeer provides an additional perspective that can support or conflict with data yielded from the PAPP—A. Most important, it provides information about an important part of the emotional climate in which the adolescent moves. For example, it can give beginning indications of whether the milieu is one of support or conflict. Is it one of similar or dissimilar perceptions?

A complementary profile, the PAPP—SFA, was designed for use when a comparison of the adolescent's perceptions with those yielded

---

*For a more complete discussion, see Chapters 4 and 10.

1. When you were together with a group of peers/agemates, did you compare with your friends on various attributes/talents? If no, why? If yes:
   a. Was it when you were with a large group? Grade?
   b. Was it when you were with a small group? Grade?
2. Did you think about the quality of your own attributes?
3. Did you think about the quality of the attributes of others?
4. Do you know how you felt about your own attributes?
5. Do you know how you felt about the attributes of your peers?
6. Do you know how you generally felt when you compared your own attributes with those of your peers?
7. Did you like or dislike being with the other people your age? How much of your time did you spend with them?
8. Do you feel you associated with your group of friends long enough?
9. Did you stop associating with them because you wanted to?
10. Did you stop associating with them because you felt unwelcome?
11. How much of your time did you spend with your family?
12. Whom do you prefer to be with? Friends or family?
13. Is this the same or different than the way it was in grade school? Junior high?
14. Do you set goals for your future? When did you start?
15. Have you settled on which attributes you yourself possess?

Figure 13.1. Peer Arena Progression Profile—Adolescent.

from secondary-field persons, by use of the PAPP—SF, is desired. The language of the instruments varies slightly. For example, in PAPP—SFA the first question reads: "When did you begin to prefer to be with a lot of friends . . . ?" In PAPP—SFP (for parents) the question reads: "When do you remember that your child began to prefer to spend more time with friends than with family?" Used in tandem, the instruments can highlight the dynamics occurring between the two parties relative to adolescent concerns. Comparison of responses from adolescents and from the secondary-field persons furnishes a measure of congruity or incongruity of perceptions about three major areas: socializing, school, and home. The degree of congruence affords insight into how wide the communication or understanding gap may actually be—information important to assessing matters such as level of stress or comfort and attitudinal conflicts.

PAPP—SF FOR ADOLESCENTS (PAPP—SFA).   Part 1 deals with perceptions of peer relationships and parental attitudes about them. The questions tap beginning points of the desire to socialize with agemates,

Part 1

1. When did you begin to prefer to be with a lot of friends rather than just a few? Were they part of a special group, or were they friends from different groups? (If the response is negative to both questions, ask if the subject had any special friends.)
2. Do you still have the same friends, or have the numbers and/or the people you are friendly with changed? If so, how? Do you have a greater number of friends, or do you prefer to be with fewer friends?
3. Do you prefer to spend more time lately with your friends or your family members?
4. How do you feel your parents feel about the number of friends you have? About the types of teens who are your friends? About the amount of time you spend with them? (If answer to # 1 was "special friends" and not "group of friends," ask the same questions about the special friends.)
5. Do you feel your parents encourage you to be in touch with friends and to participate in activities with friends?
6. Do they assist you in getting there?

Part 2

7. Do you consider your school work to be on the same level this past year as it has been in previous years, or has it gotten better or worse? If so, when did the change start?
8. Do you have any idea of what effected the change?
9. Are the attitudes and behaviors you exhibit at home now the same or different from what they were last year or two years ago? If not, how have they changed? When do you think the change started?
10. How do you feel about those changes? How do you think your family is taking them?
11. Are there any special factors that may have affected the level of your school work or the attitudes and behaviors you are exhibiting now?

Figure 13.2. Peer Arena Progression Profile—Secondary Field (Adolescent).

specifics of current social patterns, and choices of where and with whom he or she prefers to spend time. Part 2 deals with perceptions of school performance and behavior and behavior at home. (See Figure 13.2.)

This profile probes the adolescent's perception of when developmental socialization needs commenced, their nature and course, whether there was secondary-field (generally parental) support or active/passive non-support, and personal assessment of school performance and school/domestic behaviors.

PAPP—SF FOR PARENTS (PAPP—SFP).   Questions of the profile for parents very closely follow the content of PAPP—SFA, for adolescents, but the format varies. As the need for psychosocial interaction with peers grows, with its corollary of less time spent at home, parental reactions vary. Thus, the profile asks the parent very specific information not only about the adolescent's changing behaviors, but it also goes into considerable detail on the behavior and attitudes of the parent. Information is garnered on whether the increasing involvement of the child with peers has found support in spirit and/or in action, or if there have been disputes regarding the amount of time spent with peers and, consequently, with family. Parental views on school performance as well as on friendships are elicited. (See Figure 13.3.)

It must be borne in mind that noninvolvement with adolescent peers can also raise parental fears and can be as strong a factor in parental displeasure with the adolescent as overinvolvement with peers. It may be that they wish some relief from parenting time, but more likely it is based on an awareness of the inappropriateness of their adolescent's

---

1. When do you remember that your child began to prefer to spend more time with friends than with family? Was he a member of a particular group or did he choose from a variety of groups? (If parent replies that he was not in any group, ask if he had any special friends.)
2. Do you remember how you felt about the youngsters he chose to be friendly with (group or special friends)?
3. How did you feel about his spending the amount of time he did spend with them, in person or on the phone? How much time was it?
4. How much time does he spend with friends now? Is it with a large group? With just a few?
5. What are you feeling about the numbers, types, and amount of time spent with friends?
6. Does your child spend any time with the family? Do you think he should be with family more? Less? Why?
7. Do you talk with your child about his friends? How often? Why or why not?
8. How do you perceive your child's appraisal of how you feel about his friends and his relationship with them?
9. Are there any ways in which you assisted your child in getting to his friends or in participating in activities with his friends? (If the person objected to being involved, inquire as to the manner in which he might stand in the way of the child accessing friends, or particular friends. Make it a point to get an answer to both the pro and the con of the question.)
10. Has your child's school work remained on the same level in the past year as it has been in the past? Has it changed? If so, how?
11. What do you feel about what may have contributed to the evenness or change?
12. Are there any ways in which you have been able to assist? Why or why not?
13. How has your child's school performance affected family relationships with him?
14. Is your child's behavior at home this past year generally similar to what it was in the past, or has it changed? Please explain in what ways.
15. What are your feelings about his similarity or change? Have you been able to be helpful? Why or why not?
16. Are there any special factors or persons you believe may have affected your child's performance in school or the behaviors at home?

Figure 13.3. Peer Arena Progression Profile—Secondary Field (Parents).

isolation. Unsuccessful efforts at encouraging the adolescent to interact with agemates elevate the parents' frustration and concern.

Through comparing the adolescent's responses to the PAPP—SFA and parental responses to the PAPP—SFP, we are able to assess the degree of difference or similarity between perceptions. Thus, administration of these instruments affords:

1. An index of the adolescent's appraisal of peer involvement, whether she considers parents to be supportive or nonsupportive, the specific ways in which she identifies support or nonsupport, her performance at school, and her behaviors at home. Furthermore, we also tap her perception of continuity or change in school or home behavior, and some notion of when she perceives the change to have taken place. Congruity or incongruity between behavior or performance at home and at school is also revealed.

2. An index of parent perception of the same issues.

3. A measure of the distance between these two indexes.

4. Identification of the emotional tone connected with the facts revealed.

When the adolescent and the parent instruments are compared, the professional must bear in mind the range of alternative reactions held by the two generations to a given behavior, for example, conflicting opinions about the type of peer the child associates with. The instrument does not deal with how the conflicts are worked on, settled, or exacerbated. It is designed to elicit information about *what* the controversial areas are. A main objective is to assess the degree of adolescent-parent congruence or conflict in regard to relations with peers. If considerable dichotomy in perceptions or behaviors are uncovered, it is advisable to focus first on communication difficulties that may underlie relational problems.

Data disclosed by the two scales offer openings by which to intervene in current issues where adjustments can indeed be made to effect better relationships between adolescent and parent(s) or other secondary-field figures. Concentration on present conflicts and concerns is a powerful locus for intervention since the adolescent is very much involved *in the present*. Although dynamics of past relationships remain active in current issues, the past may have little relevance in a period when independence must be exhibited *now* and forged for the future. It is highly important that the adolescent demonstrate this independence both to himself and to the relevant environmental objects. The adolescent may be insulted when family members do not reinforce the adult dimensions but instead emphasize childish ways or errors that point out the adolescent's continuing dependency. A show of rebellion and even hostility to family members can be rooted in the need to affirm a shaky independence. This can explain the behaviors toward other secondary-field members besides parents. Reinterpretation alone can reduce tensions and may serve to avert future misunderstandings that can weaken the adolescent's tenuous confidence in his own level of independence.

It is also crucial to clarify to persons in the secondary field that despite outward bravado, adolescents are still in the process of achievement of a sense of self. During the growth process, they possess only disconnected fragments of a self. Outside support can offer the bolstering the adolescent needs to remain engaged with the rigorous developmental dynamics and their often-painful consequences within the arena of peer comparisons and evaluations. When family does not or cannot offer that support, the resulting negative adolescent behaviors may be an expression of hurt (expressed as anger) at the abandonment experienced. It could also be related to a subtle fear of "aloneness" at a time of general instability. If the family is not seen as supplying the needed external support, the adolescent faces the "peer arena" in a weakened condition. He is at risk of finding the intensity of the interactions too strong and may be tempted to experiment with any number of flight mechanisms (see Chapter 10).

PAPP—SF FOR SCHOOL (PAPP—SFS). The developmental dynamics of comparative acts also permeate the school setting, which is a part of the psychological peer arena. When problems with school work surface, this does not necessarily mean that materials are too difficult. Possible physical problems must be ruled out first. Then a psychosocial assessment should be made. As with other stages, developmental needs of the period need to be considered.

The PAPP—SFS is an instrument to be administered to the adolescent by the school counselor or teacher, by itself or in coordination with other PAPPs. Although the major purpose of the PAPP—SFS is to shed light on what school factors contribute to problematic school performance, some questions are the same as those utilized in investigating the adolescents' perceptions of the secondary field of home. When working with adolescents, we must keep in mind the effects of interacting forces. Simplistic notions about causes of school problems must be avoided. Hence, depth and breadth of examination are important. For example, if we explore the possibility of sibling competition, it is fruitful to remember that failing to be better than a sibling in school may also affect behavior at home *and* the level of security with which the adolescent carries on peer arena comparative acts. Disappointments become circular. The nature of the interpersonal contact with any environmental figure during the unsteady period of adolescence affects how outcomes of the comparative acts are integrated and their subsequent impact on home, school productivity, and social behaviors. Thus, the questions of the PAPP—SFS cover matters encompassing home, school, peer perceptions and relationships, and one's functioning in the greater social arena. (See Figure 13.4.)

The following guidelines specific to the developmental stage may be helpful to the school professional in formulating a diagnosis. They are diverse but pertinent.

1. Is the adolescent *overly* preoccupied with the developmental imperative of engaging in comparative acts with other teens? Is the scrutiny too continuous? Are all/most energies taken away from classroom work and devoted to developmental concerns?

2. What are the values of the smaller peer group to which the student is closely allied? Is group status enhanced or lessened by being a good/satisfactory student?

3. Are feelings of instability or insecurity exacerbated by nonacceptance from peers so that energies are occupied with coping strategies and thus not available for academic work?

4. Is the adolescent disappointing parents (in an area of their expressed values) as retribution for their attitudes toward peers they do not approve of or for their nonsupport of activities with peers?

The PAPP—SFS approach to adolescent problems is to look beyond family-centered models. If the student is an adolescent, explore peer arena issues first, to be followed (if necessary) by examination of the other, more traditional areas. The history and status of peer arena func-

1. When did you begin to prefer to be with a lot of friends rather than just a few? Were they part of a special group, or were they friends from a lot of different groups? (If the response is negative to both questions, ask if they had any special friends.)
2. Do you still have the same friends, or have the persons or numbers of the persons with whom you are friendly changed? If so, how?
3. Do you prefer to spend more time lately with friends or with family members?
4. How do you feel your parent/s feel about the number of friends you have? About the types of teens who are your friends? About the amount of time you spend with them? (If the answer to question 1 was "special friends" and not "group," ask the same questions about the special friends).
5. Do you feel your parents try to help you maintain you friendships, or do they try to change them? Do they keep you at home? If so, doing what?
6. Do you consider your school work to be on the same level this past year as it has been in previous years? Has it gotten better or worse? If so, when did the change start?
7. What effected the change? Do you feel it could be related to the atmosphere at home with family members? Any special member?
8. Could the change in school performance be due to school factors such as teachers and/or classmates?
9. Are there any nonschool factors that do not involve family that might be affecting your schoolwork? Would it be connected with any of your relationships with the various types of people you run into here at school?
10. As you think about your future, are there any connections between school subjects, activities, or the people you are friendly with and what you will do or be in your future?

Figure 13.4. Peer Arena Progression Profile—Secondary Field (School Personnel).

tioning at school and out of school may hold the key to understanding problems of under- or over-achievement, acting out, and other puzzling behaviors.

In summary, each PAPP instrument focuses on discrete areas of adolescent social participation. Any instrument of the battery can be profitably used alone or in conjunction with any instrument of the Socialization Battery. Furthermore, the PAPP—SFS can be amended by the professional to fit secondary-field members, such as siblings.

THE PEER PROGRESSION BATTERY (PPB)

The two components of the PPB, the Socialization Battery and the Peer Arena Battery, each offer important tools with which to access important information and insights into the dynamics of the psychosocial worlds of adolescents: who they interact with; the quality and character-of their interactions; and the impact of the interactions on emotional state, course of development, and overt behaviors.

The five instruments of the Socialization Battery provide data on scope, pattern, and preferences of adolescents in regard to interactions in their relevant social environment. These data offer pictures of the perceived social influence field: how it is accessed, what draws their attention in one another, depth and breadth of the desire to interact with other agemates, strategies utilized to interact with one another or indications of the inability to strategize, amount of time spent with various peer groups, and how the broad social arena is differentiated and used.

The four PAPP instruments yield data on point of developmental progress, affective responses to psychosocial interactions with peers (as displayed in prosocial behaviors or social maladaptions), behaviors and attitudes of the important members of the various secondary fields (e.g., parents, grandparents) and comparative perceptions. Furthermore, the Peer Arena Battery provides information on:

1. Whether the adolescent is participating in the adolescent peer arena period normative for his or her age
2. The extent of home-based support or negative input
3. How adolescent behaviors at home manifest an overflow of affective response to psychosocial developmental dynamics engaged in with peers
4. Impact of the outcome of adolescent psychosocial interactions with peers on:
   a. Academic performance
   b. Social behavior in school, home, and outside settings

The nine instruments that make up the PPB can be used individually or together. Used in combination, they cover the many dimensions of adolescent socialization. For example, the PAPP—A may indicate that the current 12th-grader has from the 7th grade on incrementally increased the time spent with peers and has accordingly reduced the time spent with parents. This adolescent does well in school and has participated in large groups of agemates, and socialization patterns are now showing a shift from preferences for large groups to a preference for smaller groups of others whose interests are similar to her own. If a subsequent examination of the ARGI protocol reveals the teen is (1) utilizing a number of different reference groups and (2) is generally distinguishing "peer" issues from those more appropriate to parents or other groups, the hypothesis based on PAPP findings is reinforced by the ARGI findings. Both reveal a cognitive ordering of the social influence field. (See Chapter 5.)

When instruments are used as a battery, findings from one area may reinforce or contradict findings from other areas. If initial diagnostic hypotheses are supported, treatment planning will be facilitated. On the other hand, if conflicting findings are present, planning based on weak and possible erroneous initial hypotheses may be abandoned. Valuable time and energies can then be devoted to reassessment of prior data and seeking of additional information.

Either battery may be the first administered. As a rule of thumb, the ARGI instrument is the more benign instrument to administer first since it deals with general socialization and the questions are more objective — less personal. But there is no set order of administration. Initial clinical impressions of the specific adolescent will provide direction. Begin with the instrument that appears least threatening. Be aware, however, that it is incorrect to assume that asking about other persons is less anxiety-producing than asking about emotional responses to comparative acts. Furthermore, it is also incorrect to assume that friends are a more neutral subject than parents. In fact, during this period of development, the reverse is more often the case.

Utilized together, the ARGI and the PAPP instruments provide complementary information. The ARGI gives information on cognitive organization of the social world and attendant levels of maturation. The PAPP offers subjective information on achieved psychoemotional developmental level and details of normative or irregular progression. The ARGI creates a picture of the greater psychosocial reference field; the PAPP examines the field of psychosocial interactions with peers that are crucial to development.

In a clinical setting, the adolescent should be invited to be actively involved in treatment planning. In fact, a mutual exploration and discovery process, which use of these instruments makes possible, will give concrete evidence of the professional's recognition of the adolescent as an active participant in his own growth or recovery.

A THEORETICAL KEY

This formulation holds that awareness of the peer as the key environmental other is fundamental to interpreting adolescent behaviors. The status held with peers is of top priority to adolescents. The reasons peers assume such importance is that they serve the following functions for the adolescent:

1. Their numbers provide an outward sign that the instability experienced by being a person in transition is shared by agemates. Hence, confusing emotions and erratic behaviors are reinforced as being natural and normal.
2. As peers engage in their own processes of construction of identity, they stand as models for one another and offer each other raw materials for comparison and contrast as each selects and evaluates potential "self elements."
3. They reciprocally assume new and varied roles and attributes within an atmosphere where either serious or light discussions and activities are accommodated as the moment dictates.
4. They set the standards for behaviors and attitudes. Peer responses heavily influence adolescent goal formulation, values, attributes, interpersonal characteristics, and skill development.
5. Reactions of group members are a vital determinant of the adolescent's evaluation of the current and future effectiveness of attributes and skills. In the absence of objective measurements, peer reactions serve as subjective measures. Peer responses affect one's immediate level of affective comfort or distress and the degree of self-confidence.

Adolescents intuit the need to interact with peers in order to grow psychosocially. Conforming behavior helps avoid rejection. The deep-structure imperative to engage in comparative acts with peers is outwardly reflected in a constant desire to be with peers. It is the power of these *immediate* goals that places peer activities and relationships as first priority, thus changing the nature of parent-child relationships. Other facets of adolescent life are active and important, but the central environmental figures of this period are their peers. Their influence prevails whether they are physically present or not.

This theoretical key focuses interpretation of adolescent behavior on what is relevant to adolescents, avoiding intervention grounded in outdated or irrelevant theoretical positions.

PART SIX

Applications of the Peer Arena Model

This section extends the theory, empirical findings, and instrumentation offered in preceding chapters·to avenues of practical application for professionals who work with adolescents. Three domains are specifically addressed: parenting, educating and counseling, and healing. Chapter 14 addresses the changes that parents experience in their relationships with teenagers and attendant conflicts they may encounter in their own thinking or in interaction with their adolescent. Models for flexible parenting are presented within a context of revised responsibilities—no less important than traditional parental obligations but age-appropriate and different.

Chapters 15 and 16 challenge professionals in education and mental health to adopt an updated view of adolescent behaviors within a framework that recognizes the central developmental position of the peer and allows that much of adolescent behavior must be considered as stimulated by attempts to adjust one's sense of relative status. The extent of psychological energies thus expended is explained with suggestions for handling the tensions and mood swings that result. A new therapeutic approach is introduced, providing a revised look at what is considered maladaptive behavior, and suggestions for adjustment, including even physical changes in school building structures, are offered.

CHAPTER 14

Adolescents and Parents: Alternating Currents

ROLE ADJUSTMENTS

Adolescence is a period of transition not only for the young person, but also for the parent. Until this stage of the child's life, the parent has been primary nurturer and caretaker and has been always aware, subliminally if not consciously, of the child's health, whereabouts, and progress. During the adolescent period psychological separation of the child from the parent escalates. The child makes noticeable strides toward independent functioning. This transition to adulthood begins at puberty. In Western society it is becoming increasingly longer, particularly for those who pursue extended periods of education, training, and apprenticeship.

That adolescence is a transitional period for youth is well accepted. That it is a transitional period for the adolescent's parents is not as well documented and is not often even considered. It is popularly accepted that adolescents are changing, that they are therefore moody and unpredictable, and that they like to rebel against rules that seem child-oriented to them. Sophisticated parents are familiar with the "inevitability of adolescent rebellion," and are poised for a difficult time with their youngster. How much of this difficult time is a projection of a painful, internally experienced transition is a question worth posing. Adolescents seem to claim the right to be understood as going through a difficult period of changing. Mood swings are expected and tolerated, as are even rudeness and disrespectful actions. Parents are generally not accorded an acknowledged status of transition or any of the attendant rights.

Parents also must learn independent functioning. Old habits pertinent to an active mode of parenting must be incrementally shed and new habits learned. For the child, independent functioning means functioning without leaning on the parent; for the adult, it means feeling meaningful and complete without being depended on by children. By the time the child begins adolescence, the parent has been an active nurturant agent for 10 to 12 years. Parents are suddenly called upon to extinguish their conditioned responses—which by now may have become internally experienced needs "to be needed." This is not an overnight task. More times than not it is conceptualized as getting used to feeling "dispensable." It can be a painful process.

Like their adolescents, parents are in transition between two stages—from responding to the dependence of their children to adjusting to the independence of their children. Involved is the gradual extinction of an emotional sense of indispensability and acceptance of limited dispensability. The process may bring great costs to self and relationships with the adolescent or other family members.

Years of nurturance bring the offspring to the desired goal—a level of maturity appropriate to adolescence. A parent who has guided the offspring to this point has been successful. Now the child is ready to grapple with demands of the next growth period. The chief rival for the child's time, interest, and adulation becomes the adolescent agemate or near-agemate. The agemate is the "other" who becomes increasingly crucial to the offspring. Influence positions on issues such as apparel and leisure activities are transferred from parent to peer, increasing the parental feelings of irrelevance. Furthermore, the strong adolescent wish to be with peers is paramount and competes with even the most alluring family opportunities. Parents experience new boundaries. The period of active parental nurturance ends, at times abruptly, with onset of adolescence.

In Western society, however, the child is not asked to assume adult roles when he reaches teenage years; societal expectations lag quite far behind physical readiness. Thus, adolescent desires for independence reignite conditioned protective responses in parents, but the adolescent no longer responds. Parents recognize that the adolescent is not yet mature and are confused. They do not perceive a finished adult; hence, they see their job as not yet completed. Perhaps if Western society practiced the customs of simple and primitive societies, with abrupt cessation of childhood and equally abrupt assumption of adult roles, the reduced level of responsibility of the parent would be more clear. (Mead, 1928; Benedict, 1954).

Parents in Western society have generally not been advised that transition to peers is the developmentally appropriate next step. The peer is the *primary* environmental other in adolescence. The peer is also the nurturer. But unlike parental nurturance, it is *not* protective nurturance. This sustenance for the adolescent is quite different. Adolescents nurture one another by their physical presence. Looking at agemates in similar conditions of uncertainty and transition reassures. Furthermore, the psychosocial task of the period is to establish an identity (Erikson, 1956). A major part of the process is deciding on the contents (elements) of one's "self" structure. Attributes, opinions, and behaviors of peers are raw material to be closely examined, compared with, evaluated against, modeled, and copied. The parent is at this point no longer caretaker or model, no matter how devoted. Peers are models, and adolescents are becoming their own caretakers.

It is essential to eductate parents to help them accept that the primary figure for their adolescent offspring is the age peer. Informed and forewarned, parents can better prepare to one day curtail parental functions that have become obsolete. Parents who understand that the years of *active* nurturance are limited to preadolescence will reorganize their concept of parenthood accordingly. A continuum of different stages of altered parental functions is the appropriate model.

The distinct brand of parenting best suited for adolescents involves passive and invited nurturance. It is what adolescents need from parents. Passive nurturance continues through adolescence in the form of financial provisions—shelter, food, clothing, education, and other basic needs such as health care. Invited nurturant functions are of equal importance. They are specific, as opposed to the global needs expressed in younger days. Invited nurturant functions include advice pertaining to job/college, qualities to seek in others, and moral issues. In general, they are delivered within a cognitive context rather than the context of emotional need of younger years. These functions the parents serve are no less important than their previous ones. What is confusing is that they *feel* less important and make parents view themselves as less central to the adolescent. This emotional sense of decreased centrality is based on fact. It becomes clear that the adolescent agemate—the peer—is given the prominence previously accorded parents.

REBELLION: AN OUTMODED CONCEPTION

Parents do not always understand which changes are appropriate to the transitions of adolescence. They need assistance, particularly since outmoded theoretical conceptions are still prominent. For example, the outmoded and limited model of adolescent rebellion is still strong. However, what psychoanalytic followers see as rebellion is seen by other perspectives as independence seeking (Freud, A., 1936). Depending on which theoretical frame of reference is adopted, the same behavior can be interpreted differently. Followers of the notion of continuous development emphasize the continuity of growth and view rebellious behaviors as a manifestation of independence seeking rather than true rebellion (Offer, 1969). But if the parents choose to buy the notion that parents remain the primary libidinal force and that the adolescent must battle against unconscious impulses to tear themselves loose and attach to age-appropriate others, they will fit the adolescent's behaviors to the menu and still feel "rebelled against." This theoretical format implies acceptance by the parent of adolescent untoward behaviors reflecting rebelliousness as a developmental necessity. The designated course of action is to hang on tightly to the continuing posture of major emotional other and "wait it out."

Accepting the notion that when the child becomes an adolescent the parent's primary emotional nurturance years are over, and developmental nurturance is transferred to another source (agemates), fosters a more impersonal view of the erratic, unpredictable, and often chameleonlike behaviors of adolescent offspring. This knowledge can eliminate convoluted interpretations and consequent lengthy discussions or arguments, not to mention emotional disfigurement of the persons involved and misinterpretations of attendant dynamics. In fact, it may even be comforting for parents to assign responsibility for the ups and downs the adolescent exhibits to relationships with others.

Thus, it is crucial to bring to parents the "peer arena model" of development, which establishes the peer as the central nurturant figure of adolescence. With this perspective, rather than feeling antiquated, the adult can intelligently guide the offspring to access the others he needs. Extremes of mood stand a chance of not being attributed only to family-related home tensions. The model establishes that the home may function more as haven than as arena.

SUPPORTS

Two parents can serve as a support system for one another and for other parents. When parents are familiarized with the passive nurturant role, they will be able to discuss with openness (rather than quizzical cynicism) the emotions experienced as their children transfer former loyalties to agemates. Furthermore, the discussion can profitably deal with nonverbal parenting postures that need to be assumed.

Findings from the ARGI instrument reported in this book can be utilized most effectively with parents in parent education groups to illustrate how they retain an important influence position. In a therapy situation, each adolescent can be administered the ARGI, and the findings can be shared with parents. In well-adjusted families, findings should not vary too much from those of the sample reported in Chapter 5. Findings will prove helpful to parents in at least two respects: (1) They will disclose the areas of importance they still occupy with the more mature offspring (e.g., ARGI findings reveal parents are the reference group of choice for furture-oriented issues and matters where experience is an important factor). (2) They will identify other groups who are part of the greater reference field of the adolescent and their respective areas of perceived expertise. Parents may relish concrete evidence that the sometimes petulant or childish individual who lives with them (and for whom they still supply the primary emotional haven) has gained an expanded sense of the world and the relative places of the variety of others in it.

Creative use of findings from the ARGI brings the parent into the adolescent world rather dramatically. It counteracts the notion that the adolescent's psychological world is made up of just family or peers. A productive strategy may be to administer the ARGI to parents and ask them to indicate the groups they believe their adolescent would select. Responses to the two inventories could be compared in family session.

Information transmitted to parents from ARGI findings can depressurize and reassure. When the adolescent's world is conceived as moving back and forth between only family and peers, parents can assume they are in competition with the adolescent's peers. Relationships with members of these two groups are primary, but are more correctly understood within a framework that includes a broad array of others.

VERBAL/NONVERBAL PARENTING MODEL

Parenting young children involves a skillful balance of verbal and nonverbal exchange and action. The situation is no different from parenting older children. In adolescence, however, the following general guidelines can be helpful. The verbal is pitched to the adult dimensions of the adolescent; the nonverbal caters to more childlike needs. Expanding cognitive capacities of the adolescent allow the imagination to soar and stimulate thought processes that can encompass a most ambitious, and often unrealistic and pretentious, set of aspirations. Adolescents need serious discussion of their ideas on an egalitarian basis—adult to adult. Parents who too quickly declare the ambitions impractical will find that the adolescent withdraws. More advisable is engaging the adolescent to explore the dream and contributing appropriately worded issues for the adolescent to search out. In other words, parents should be encouraged to lead the adolescent to discovery rather than to "tell." Whether it be plans for the young person's future, the prospect of new relationships, or insights into situations that are new to him or her, all parties benefit from communication that stimulates elaborated thought and advances the adolescent toward adulthood.

By contrast, when the parent intuits that childish needs are surfacing, nonverbal attention is best offered. The adolescent gratefully receives this brand of understanding. He may far more gracefully deal with his own changeable nature when the part of him that is still child is responded to but not talked about. Alternating these two approaches is the best way to deal with the dialectical character of adolescence.

PEERS AS DEVELOPMENTAL RAW MATERIAL

A major issue for parents of adolescents is dealing with their displacement as the major influence force in their children's lives. Not only does their influence decrease, but it goes to youthful and/or unknown individuals. Expended efforts of child rearing appear jeopardized as their offspring lend themselves to the influence of peers. Educating parents as to how diverse peers differentially contribute to the many aspects of their children's social maturation can reduce anxieties over relationships that are important to the youth but frighten parents. Parents need to be advised that peers represent a range of possible personalities from which their children choose. Adolescents are engaged in an exciting period of deciding who and what they wish to be in future life. It is understandable that parents feel safest if they see the child doing what they themselves do.

Close relationships with peers who are quite unlike the family or who represent what appears "dangerously new" stimulate parental discomfort and fear. Compounding what the parent sees visually is what the parent hears teens talking about. Understanding that adolescence is a period of "tryout" does help parents tolerate some of this behavior, but it does not allay the concern. Helping parents to understand the psychological "borrowing" the adolescent must do in the course of his psychosocial development can reduce the stress.

"Borrowing" is a more psychologically intense activity than "trying out." Borrowing implies a temporary identification. The personality element (attribute) that is admired in the peer is experienced as one's own, is inserted into the "self," and operates as a facsimile element. As the adolescent manifests the borrowed quality, she must continue to be physically with the borrowee to be able to check for acccuracy. The individual needs enough feedback from self and others to assess whether the element is experienced as consonant or dissonant over time. This process may involve borrowing one or more elements from the same person, a few others, or many others. The length of time necessary to arrive at decisions will be short for elements where conclusions may be quickly reached and longer for more complex elements.

Parents who are advised of these developmental dynamics will better understand the basis for the new behaviors new friendships stimulate and will see that this kind of tryout is necessary for full psychological growth. Friendships in adolescence serve stage-specific functions very different from those in adulthood. The various peer groups make others accessible for close and silent scrutiny. When one or more characteristics are selected for borrowing and tryout, peer groups are the arena where the target others are regularly accessed. It is important that parents be sensitized to the complex and enervating dynamics of the peer arena, the potential ups and downs that can befall their offspring, and their children's emotional responses to the outcomes of displaying the new personality element(s) they are borrowing.

Parental intervention is very important at these times. However, it requires great sensitivity to know when the adolescent should be encouraged to communicate and "talk about it" and when it is best to gracefully acknowledge the importance of an "alone" period in which the teen can recover from disappointment in self, reevaluate, and regroup energies. The latter kind of parenting is subsumed under the rubric of *nonverbal nurturer*.

Adolescence is a period when personality elements are being worked out and developed. Some fit; some do not. It is important to advise parents that there are periods when fewer elements feel consonant and integrated and other periods when the number of congruent elements seems greater. In the former periods, the adolescent feels less sure of himself. At these times "borrowing" additional elements from others not only offers new opportunities for tryout, but it makes the personality feel more stable. Empty spaces are filled. Outside parties may find the adolescent "different" and very changeable—chameleonlike. What they see are overt manifestations of internal tryouts. Although parents are generally aware that adolescence is a period of rapid change, they generally do not know that it is also a period of instability. Introducing instability in adolescence to them as normative, and not maladaptive, assists them to accept strategies, such as borrowing, that serve needs for both change and stability.

Necessarily, there will appear to be challenges to basic parental values. They are not necessarily permanent. As the adolescent continues through the period, he will reengage the dynamics of the adolescent dialectic and will repeat the process of borrowing. He will experience more and more new elements and will engage comparative act dynamics to assess and evaluate their fit and utility. If the outcome is positive, the element will be retained and integrated. He will borrow and try out many foreign elements until he has filled the spaces in the self structure with elements that have been reworked as his own and are no longer borrowed. Many adolescent years will be spent engaging these psychological processes toward the end of assembling a coordinated set of elements constituting the self structure. The need to engage with a wide variety of personality types needs recognition as a prevailing adolescent theme. This basic developmental need also explains why an adolescent may desire to be with a particular (often very different) other *almost constantly.*

Statements by others that a particular attribute is negative or is positive are not blindly accepted by adolescents. This is not indicative of an oppositional stance. This evaluation is a function of development they need to accomplish *on their own*. Otherwise, it would be experienced as superficial and not fully worked through. In fact, it would be regressive. Adolescence is the period of life when attitudes and opinions of others and their relevance to oneself must be *hammered out*. Otherwise they are not meaningfully integrated as "self "; they remain facsimile. If the adolescent eventually adopts the same conclusion about another's character or attributes that a parent has expressed for months or even years prior, it is an experienced perception and not an assumed one. The adolescent has "lived" the element and experienced its cognitive and emotional dimensions. Whether or not to adopt an attribute modeled by a friend as part of one's own set of elements is a product of intensive effort, not another person's advice.

RECIPROCAL SHIFTS

In essence, the primary agent of psychosocial development is now *out of the home*. Notwithstanding all other adjustments, this change is perhaps the most radical change of the period and the most difficult for the parent. To the adolescent the home will most often be used as:

1. A release valve to the constraints on behavior that are maintained when with peers
2. A place to privately regroup energies necessary to continue peer arena interactions. Here the adolescent can be alone. Often this behavior is misunderstood as negative in orientation. Parents and

other family members feel ignored. In reality, it represents a positive use of the home field to recharge.

3. An anchor, whether the adolescent is physically at home or not

In adolescence, the home is no longer limited to its physical definition. With the added intellectual growth, which has fostered structures for abstracting, the "home" is now carried cognitively even when the adolescent is physically away. Parents and siblings merge into a concept of home; their physical presence is no longer necessary.

Parents must work hard to accept and integrate these changes—and the adolescent's advance in formal operational thought helps. The new ability to abstract on abstractions allows a host of common interests between generations. Discussion can now capture some of the relationship that was previously entirely emotional. Close relationship can continue if parents find *new cognitive dimensions* to energize the relationship, even in the most mundane daily encounters. Remarks such as "I understand that Macy's offers specialized sales service to assist in fitting their suits well" should replace "I don't like the way that suit fits you." The latter dismisses the adolescent's growing capacity for judgment and represents a parent–small child relationship; the former offers information (which the young person can choose to use or not) and reflects adult-adult communication.

Understanding that the desire to spend more time with peers than with parents is developmentally appropriate allows parents to encourage, not sabotage, their children's direction, enabling the adolescent to deal primarily with his own ambivalence about leaving the comfortable dependencies of childhood. If parents can assume this perspective, they can recognize that their physical presence and emotional support, *if* needed, is invaluable. Verbal exchange is not always necessary. Physical presence suffices to offer a graphic picture of support.

HOME AS HAVEN

Except for troubled families, home is the adolescent's arena for rest and recuperation from the day's task-related and developmental work. It also is an outlet for bridled negative feelings, residues of the day's interactions. Since the comparative acts that make up the developmental work are subliminal and not deliberate, their emotional after effects are generally not understood or interpreted correctly. Furthermore, even if they are understood, expression of negative emotions toward peers is risky. Relations with peers require careful handling. Angry exchanges serve to distance, and rejection may result. Hence, at day's end a variety of unexpressed emotions are brought home. Since these negative feelings are not understood as emotional reactions to comparative act dynamics with peers, they frequently find a target in a family member by whom the adolescent does not risk rejection.

These negative behaviors have been commonly taken at face value and have reinforced notions of adolescent rebellion. This approach reflects the philosophy that the parent-teen dyad needs to be adversarial in order that separation issues be worked out. The peer arena model not only discounts the concept of parents as adversaries but argues that they offer support and comfort to the developing teen. This is clearly contrary to the psychoanalytic position, which holds that other adolescents and the peer group offer teens the haven from the hardships of their libidinal struggles to separate from parents (Erikson, 1956; Josselyn, 1952). We suggest that the home is the haven and that peers in peer groups constitute the arena that often yields dissonant and disappointing results affectively hard to integrate. It is not the dynamics of the parent-child separation issues but the *results of comparative acts with peers* that account for the psychological unrest. DFI sets the parent forth as less emotionally potent and less important to the adolescent than peers. Hence, the teen is safe to act out emotions with them, ridding herself of tensions to facilitate reentry into the peer arena. Parents and other family members, in most cases, continue to offer emotional love and support in spite of the pain they experience as "safe outlets" for hostility.

CLARITY FOR PROFESSIONALS

Outdated theoretical positions that still form the basis for a great deal of professional work with adolescents confuse professionals, not to mention the lay public. Thus, parents continue to personalize the hostilities expressed by teenagers instead of understanding adolescent angers can be peer-stimulated. A cycle of negative interactions ensues. In so many cases, the emotional connections eagerly sought by all parties become tangled in a web of misdirection and misinterpretation.

If professionals can supply parents with this broadened perspective of comparative acts and affective responses ranging from pleasure to deep pain, parents could understand that upsetting behaviors and even anger displayed by the adolescent are usually not manifestations of negative sentiment toward them. They are more likely affective responses to developmental dynamics and are not understood even by the adolescent.

Layperson and professional alike often assume that adolescents deliberately withhold information in order to individuate. At times this is true. Nevertheless, much is withheld because it is not cognitively clear to the adolescent herself. Furthermore, it would assist the parent to pick the appropriate time of day to raise painful issues. A negative outcome to an argument due solely to poor timing could thus be avoided. Very simply, parents must have a general understanding of "a bad day at the office." With this understanding personalization of anger is reduced, even though the experience is painful.

We have combined these conceptions into a *bigenerational task model* to complement the psychoanalytic model of parent-child separation (Seltzer, 1982). Our model depicts parents moving from an active parental stance to a specific latent model. In other words, the global parenting functions appropriate for smaller children are supplanted by specific tasks appropriate to the parent of an adolescent. There is a change from directing and managing to guidance, information, and suggestion. It is not a passive role of "adjustment to the changing child." Rather, it is an active model of *realignment* of function where the parent actively engages in changing his or her behavior to meet the new needs of a maturing adolescent.

Cognitive strides have changed the psychosocial world of the adolescent to encompass a much larger society, and restricting the adolescent experience to a two-dimensional model of "parent-child" lacks the scope necessary to be effective in adolescence. The expanded model is multidimensional. Included are parent and family, adolescent peer groups of the peer arena, and a variety of other reference persons who represent diverse age groups accessed according to perceived need. Familiar concepts of adolescent separation, rebellion, individuation, rejection, and escape represent only a fraction of the dynamics involved for adolescents and families. Our more expansive model highlights new conceptual notions of peer arena, frameworklessness, the adolescent dialectic, comparative acts, the dissonance-consonance continuum, bigenerational tasks, relationship realignment, nurturance postures, relevant models, active and passive support stances, maturation versus stagnation, domains of development, differing profiles, etc.

In essence, if both adolescents and parents redistribute their energies in accordance with their respective developmental stage and posture, growth advances. Entailed are role and relationship realignments. Driven by developmental imperatives, adolescents choose to choose each other. They are one another's developmental figures against a background of parents and home. This background is an anchor. The more stable and dependable it is, the more it helps the adolescent to navigate out and psychosocially engage relevant agemates. Bringing the parent to recognize and value his or her high importance as anchor facilitates efforts to let go of old parenting habits and postures and to creatively shift to guide, informant, continuing support, and model.

CHAPTER 15

The School Experience: Peer Arena Issues and Implications for Educators and Counselors

The educational arena is responsible for socializing children into adults who will take on responsible adult roles. Its task is the transmission of the society's culture to ensure its continuity (Spindler, 1974). Within our conception of the peer arena as the psychosocial aggregate of any and all interactions in any and all peer groups, the school is seen as the locus for a large percentage of this psychosocial exchange.

THE SCHOOL AS A MAJOR COMPONENT OF THE PEER ARENA

The school can be considered as the focus for major exchange of psychosocial energy. Here adolescents encounter hundreds of agemates daily. They interact physically, verbally, and nonverbally. They have opportunities to compare on appearance, abilities, personality attributes, interpersonal skills, and possessions. Since they are available to one another five days a week, nine months a year, there is opportunity for their protracted study of one another. Each adolescent is also the object of other adolescents' looking and listening. An unexpressed sense of mutual need for one another as raw materials of development exists.

Comparative behavior begins on the way to school and continues in the hallways, classrooms, lunchroom, gym, swimming pool, athletic court, at after-school functions, and on the route home. The dynamics are engaged subliminally and continuously alongside the socializing and learning activities seven or eight hours of the day, as well as two additional hours before and after school.

The school is an *intense arena*. One cannot leave at will or decide not to attend for any length of time. Paradoxically, the role of school as a major component of the peer arena is not seen as a school function. The activity at school is academic production. In sharp contrast to academics, psychosocial development is not discussed in class, but is a private and silent enterprise. How one is progressing developmentally is not a school issue. Neither is how one feels about oneself and how that affects motivation, academic production and conduct. Most adolescents manage to cope with the difficulties; others cannot. Still others do well most of the time and falter some of the time.

As discussed earlier, adolescents need to let go of the former guideposts provided by parents and exist in a "frameworklessness" condition until they arrive at their own mature perspectives. Along the road to adulthood, they look to others in a similar condition as models. They measure themselves through comparisons. When the results are discouraging, anxiety about self and self in relation to others surfaces. Sometimes it is controlled, and the adolescent continues to maintain sense of self at an acceptable level. At other times, the anxiety can be overwhelming, and the need to protect oneself takes varying forms.

Academic production can be affected by developmental activity. Outcomes in one area have emotional ramifications for the other. For example, a lower mark on a math test than that received by a friend perceived to be less talented at math brings more than academic disappointment. The realignment of perception on relative standing on math ability affects the future. For example, previously the adolescent may have considered math as a profession based on the perception of his or her own high performance relative to that of others. Such emotional letdowns occur over and over again as the early to middle adolescent works to achieve a self picture in terms of academic and social attributes, their relative merit, and their future potential.

Academic Problems

That academic problems can be exacerbated by distressing results of psychosocial comparisons is not often recognized. Miscellaneous types of school problems may result, for example, underachievement. Certainly, the cause of underachievement may be associated with academic inability, but some underachievement is a response to developmental dynamics of comparative acts.

Another familiar problem is the preoccupation of a young male adolescent who experiences insecurity (or a new sense of security) about his masculinity. He diverts attention and energies from school work to compare himself with other males and arrive at some notion of relative standing on masculinity. Perhaps he then thinks about females he would like to experiment with. Many energies may be expended in assessing the females in relation to one another, deciding which one is appealing and which would be most helpful to his quest about himself in relation to perceived competitors, etc. All this goes on in English class. He may be able to contain this need, or it could go forth into the rest of the day or week or even beyond. Academic success may be important to this particular student, but at this time the new feelings of maleness may be more prominent and more immediately relevant. Such preoccupation may occur with hundreds of characteristics and attributes on which youth compare themselves.

The peer arena experience for an overachiever might also be painful. Overinvolvement in academic activity represents an avenue one can take to avoid exercising painful comparative and evaluative dynamics and shield self from evaluation and relative placement. Overinvolvement in academics with little time to socialize may serve two purposes: (1) protection from disappointing conclusions and accompanying emotional responses connected with comparisons of self with others in the arena, and (2) support of the faltering ego with reinforcements from the subject matter itself or the marks achieved. Both under- and overachievement are defensive initiatives adopted in service of ego, but the extent of energies diverted to these defenses may bring an overall developmental disadvantage.

The Axle of Adolescent Life

Peer relations are the axle of the wheel of adolescent life and represent the hidden agenda underlying adolescent behaviors. Skills and talents at this stage of development are judged by the positive or negative response they stimulate from the group. This must be kept in mind at all times in work with teens. Most important is whether or not the attribute will bring prestige and status with peers. A productive outcome may be reached more quickly if the school counselor can acknowledge the importance of the interpersonal dimension.

The essence of appropriate counseling of junior high and high school students is a basic understanding that adolescent behavior must always be regarded within a developmental perspective and that actions are motivated by self-interest but mediated by peer response. Opportunities for the student to relate to the counselor the effects of new "trial and error" efforts with peers should be formally structured. Discussions centered on estimates of how the group perceives the adolescent, his or her emotional response, and how these feelings are dealt with should be cornerstones of any treatment plan. Questions such as how and why behavior in one group is similar or different to behaviors in other situations and/or in other groups is very useful. Chances are that the student will feel understood and may be more ready to risk letting down interfering defenses.

STRATEGIES FOR EDUCATORS

If school personnel are to adequately and sensitively meet the needs of adolescents, in-service training programs and flexible policies are necessary to educate them in the specifics of peer arena developmental dynamics and their course and manifestations, and to service both socioemotional *and* educational needs of students. Four strategies are recommended:

1. In-service training programs for teachers and administration:
   a. Information about how the school is an important component of the developmental peer arena
   b. Instruction on the specific dynamics of growth that are activated when adolescents are together, the normative nature of these processes, and the general course of progression
   c. Training to recognize peer-related developmental problems or deficiencies with subsequent referral to school mental health professionals

2. In-service training for school counselors to:
   a. Sharpen diagnostic skills to detect and diagnose academic problems such as truancy and dropout, under- and overachievement, acting out behaviors, and even drug and alcohol problems as possible responses to peer arena problems
   b. Provide necessary theoretical information and pragmatic tools to enable them to institute preventive strategies
3. Revision of school schedules to allow for flexibility so that adolescents' beginning psychosocial work can be well underway before academic assignments and schedules are firm or demanding
4. Redesign of building plans to include private "time out" rooms for students where verbal communication is not allowed, which would concretely recognize and sanction the adolescent need for occasional retreat from the school arena for psychological developmental needs to regroup.

Focusing Interest

School personnel would do well to establish a peer arena developmental framework for understanding their students. School personnel should be educated to expect adolescents to manifest behaviors connected with their unsettled state—particularly the early junior high students, newly embarked into adolescence. Uncertainties about self are both calmed and sparked by being with similar others; thus choosing to act and dress alike should be seen as overt manifestations of a deep-level psychological process—"borrowing of elements" from one another. This dynamic is strongest in the earliest years of adolescence, when youngsters relinquish the borrowed identities of parents. Now, en route to identifying their own self elements, they need to temporarily fill in the empty spaces with facsimile elements that are *not* those of parents. Consequently, they psychologically identify with the attributes seen in their peers. This explains a magnetic attraction to be near to them and to inspect them carefully. Thus, particularly in the beginning stages, when they need to borrow a number of elements from agemates, these crucial environmental others must be close at hand. They also need variety to select attractive elements. Hence, whenever possible without violating academic objectives, school personnel who plan for the early junior high grades should design programs for large groups with preplanned strategies to keep teens interacting. Teachers of the seventh and eighth grades need to be made aware that during these developmental years (the real beginnings of adolescence), needs for exchange of raw materials are strongest. They should be alerted that students' interest in one another may far outweigh interest in school assignments.

Curricular programming can easily incorporate intellectual and social needs. Encouraging classroom joint projects among friends as well as random assignment to other joint tasks will provide a basis for interacting with a mix of old and new people. For example, a course on cultural differences could be structured so that assignments and discussions focus on differences and similarities in individuals and in group mores. In this manner, educational materials would tap a primary interest on the deep-structure level—the need to become aware of different varieties of attributes, to have a supermarket of characteristics to choose among. Academic study and deep-structure developmental need can thus fuse. This kind of curricular programming, which truly takes account of who the programming is targeted at and makes use of developmental timing, will reinforce, not discourage, maximal utilization of the educational institution.

Amount of Energy Expended

Concrete information on peer arena developmental energy demands and the impact of this energy displacement on school performance constitute an important area of study. Subjects to be covered include:

1. The subliminal developmental work that goes on at the same time as school work
2. The amount of energy expended all day long in dual demands of intense social and academic development
3. How performance in one area of development affects the other
4. The importance of relative status—their own and that of others
5. The primary position of peers as texts for developmental maturation and growth

An Assessment Tool: The PAPP Battery

School counseling personnel should be trained in the use of the PAPP. This instrument yields the data necessary to assess whether a youngster is developing psychosocially on schedule. Use of the generic version establishes the point of developmental progression—which of the two peer arena stages the child is in. It also provides data on the affective component of peer-related experiences: defensive overinvolvement or underinvolvement, degree of comfort or pain connected with comparative activity, etc. To assist in understanding the appropriate pace of development, the following general guidelines trace the adolescent's developmental progression in junior and senior high school years.

1. In early junior high school years, developmental demands will divert a great deal of energy from school work to school peers.
2. In grades 9 and 10 the intensity reduces somewhat. Some psychosocial integrations that have taken place allow a lessening of cathexis with peers (who represent facsimile elements) and a freeing of energies for school work.
3. Grades 11 and 12 show a continuation of the trend. Enough elements have been tested out and identified as one's own so that a temoporary self structure is organized. The youth has a temporary self framework, that is, a general idea of where talents and weaknesses lie, a picture of where he stands relative to the other members of the class, some notion of general future directions (college versus job bound and a sense of the general area), and only an occasional desire to be with very large groups of others. Interest in smaller, more similar groups grows.
4. Youths of grades 11 and 12 are completing the first peer arena period and will soon enter the secondary peer arena period, where refinement of and closure on the final set of elements that make up the self structure takes place. To complete this task, fewer friends more similar to self are sought out.

Data yielded from the PAPP reveal whether the adolescent has had a satisfactory peer experience, has not successfully accessed the group, or perhaps has even experienced very painful rejection. The PAPP questions directly involve the student in identifying the real areas of concern. For example, resistance expressed as lack of interest in the activity of the group may in reality be fear of rejection. Connections can be drawn from what the activity of the group is to the deep-structure concern about *who the others in the group are* and their anticipated response to the student. The structure of the PAPP prevents the counselor from being diverted by non–peer-related matters, which often are white elephants, and prevents inquiry from being restricted to "do you like the activity?" which stimulates an evasive response or a simple yes or no.

Use of the PAPP and these general guidelines of development yield data for assessment of the point of psychosocial development or the point of development where trauma was so great as to encourage defensive flight behaviors.

SCHOOL AND SOCIAL PROBLEMS

Truancy

Explanations for truancy and high absenteeism range from the psychological, which emphasize disturbances within the child, to the sociological, which focus on environmental factors. Family conditions such as low socioeconomic status, financial need, and situations of divorce or separation with attendant use of the adolescent for care of younger siblings, often cause or aggravate the situation (Cnaan & Seltzer, 1989). There are other outside factors that encourage truancy, such as monetary payment for work, feelings of independence and maturity, and avoiding embarrassment caused by inadequate academic performance. Although allowing for these factors, our focus stresses the impact of multifaceted peer arena factors in the classroom—a setting par excellence for studying the psychosocial pressures of development.

Some students find the classroom dynamics extremely painful. Since classroom groups are assigned and not selected, comparative acts and evaluations may be engaged with others who are similar, but also with others who are quiet different. If students rank themselves "as good as" or "better than" the majority of the group on only a few attributes, or on none at all, it becomes extremely painful to confront the same setting day after day and have the low self-image reinforced. Counselors who understand that the adolescent developmental condition is one of a present-future orientation will be aware that this type of experience yields disappointment not only in the present, but it raises anxiety about adequacy in the future, too (particularly for the high school student).

Discouragement can readily turn into depression if characteristics of others appear to be unattainable, qualitatively or quantitatively.

A particularly common—and cogent—example is how comparisons based on economic differences may have an impact:

1. Children provided with material possessions that result in attribution of status at school may be seen as generally superior by costudents not similiarly provided for.
2. When a child of a lower class compares himself with one of a higher class at the same academic performance level, the road ahead for the latter may be college and a career, for the former it will likely be a job.

In early adolescence, the present experience is prominent. Therefore, the effects of comparison 1 may be immediately felt in low self-evaluation. Later on, perceptions of future opportunity may bring even more pain (comparison 2). For some the struggle is too great. They truant and leave, perhaps to find others with whom they feel more comfortable.

The preceding examples describe the impact of the classroom as a prominent setting of the peer arena. Junior and senior high schools are not benign havens of similar others; they are arenas. All present participate in its comparative act dynamics. A counselor must not focus only on the "facts of the situation" (e.g., "the work is too hard" or "I don't wake up on time") but should use a developmental framework to understand what the psychosocial demands of the period are.

A preliminary study was carried out in 1986 with four high school students who participated in an educational and counseling program designed especially for truants (Klein, 1986). In individual interviews each of four students told how relations with peers affected his or her truancy. The impact on each varied. One male and one female stated they felt *different* from their peers at school. The female had a positive relationship with peers until eighth grade, when she became a cheerleader, fought with her friends, and lost her best friend. She soured on school and began to truant. The friend who "deserted" her joined the opposing group. In spite of her lighter skin color, which was at one time "the object of envy," she had a very low opinion of herself, and the loss of this friend decreased her ability to withstand the criticism of classmates. It is possible that this best friend supplied the facsimile elements that provided her temporary stability, without which she could no longer cope with the stress of interacting with other peers. So she left school.

The male student said that daily harassment led him to become truant. He was quiet and kept to himself, arousing distrust and suspicion in his peers. He felt different from his peers. He had no special friends. Further probing was met with a shrug of the shoulders.

A second female student talked about comparing herself with her peers on what was most important to her: "clothes and appearance." She said she feld "bad" when comparing herself to others in school because "people have things you don't have." The experience of "not feeling as good as" was dissonant and troubling. Association with the neighborhood group was consonant since they were like her. A small group of neighborhood female friends were truanting and encouraged her to do the same. This student chose to leave the pain of the school classroom.

The fourth student, a male, attributed his truancy to being part of a gang for which the norm was truancy. He resisted all efforts on the part of the interviewer to deal with his perceptions of self in relation to school peers, but he freely answered questions about his family. It was easier to talk about family because, clearly, they were not the problem area; peers were. Talking about family *was not hard.*

Three of the four students had insight into painful peer-related factors that contributed to the decision to truant. Two students had a comfortable gang to go to on the outside. In fact, the last student attributed his truancy entirely to gang conformity pressures. He either had no insight into his other peer experiences or he did not choose to share it.

Drug and Alcohol Abuse

Developmental factors must also be a primary focus in dealing with problems of drug and alcohol abuse. Our developmental framework suggests that addictive behaviors can be a defensive flight from difficulties encountered in handling the intense dynamics of the peer arena. Perhaps prior estimates of self have been challenged or attacked, or increased efforts toward new aspirations have not yielded expected results. The adolescent needs relief from pain. Physically or psychologically dropping out of the peer arena would relieve the pain. However, since the adolescent is subliminally but keenly aware of his need for peers, leaving them is difficult. An opportunity to protect oneself and yet continue to see oneself as part of a group would be very attractive. For groups based on drug use, there is only one criterion for acceptance—participation in the group activity. If this criterion is met, there is automatic and immediate inclusion.

Some adolescents see this sole criterion as a means to psychologically leave the classroom and other groups that make up the peer arena. Others choose to abuse drugs or alcohol and try to remain connected with the psychological peer arena. However, once one is involved, these nondemanding associations become more and more seductive. Self-scrutiny is highly reduced—in fact, it is almost absent since true comparison with others cannot be engaged. No one is held responsible for his or her behaviors. *The drug is held to be the causal agent.* There is an intrinsic consensus that the real person is not evident; thus, the adolescent can really relax in the group. This, perhaps even more than the effects of the drug, may make continued participation desirable. The "twin blessings" of (1) being part of a group and (2) not dealing with the hazards of peer arena dynamics are powerful motivators to engage in drug/alcohol use. For adolescents who experience pressures of painful comparison constantly and intensely, the risk is high that the wish for this relief will become even stronger and that the degree of drug/alcohol abuse will increase. The ubiquitous presence of drugs in the school (Kandel, 1985) and the "mature" image attached to consumption of alcohol make these two potentially addictive avenues most accessible and very attractive.

Peer Approval

The quest for peer approval is well known to be a powerful force manifested in conforming behavior. But conformity in adolescence goes beyond "being accepted by others" and being part of a group. Understanding of the behavior reveals the connection to their psychological state of frameworklessness and their search to feel "OK". During adolescence, when few objective measures are available to reassure the adolescent that he is "OK" it is the group response that provides this information. Hence, a statement such as "I don't want to be the only weirdo who studies" reflects the desire to feel similar and accepted as part of the group. It may have little to do with lack of academic motivation. Reassurance of being OK is the operative dynamic.

A small, preliminary study carried out in 1986 focused on drug abuse with 14 teens (9 male and 5 female) from a middle-class, small-town public school in Maryland, grades 8–12 (Morrell, 1986). Most were good students. All disclosed an acute awareness of each other. All were aware of their academic standing relative to their peers, who were perceived to do better work than they. Each teen was interviewed separately. All but one male felt school relevant to their future and liked school. All used drugs. "Alcohol is easier to get, but it's pot that's easier to get away with." The reasons for soft drug use varied: "It feels good," "Nothing better to do," "Because my friends do it." Three adolescents stated that soft drug use was a social tool used to feel comfortable and convivial. They were particularly concerned with what their friends thought of them. "If we're working on a group exercise it's really important for my friends to approve of me, and I want to do my work so they won't look down on me." Another teen picked up on the comparative component of the motivation but then denied its impact: "I find myself picking up on someone else's drive and motivation, but their approval is not that important." "I don't want my friends to look down on me as different . . . or dump me." Some teens spoke of peer approval as having no influence, but, in reports of their behaviors, they all described action stimulated by peer judgment.

A Vulnerable Condition

Clearly, each adolescent's condition is determined by a different set of contributing factors. But, what is common for adolescents in school is that every day they interact in an arena of agemates, which stimulates the powerful dynamics of comparative acts. This dynamic activity is operative throughtout their day. The adolescent studies what is acceptable, valued, or rejected because it is perceived to be valuable *not only in the present*, but also for future functioning and interpersonal relationships.

It is true that in every stage of life, painful interactions with peers are experienced. However, the impact and how it is handled differ.

In childhood parents comfort, and "the person" does not feel attacked. The mature person can recognize the boundaries between self and others and can try to understand the source of the problem. Furthermore, the mature person is able to attach the insult to a specific *portion* of self. But in adolescence boundaries between self and others are not clear since the self is *in formation*. Whatever portion is present is temporary and unstable and can easily be reduced in strength. Hence, each negative charge or appraisal reverberates with a strength unique to this transitional period of life. Truancy, drug and alcohol abuse, and other antiself and antisocial behaviors provide relief from pain and frequently, as we sadly see, also environmental supports and reinforcement.

This core dimension has not been recognized in many distinguished prior models that interpret adolescent social problems. Valuable theories of adolescent growth behavior and therapeutic modalities directed toward amelioration of difficulties would be strengthened by incorporation of this central insight. Clearly, diagnostic models based on only conformity and/or rebellion are limited and miss what is seen here to be the essence of adolescent dynamics.

Impact of New Settings

The student who returns to the same school at the beginning of a new school year has far less to be concerned with than the student new to the environment. Although every student is involved in carrying on two complementary areas of development—academic and social—planning and scheduling generally reflect academic concerns, not psychosocial needs. But before the adolescent can give real attention to academic tasks, she needs to come to some beginning resolution as to how she rates relative to others.

Comfortable emotional functioning and effective academic learning affect one another. Effective planning for new students involves recognition of the activity of development—the automatic comparative acts that are stimulated in adolescents by being with new and strange others. Adolescents have not yet developed a stable self that they can carry from group to group with minimal adjustment.

In actuality, not a great deal of time is necessary to regroup, to reorganize, and to establish one's current place among peers. But during the initial period, little energy is left to the new adolescent to attend well to school work. Once initial positioning has been completed, energies are freed for academic learning.

However, special situations do exist. For example, adolescents who enter a new school, particularly in midterm, are in critical need of this social self-positioning time. They must familiarize themselves with general customs and mores. The comparative act dynamics of comparison, evaluation, and initial ranking are strong. During the beginning period of these school years, expectations should be flexible, not rigid, particularly for students in transition to new settings (e.g., movement from grade school to junior high or junior high to high school).

College entrance for most students involves many of the same dynamics that the "new girl or boy" experiences in public school. With entrance to college comes exposure to an unfamiliar group of others. The adolescent new college student feels uncertain. The validity of the temporary self structure recently forged may be seriously threatened. In this new setting, the newly assembled persona may be vulnerable. Temporary regression to primary peer arena needs and behaviors may be stimulated by this totally new environment. Still, it is developmentally important to incorporate findings from comparative acts with new others who have a wider range of competencies. But although a few adolescents are blessed with sufficient insight to understand what is happening, most do not possess the cognitive perspective with which to mediate and sooth harsh emotional responses. For certain students, the "freshman orientation week" activities are of sufficient length for them to complete the psychosocial gymnastics and make their readjustments. Others need longer and are thus disadvantaged when the academic year begins. These students need more developmental reorganization time. Again, more flexibility in beginning expectations based on an understanding of the period would ease the transition.

High school academic counselors can be of enormous help in preparing students for transfer to the college setting by eliciting from their graduating seniors: (1) verbal descriptions of the attributes they feel they possess and how they interface (the integrated clusters) and (2) some discussion of what the move to a new milieu will mean in relation to the current concept of self. This process serves to cognitively reinforce the development on a nonverbal level with insight awareness. Further concentration on how this "persona" will serve the student now and in the future stimulates reality testing. This approach, which extends far beyond academics, readies the student for the inevitable reexamination of self and self-attributes in a new milieu where relative values may differ from prior ones. Having been forewarned, they may at least intellectually recognize that painful comparisons are in some sense universally experienced and are to be expected.

College preparatory counseling in the high school can thus be preventively oriented. College personnel as well need to recognize:

1. Peer arena dimensions of the freshman experience
2. The possibility that some students may temporarily regress to primary peer arena needs
3. That energies will for a time be siphoned away from academic pursuits
4. That initial energies must necessarily go to regrouping
5. That the temporary self structure must be reclaimed before energies can be redirected from its reestablishment toward academic pursuits.

This information about the precariousness of the entering college student should be translated to academic planners on both the secondary and college levels.

STRUCTURAL INNOVATIONS

Most schools are designed with appropriate classrooms, libraries, gymnasiums, auditoriums, offices for administrative personnel, and service areas such as lunchrooms, kitchens, and lavatories. Students can usually use classrooms after school for club meetings. In some of the newer buildings there are informal lounges for students to relax and chat with one other. Sometimes they are equipped with current books and magazines.

We have pointed out the amount of psychological energy expended by the student who must simultaneously pursue academic and developmental tasks and deal with the ups and downs of ego. These experiences are intense. The individual needs a time and a place to regroup energies—to muse on information gathered about others or self, to think through and evaluate results of comparative acts, and to intergrate new knowledges. Any number of developmental insights, adjustments, and integrations are continually in process. Students need time to process them thoroughly. They cannot always be put aside until "after school."

What is necessary is not time with others but time alone. Students need a place to withdraw to in the middle of the school day. "Musing rooms" accomplish two goals: (1) They *legitimize* the need adolescents have for time alone as natural and as important (2) They provide the private setting where developmental activity can be processed and integrated. Musing rooms allow sitting with no literature and no apparent task. Whether the youth uses such a room to "get away" from the intense atmosphere of peers and rest from all the stimuli or to "just think" is seen as an entirely private matter. Libraries do not serve this purpose but have a specific function: to provide students with the opportunity to look up materials and learn from them. Libraries do not encourage the student to feel free to "muse."

Provided a musing room, students can elect to separate from peers for short periods of time and regroup before they are further exposed to new academic and developmental stimuli. If the need to retreat from the stimulation of the peer arena is unmet, other strategies will be adopted—for example, feigned or real physical symptoms may provide the outward rationale for leaving school at midday or not attending at all. In situations of extended stress, truancy is a way out. Small rooms for just a few students sprinkled throughout the school building may allow some students to continue regular attendance.

MISDIRECTED STRATEGY

Ironically, a popular strategy utilized by school counselors to respond to perceived stress in students is to organize a "rap group." The rationale is for students to get away from the formal classroom setting and communicate with one another about common issues or difficulties. Implicit in this approach is that the teacher and the formal academic expectations are the stressors. That the peer is *the relevant other*, not the teacher, and that relations with peers stimulate the stress are missed. If planning for a more benign school atmosphere is dominated by this misconception, the essence of what is psychologically most important to the adolescent will fail to be addressed.

The level of production in school work is meaningful primarily in terms of what it reveals about self in relation to agemates. How academic performance impacts public status with peers and the private assessments of one's skills are the crucial factors. It is essential for the school administrator, teacher, and counselor to acknowledge the impact of the adolescent agemate as the most relevant environmental figure of this period. If the agemate is seen as both stimulant and stressor, it stands to reason that opportunities must be provided *within the school day* for teens to be alone. Programs that erroneously provide for *more time with peers* to relieve stress should be eliminated.

There is an unrecognized resistance to acknowledging peers to be of primary importance to one another. To do so in an educational setting involves a reevaluation of the roles of key education personnel.* Educators have trained long and hard for their professions. A major attraction is the important role they can play in their students' lives. It is most helpful for educators to keep in mind that the framework within which they can indeed play a major role is educational development. Those educators who accept their function as "setting the stage for learning" and establish an atmosphere that respects adolescent peer arena needs will achieve a lasting influence on their students. They have the opportunity to generate excitement and interest in the variety of knowledge areas.

---

*Findings from the ARGI underline the importance of school personnel for educational advising; however, these personnel were not sought out for other matters (see Chapter 5). Thus, not only parents but teachers must cope with the reality that the emotionally relevant other of this period is the agemate.

CHAPTER 16

Peer Arena Therapy: A Relevant Intervention Model

Peer arena therapy focuses on the adolescent. The goal is to rehabilitate the adolescent so that he or she can continue the necessary developmental work of the period notwithstanding what may be a difficult, painful series of interactions with peers. The fuller the participation in the dynamics, the fuller the personality that will emerge. This chapter covers a variety of therapeutic methods and some instruments for determining the treatment of choice. We will introduce the Peer History Profile (PHP), a valuable tool with which to gather data on how the adolescent has managed relationships with peers. Since we hold peer interactions to be the building blocks of adolescent development, such information is crucial to decision-making as to the therapy of choice. Some adolescents respond best to therapy on an individual basis, others to group therapy. At specific stages in adolescent development, small groups are the treatment of choice. At other times larger groups better serve growth needs.

A family history is important and should be carefully taken. Certainly, positive family life offers the security that allows the adolescent to focus energies on solving developmental tasks, and absence of a sound family support system is a serious hindrance. But in and of itself, a family history is insufficient. Primary psychosocial dynamics of the period are carried out with peers. Data on peer preferences provides information about developmental level, which facilitates decision-making as to the optimum therapeutic modality. A "peer history" gives data to evaluate the subject's point of development as well as developmental lags and complete or incomplete developmental tasks. The broad definition of "adolescent peer" used here refers to friends drawn from a variety of subgroups of peers. Some are encountered in school, some in the neighborhood, some at discrete activities, etc. But no matter where or when encountered, the peer becomes a "relevant environmental other." In important ways, peers are compatriots who serve social needs and act as important developmental models. If the peer history is revealed to be age-appropriate, it is likely that the presenting difficulty is temporary. The treatment period will most likely be minimal. If the peer history reveals deprivation or indicates troubled behavior to be regressive, remediation efforts will take longer. We urge that both a family and a peer history be taken; however, since the literature is replete with family history models, our discussion focuses on introduction of the Peer History Profile.

THE PEER HISTORY PROFILE

The Peer History Profile form should be administered prior to decision-making on treatment modality—individual versus group therapy—or placement out of the home. What follows is a brief listing of the three sections of the PHP.

Part 1

The first part of the PHP deals with peer group involvement. How much time is spent with peers? Is it more or less than it was in the past? At different ages, it is appropriate to prefer different numbers of peers. In early adolescence, developmental demands stimulate adolescents to seek out large groups of peers. In the earlier stages, great heterogeneity of friendships is necessary to meet needs for variety of comparison and broad scope of evaluation. Later developmental needs require fewer, quite similar friends.

BROAD VERSUS SPECIFIC COMPARISONS. How the adolescent views the interaction with peers adds data that will help to establish the current stage of adolescence. Do comparison and evaluation continue with each peer? Do peers continue to be used as models for new characteristics, attributes, and skills? Or has the scope been narrowed to focus on specific attributes and characteristics? The latter indicates a more advanced level. Are agemates seen as separate individuals, or are they viewed primarily in the context of their reaction to the adolescent? The former is more advanced. These different styles of interrelating exemplify different levels of development. The broader, more superficial kind of relating is indicative of first-stage comparison functions aimed at establishing a temporary self framework. The goal of this stage is to give the adolescent a "ballpark" notion of what he or she is like. Activity with a reduced volume of others, coupled with a more intensive relating to those perceived as quite similar to oneself, is evidence of progression into the second stage of adolescence, the period of secondary peer arena. This occurs when a temporary first-stage self structure has been constructed and the process of refinement of self elements has begun. This activity represents an advanced stage of development. The adolescent who has reached this point should be assigned to work in small groups in order to approximate his level of functioning in the real world.

SMALL VERSUS LARGE SETTINGS. Preferred meeting places provide another source of data. Adolescents in earlier stages will look to settings that accommodate very large groups of agemates. In addition to providing a variety of models for comparison, large numbers also offer opportunities for a more removed appraisal, for greater anonymity. Adolescents further along in development seek to study specific characteristics and skills in depth. Therefore, they look for smaller settings where they can achieve closer interaction with fewer numbers. Furthermore, emotionally they are ready for experimenting with more intimate relations. If past and present preferences show no differences, the adolescent may be "stuck in a stage," or the development might have been foreshortened or foreclosed.

PATHS FOR ACCESSING PEERS. Has the level of dependency on elders increased, decreased, or remained stable? Has the adolescent found a means to access friends on his/her own, or is there still considerable dependency on parents? The latter is generally problematic and necessitates also looking into parent actions: What are the past *and* present attitudes of parent(s) toward peers? These questions assess the extent of parental encouragement/discouragement of interactions with peers. This information can be used to determine if normative attraction to peers was supported or if the home environment may have contributed to developmental problems. Was the movement toward peers interpreted as rejection of parents and other family members? If so, questions arise as to the extent to which the adolescent was able to manage.

Part 2

The next section of the form deals with problems encountered with peers. The areas of inquiry are as follows:

1. Problems currently encountered with peers
2. Parent and family attitudes toward current problems with peers as well as their past attitudes toward problems with peers
3. Present and past factors contributing to problems with peers
4. Current and past factors contributing to positive relations with peers
5. The adolescent's perceptions of status and course of interactions with peers, parental input, and self-management

Part 3

The last section of the PHP form deals with patient perception of continuities or changes in:

1. Numbers
2. Function
3. First meeting place
4. Access point
5. Parental attitudes
6. Peer problems over time
7. Peer consonance over time
8. Changing relationships
9. Stability of others' conduct toward oneself
10. Self-evaluation
11. Evaluation of one's own behavior

The Peer History Profile form is shown in Figure 16.1.

Utilizing the Data

Data from the Peer History Profile form stimulate initial hypotheses and provide a framework within which to assess current functioning with peers. The data provoke insights into the dynamics of the family system, which might otherwise take much longer to be exposed. For example, the following questions can be answered by the data.

1. Is the social overinvolvement or underinvolvement continuous behavior, or is it new behavior? If it was seen in the past, too, an assessment should be made of its appropriateness and why it continues in the present. If there has been change, investigation into the causes or circumstances for the change in characteristic pattern may disclose important environmental, situational, or internally based data.

2. What is the ratio of same-sex friends to other-sex preferences? Is the ratio age-appropriate?

3. If peers represent different end goals from those of the past, are these new goals age-appropriate?

4. Is the adolescent seeking out friends in groups that are not age-appropriate (too young or too old)? Is the choice reflective of regressive behavior or of a compensatory need to feel adult? If so, a careful investigation of the degree of comfort or discomfort experienced with agemates would be in order.

5. Have parental attitudes supported or inhibited freedom to naturally transfer most-relevant status to peers? If there has been change in the perceived level of support, is it caused by parental reaction to the type of friends the adolescent is selecting, or is it a reflection of stress in the parents' psychological world?

6. Is the nature of problems encountered with peers the same as before? If so, insight therapy into the persistent interpersonal malfunctioning is in order. If current problems are of a different nature from prior years, inquiry into peer arena experiences may reveal conditions that caused the changed behaviors. Later, if necessary, examine prior behaviors and home conditions. It may be that problems are state-specific and not characterological.

7. Are there persistent defensive attitudes on the part of family members that the adolescent is either the victim or the cause of problems

---

Part I: Peer group involvement

A. 1. Do you usually hang out alone or with friends these days? How many friends do you usually hang out with? How many are the same sex as you? Different sex? (If the above yielded negative responses, ask: Since you do not hang out with friends these days, what do you do for company?)

2. When you were younger, did you usually find yourself with friends, or were you generally a loner? How many friends did you generally hang out with? How many were of the same sex? How many were of the opposite sex? (In case of negative response, ask: Since you did not hang out with friends in the past, what did you do for company?)

3. What type of teens do you like to spend time with these days? Tell me a bit about what they are like and what you like about them.

4. What type of friends did you used to enjoy being with when you were younger? What were they like, and what did you enjoy about them?

B. 1. What do you think the teens you like to be with these days offer you? (If necessary, prod very gently, offering as little lead as possible—e.g., "learn from them," "lot of fun," "keeps me from being lonely," etc.)

2. What do you think the friends you liked to be with when you were younger offered you? (Again, if necessary, prod gently.)

3. Do you find yourself aware of the attributes your friends possess? Do you ever compare your own attributes with theirs? Or try out new things together?

4. Do their personalities offer you ideas about what you may be like or wish to pursue?

5. Have you found you are doing more or less of the above lately?

6. Do you find that what you are interested in about your friends is the same or different than in the past? In which ways? If it changed, about when?

7. How do you determine what is unique about them? About yourself?

C. 1. Where do you and the people you enjoy being with generally meet and get together? (If the answer is "many places," prod gently for specifics.)

2. When you were younger, where did you and the others you enjoyed being with generally meet and get together? (If the answer is "many places" or is nonspecific, prod gently for specifics.)

D. 1. How do you get to meet the friends you generally enjoy being with in the first place?

2. In the past, how did you get to meet the friends you liked being with in the first place?

E. 1. What do you think your parents think about the friends you generally like to be with?

2. What did your parents think in the past about the friends you liked to be with at that time?

Part 2: Problems encountered

A. 1. Are you having any difficulties in your relationships with the teens you select to be with? If so, could you tell me a little about what they are? If not, why do you think this is the case?

2. In the past, do you think you used to have difficulties with the friends you chose to be with? If so, could you tell me a little about what they were about? If not, why do you think this was the case?

B. 1. What do your parent(s) and family think about the problems you are now encountering with friends you generally like to be with? (If the response is noncommittal, probe gently to gain information on who the parent(s) and family perceive was at fault and whether they had remediation suggestions.)

Figure 16.1 The Peer History Profile Form

2. What did your parent(s) and family think about the problems you encountered in the past with friends that you generally preferred to be with? (If the response is noncommittal, probe gently to gain information on who parents and family perceived was at fault and whether they had remediation suggestions.)

C. 1. Is there anything happening these days that would be contributing to the difficulties you seem to be having with the people you generally like to hang around with? (If response is noncommittal, probe gently as to parental, peer, or other family involvement.)

2. Was there anything happening in the past that would have contributed to the difficulties you had with the people you generally liked to hang around with? (If response is noncommittal, probe gently as to parental, peer, or other family involvement.)

D. 1. Is there anything happening these days that would contribute in some way to the pleasant relations you are having with the teens you generally like to hang around with? (If subject is reticent to answer, probe as above.)

2. Do you think there was anything happening in the past that helped you to have pleasant times with the friends you generally liked to be with? (If subject is reticent to answer, probe as above.)

Part 3: Perceptions of past and present (continuity and change)

1. Do you think you generally like to be with more or less people than you used to like to be with a year ago? Two years ago? Four years ago? How many more, or less, than last year? Two years ago? Four years ago?

2. Do you think you are friends with people for the same reasons you used to be friends with them? Last year? Two years ago? Four years ago? (If subject is reticent to mention the ways in which there is continuity or change, probe gently.)

3. Do you generally still meet friends you enjoy in the same locations as you did last year? Two years ago? Four years ago? (If there is change, probe gently as to where the differences are.)

4. Do you meet for the first time people you wind up wanting to hang around with in the same places as you used to in the past? Last year? Two years ago? Four years ago?

5. Do your parents and family still have the same general kind of attitude toward the people you like to hang out with as they used to in the past? Last year? Two years ago? Four years ago? If so, why? If not, why not?

6. Do you think the same factors exist as did in the past that contribute to the difficulties you are having with friends you usually like to hang out with? Last year? Two years ago? Four years ago? If yes, please let me know what they are. If not, why not?

7. Do any of the same factors that helped you in the past to get along well with friends you liked to be with still exist today? Did they exist last year? Two years ago? Four years ago?

8. Are any of the people you like to hang out with today the same as those you used to hang out with in the past? Last year? Two years ago? Four years ago?

9. Do these people who were friends in the past and still are today act the same or differently toward you now than they did then? If yes, why? If no, why?

10. Do you feel you are the same or different now than you were in the past? Last year? Two years ago? Four years ago? If different, how and why? If the same, how and why?

11. Do you think you act the same or differently with those people you like to hang out with than you did in the past? Last year? Two years ago? Four years ago? If differently, how and why? If the same, how and why?

Figure 16.1 The Peer History Profile Form *(Cont.)*

with peers? Such attitudes indicate a far different family milieu than do responses disclosing a family that differentiates specifics of each situation and responds accordingly. The former implies a rigidity that may infect child rearing practices and hinder the flexibility required in parenting adolescents. On the other hand, too much fluctuation denies the adolescent a stable, dependable base. Clearly, a middle ground of stability, without rigidity, and ordered flexibility is closest to ideal.

8. Do situational factors exist that are stable over time and facilitate either positive or negative experiences for the adolescent with his peers? For example, dealing with poverty, alcoholism, explosive domestic relations, overcrowding, death of or separation from a parent, or terminal illness adds stress and increases feelings of instability. What is particularly critical in adolescence, a time when conformity and similarity contribute to security with peers and continuing membership in the peer group, is that any one of these factors can make the adolescent feel different and insecure. Difference is desirable if it is one the group values, such as an unusual athletic skill or a rare gift of beauty, but undesired differences such as those listed can stimulate compensatory behaviors or exit from the peer group. Maladaptations discussed earlier may ensue. On the other hand, a secure family background with loving family members who meet basic needs supports energies devoted to expansion of knowledge and skills and allows the adolescent to better handle the ups and downs of the peer arena comparative acts. Notwithstanding factors of heredity and temperament that mediate existing conditions, environmental circumstances act to support or impede smooth developmental progression.

Responses to the PHP provide tips on whether the adolescent can best be approached initially on a cognitive level or if a pragmatic, behaviorally based method will be more fruitful. Whether the adolescent perceives current functioning with peers to be the same or different from that in prior years provides an index of the adolescent's insight into deep-structure dynamics. Is she aware of the comparative processes in which is she engaging? Is she able to verbalize the emotional responses that result? Does she learn from friends? Does she reveal any of the aspirations, comparisons, or competitions she may be engaging in?

These data will disclose if the adolescent is involved in the maturational process on a conscious basis.

PEER HISTORY DATA AS CRITERIA FOR TYPE OF THERAPY

Individual or Group

Point of cognitive advance is an important criterion for therapeutic placement. Data from the Peer History Profile can serve in determining whether the adolescent is best suited to preparation for group session or for individual session. If not overwhelmed by neurotic oversensitivity, individuals who demonstrate cognitive insight generally are good group therapy candidates. Others need a minimum of preparatory individual insight work, following which they can be assigned to a group. Those who are more defensive may well be assigned to a group of like others where behavioral techniques and concrete examples are utilized initially. For example, dramatic presentations and role play can utilize concrete situations to assist adolescents to describe similarities to their own experiences. Considerable time may be devoted to these beginning strategies to allow defenses time to slowly weaken. Once insight is increased, the client can be readied for transfer to an intermediate group, where a greater proportion of insight therapy can be combined with the behavioral techniques. During this period, encouraging peer support from others in the group is an invaluable therapeutic aid to bolster confidence. The last step is to groups where the cognitive approach is exclusively available for insight therapy.

Point of Development

Level of maturation is a second criterion in planning treatment. There is considerable maturational variability within a narrow chronological range. In addition to the data of the Peer History Profile, the PAPPs provide information as to whether the adolescent is in the beginning stage of adolescent psychosocial development or in the second of the two peer arena periods, where finishing touches on the self are underway. Adolescents who are still in the first stage of development require placement in large groups. Those further along require groups that are smaller and composed of others with whom they feel some similarity. Identification of the level of development is essential since the therapy group will serve as a microcosm where initial peer group experiences are relived.

Goals of the group therapy experience are both educational and experiential. The educational component introduces to the adolescent how natural and normal it is to engage in comparative acts. Competition and comparison are healthy and to be desired. Furthermore, adolescents are advised that emotional responses of pleasure or pain to the findings of comparison and evaluation are also normal and natural. Although the educational component will initially be perceived as remote and abstract, as the adolescents begin to deal with their own experiences, the cognitive interpretation and the experiential will come together. The therapeutic plan should be geared to simulate the point of trauma so that the defensive flight into maladaptation can become the focus of therapy.

OVERVIEW OF THERAPY

In initial meetings, it should be anticipated that adolescents in all therapy groups will more freely talk about past experiences with other adolescents than about the comparative dynamics they are currently experiencing with one another in the group (Seltzer, 1980). This is entirely appropriate for stage 1 of therapy and should be supported by the professional. Further along, in stage 2 of the therapy, adolescents should more readily respond to probes centered on their reactions to one another in the group. This is the heart of the therapeutic experience; stage 1 is preparatory. Here, painful dynamics are reawakened. Steady and skilled facilitation by the professional should result in each adolescent feeling the support essential for them to risk comparison and evaluation dynamics anew. In the original traumatic peer arena experiences from which he retreated (either physically, psychologically, or both), the pain of the comparison results was too debilitating to bear. Moreover, the adolescent had no notion that these experiences of pain were not unique to him, that *all* adolescents experience some disillusionment as a consequence of comparison. No one escapes, and those who confront the painful stimuli may be stronger and have better support systems. A therapeutic group milieu should be one of honesty banked with acceptance, empathy, support, and encouragement to risk further. An atmosphere of openness, where contribution by all and response by all has been established as a group norm, will facilitate therapeutic action.

Diverse Issues

Depending on developmental stage, different issues will be involved. For example, we know that it is important that early adolescents be exposed to diverse others and to a variety of potential self elements and directions. But the more fragile the adolescent's sense of what he is, the greater the anxiety when he is confronted by difference in others. Inasmuch as development will not progress without this involvement, the adolescent must deal with this increased level of anxiety. Most youngsters rise to the challenge. However, others can do so only within the safe parameters of a therapy group. Still others may need to break for some individual sessions and then return to the therapy group to continue with the group experience. In the individual sessions, the adolescent has the option to privately risk before publicly risking. He may need help in handling dissonance either from others or with respect to surprising self-evaluations.

Greater difficulty in dealing with first-stage primary peer arena developmental tasks will be experienced by the adolescent who struggles with difference and clings excessively to similar others. The stage is completed only when the adolescent has engaged differences in others, has tried diverse elements out on himself, and has determined whether they fit or not. These dynamics are engaged over and over again with a myriad of characteristics, skill, and opinions.

THE PROCESS

Stage 1

The therapeutic process involves engaging these dynamics within a protected setting, guided by a professional who enlists support by the others in the group *and* invites candid observations about how the adolescent handles the challenges. The target adolescent's problems in the past are reenacted and discussed in the present. She is asked to consider what may have been the operative forces within and without that determined her responses and precipitated compensatory defenses (e.g., withdrawal, drugs). During this process she is also participating in the "life" of the group and must analyze and discuss the psychosocial operations she is currently engaging in relation to the others in the group. The group work is to together focus on each individual's developmental challenges. Individual challenge is experienced as a common pursuit.

It can be anticipated that the majority of the adolescents who come to treatment will be those who encountered problems early in development. They may be of various ages, but their developmental stage will be similar. Thus, together they will offer the numbers necessary to approximate the large arena problematic to them. Part of the treatment will entail activities scheduled for large groups. In the beginning, the experiences may be very painful because they simulate what caused them distress originally. Experiences in the large groups should be reexamined and interpreted in small-group sessions of 10 or 12 adolescents, where focus is on anxieties stimulated in the larger group.

The therapeutic process for adolescents in stage 1 is the same as the process for those in stage 2, shortly to be described:

1. Recall of the original experience with other agemates in other groups
2. Identifying how assaults to ego were experienced
3. Identifying the defensive response
4. Determining the impact of the defensive response and connecting it with the behavior manifested
5. Discovering a prosocial, non–self-destructive approach to dealing with the unpleasant outcome of comparisons and ego assault

Stage 2

Stage 2 of the therapy includes some large groups and a majority of small-group sessions for closer interactional work. The adolescent who begins therapy in stage 2 will be a different type of individual from the one who entered at stage 1. This adolescent will have already begun to identify a temporary self structure. He has tried out some elements of self, evaluated them, and may have achieved some integrated grouping of elements.

The PHP discloses which individuals have already arrived at a temporary self structure. Generally, they have described their past interactions in large groups of adolescents and now prefer smaller groups. Most must reach an age of at least 16 to allow sufficient time to complete the developmental tasks of the first stage and identify a temporary set of self elements. The primary task of second-stage peer arena development is to refine the self elements, to make certain of their relative places in a self structure, and to integrate them in a flexible, complementary relationship. This is accomplished in small-group comparative act dynamics.

Some adolescents who have managed the early stage find the close scrutiny and smaller-group relationships very stressful. These adolescents have been able to deal with diversity, they have managed to engage in the difficult trial, error, assessment, and evaluation period, and they have assembled who they think they are. The next step, restricting the comparative act process to others perceived as very similar, causes intense psychological pain, and they exhibit flight behavior in defense against this pain.

These adolescents usually do possess insight. In fact, their insight makes the comparisons clear—and the results painful. Because they are responsive to intervention based on insight, beginning with behavorial strategies is not necessary. The therapeutic task entails helping this adolescent to discover the full contours of her attributes and skills and to accept their limitations.

THERAPEUTIC GOALS ACCORDING TO STAGE

Presenting problems vary. They include addictive behaviors, sexual acting out, delinquency, withdrawal, extreme aloneness, under- or overachievement, and cause extremism. Presenting symptoms and chronological age are but two of a number of factors that determine the treatment plan. Type of therapy recommended should be based on data obtained from the Socialization Battery, the PAPP forms, and the Peer History Profile. Collectively, these data give a full picture of the subject's peer arena functioning. Based on these scores, a treatment plan and attendant goals are designed.

The therapeutic goals for first-stage adolescents are:

1. To bring to consciousness the deep-level developmental dynamics they are engaging
2. To assure them of their normality and the universality among agemates of these dynamics
3. To allow them a forum in which to discuss and compare their experiences and their feelings
4. To place these responses within a developmental framework

Using that framework, the pain they have experienced and fled from is identified and analyzed. The cognitive and emotional components are identified and reviewed *in session*. Insight into one's patterns are gained through analyses of interactions with the others in the immediate group present. The self-destructive nature of the behavior is pointed out by the therapist in private session, or by other group members and the therapist in group session. Thus, group members make up a living counterpart of the peer arena from which the adolescent sought defensive shelter. In this safer arena for experimentation, they help one another to assess and evaluate. They structure objectives and schedule behaviors to actualize those ends. For example, an objective for an early adolescent might be to keep track of tendencies to invoke self-destructive defenses. A strategy may be to keep a list on 6 × 8 cards, filled in nightly, of painful experiences, reactions, desires for defensive flight, and reports of how they were coped with. Open discussion of these cards in the group follows.

While individual therapy is indicated in a number of cases, for most adolescents peer arena group therapy is the model of choice. It simulates the context in which the symptoms were manifested. Being a member in a therapeutic group reactivates the dynamics of group experience. These dynamics reawaken the forces underlying the adolescent's struggle in outside groups. Successful handling of the impact of these dynamics is the unfinished business of development.

Adolescents are more able to deal with the dynamics of comparative acts when they are with others who are also dealing with them. They can see that they are not alone in finding them difficult.

The adolescent often feels he or she is "the only one" who is experiencing difficulties. In addition to providing the necessary "reliving" of peer arena experiences, similar others give concrete evidence that the rocky road is not a singular experience. Group consensus that the adolescent seems ready provides support for leaving the therapeutic group. Then the adolescent uses the therapy group on a decreasing time schedule to deal with projected difficulties. Therapy ends for participants when they feel strong enough to manage the real-life peer arena.

Similar goals exist for the adolescent who begins at a more advanced stage. He too leaves the therapeutic group when he has achieved enough insight into how he responds with self-destructive defensive behaviors to ego assault and has developed a coping strategy. Gradual weaning from group participation follows. No matter what the point of developmental progression, the criteria for ending work with the group are the same: The adolescent feels strong enough to endure the ups and downs of peer arena involvement, anticipates vulnerabilities and recognizes his own characteristic response patterns, develops a set of strategies for dealing with those vulnerabilities, and finally, has set incremental goals and has specified the behaviors necessary to achieve those goals.

HELP TO PARENTS

The adolescent does not live in a vacuum. Parents and siblings are most influential. Often they are also the most accessible targets for anger and hostility that stem from difficulties in the peer arena but are not understood as such. Because parents and significant others generally are also the most caring environmental figures, they do not reject the adolescent and thus continue to be available for verbal or nonverbal abuse. They also worry a great deal. Therefore, a peer arena therapy model would be incomplete without services to them. Most parents need factual information about the adolescent period to understand their child's behavior, and parent education classes would meet these needs excellently. They can be affiliated with school, church, or community, or they may be privately sponsored. However, parents who experience anxiety levels that are deeper or whose children engage in behaviors that are very worrisome may require a more individualized and intensive approach.

It is advisable to draw a beginning profile of parent-child interaction from the battery of indexes administered to the adolescent in the diagnostic period before meeting parents. The ARGI offers important information about the extent to which the parent is a perceived influence figure for the child and in what areas. The PAPP forms offer information on whether the parent supported, inhibited, or was neutral about the adolescent's desires to be together with peers. The group preference data may reveal whether chosen groups are those that appear to be parental favorites. In many cases enough data are provided by the batteries to assign parents to either parent education didactic classes or parent therapy groups.

Group therapy is not the treatment of choice for all. It does offer the comfort of other parents who are dealing with greater or lesser problems, but the group affords opportunities for comparisons that may elevate or deflate feelings of comfort. The potential effects must be considered carefully. Settings known to raise anxiety levels are not appropriate for all individuals. Individual therapy is the treatment of choice for the most stressed, who may not be able to tolerate the added strains stimulated by dynamics in the group. Another type of parent is one whose defenses are so tightly organized that, initially, one-to-one therapy is necessary to reduce defenses so that they may participate in parent groups.

Enlarging Parent Perspectives

The focus of parent therapy and parent education is to facilitate the adolescent's completing developmental psychosocial tasks. Concentration should focus on what aids normal progression and what impedes development. Educational objectives of therapy include knowledge:

1. That the psychosocial task of the period is achievement of a sense of identity in love and in work (direction in life)
2. That completing a sense of identity is the product of hard work at determining the elements composing a unique self structure
3. Of the psychosocial dynamics of the adolescent dialectic and their sequence
4. Of the functional role peers play in providing raw materials for development

5. Of the extent of the emotional toll of disappointing self-evaluations in relation to peers

6. That escaping this pain by defensive flight behaviors is a very attractive option

7. Of projection onto parents and other close figures angers and frustrations experienced with and held back from peers since adolescents are reluctant to alienate peers

8. Of the importance of conforming to standards and norms set by adolescent peers so as not to risk rejection and to assure oneself of the continuing:
   a. Company of others in the same position
   b. Access to peers as models and comparison figures

Finally, parents should be educated that attitudes and information are more effectively transmitted as guidance, *not* direction. This represents a dramatic reorientation from a position of indispensability and authority to facilitator and guide. The transition is difficult and at times very painful. Parents can feel unwanted, outmoded, and even rejected. Support that values their achievement in having raised children to semi-independence is crucial.

These quasi-educational and quasi-therapeutic goals deal with adjustments parents must make to their new status. Achieving these objectives is not a simple task. It is particularly complex when problem behaviors are exhibited by their children (e.g., drugs, alcohol, promiscuity, truancy, failure in school). In such cases, parents should avail themselves of more intensive group peer arena therapy. Here parents help one another. The professional focuses initially on maladaptations as stemming from serious ego assault encountered during the course of stage-specific developmental work. Although a continuing therapeutic effort needs to be aimed at helping the parent understand the demands of the developmental process, the cognitive and emotional ups and downs, and the origins of defensive behaviors, parents also must be helped to face troubling behaviors as symptomatic of a more serious situation—interruption of the process of normal psychosocial development. If not treated in time, interrupted adolescent development portends a troubled adulthood or a protracted adolescence. The course of peer arena therapy emphasizes to parents this crucial message.

DIFFERENCES FROM GROUP THERAPY APPROACHES

The essential differences between peer arena therapy and other group therapies are:

1. Focus is on cognitive comparisons and the affective responses to the comparative acts.
2. Problem behaviors are interpreted as defensive flight from the dynamics of the peer arena.
3. The diagnosis and treatment plan draws heavily from information from the Socialization Battery, the Peer Arena Battery, and the Peer History Profile.
4. The group to which the adolescent is assigned becomes a peer group in microcosm; original difficulties are eventually reexperienced.
5. Dynamics identified for examination are the comparative act dynamics of the adolescent dialectic.

This is not rap group therapy, nor is it only experientially oriented. Its focus is on developmental dynamics. Problems are conceptualized as symptomatic of peer arena malfunctioning. Therapy is geared to uncovering and remediating the forces causing the malfunction. Adolescents will be helped to deal with the anxiety of engaging closely with peers during the course of the peer arena therapy by:

1. Examining developmental functional dynamics that come into play during this period of life
2. Discovering and examining how they have handled them in the past
3. Determining more constructive patterns of behavior

Thus, adolescents will be asked to concentrate on:

1. Increasing insight into early and continuing stress factors
2. Identifying links between personal history and stress points
3. Identifying common defenses and what type of stress stimulates each defense

4. Examining the functional or dysfunctional impact of these defenses
5. Setting forth potential dangers inherent in not employing the defenses
6. Developing strategies for handling these dangerous outcomes
7. Assessing level of development
8. Remaining acutely aware of the primary task of achieving "a sense of identity"
9. Establishing achievable goals for interactions with peers

These objectives apply to the individual who requires initial individual sessions as well as to the individual who participates in peer arena group therapy from the beginning. Participation in a group requires:

1. Recognizing that each group member is involved in the same set of developmental processes and goals
2. Agreement that engaging the developmental dynamics of the adolescent dialectic is essential to psychosocial progression to adulthood
3. Examining how each of the developmental dynamics works in harmony with the others (e.g., "What do I like in Jim? Do I have that quality? How good is it? How does everyone in the group score on it? How does comparing myself with them make me feel about it?")
4. Maintaining the conviction that accurate self-knowledge is desirable and is functional to the decision-making independent people must do
5. Consultation with group members on how achievement of peer arena group therapy goals can help one to aggressively take on tasks of life and not strive to escape them
6. Consulting with group members when the member feels ready to leave peer arena therapy as to whether graduation criteria have been achieved.

We have discussed the important contributions of personal family history and family relationships to current functioning. But the individual at this stage of development must primarily engage in psychosocial dynamics with peers, which stimulate growth and maturity. Since crucial developmental figures in adolescence are peers, the peer arena models of therapy, whether individual or group, focus on peer interaction. The group model allows the adolescent to reexperience the impact of the group, to become aware of his emotional responses to such interaction, and to gain insight into the avenues of flight he has selected, regardless of the external rationale. Living with anxieties, *dealing* with them forthrightly with the support of therapist and peers, and constructing strategies for coping with them *in the arena* constitutes the therapeutic outline.

End Note

Our model of adolescent development demands recognition that age-mates are mutually instrumental to the course of their development. Peers are *the* central environmental others during this period. Although family members continue to be very important for far more than bed and board, peers set the pace and establish the priorities for the adolescent. Their interest in one another is not only intense but is very broad; no dimension is left unexamined. Looking at one another, assessing one another, and then evaluating self against other is the primary psychosocial dynamic of the adolescent period.

Data presented in this book document the theoretical model of the peer arena and reveal that peers are the reference cluster of most importance, that distinct "peer issues" exist, that the most interesting other is the agemate, that this agemate is examined in detail (whether in large gatherings or in smaller settings for closer contacts), and that adolescents draw their companions from a variety of different settings, which together make up the peer arena. We suggest that the "peer group" is too imprecise a formulation since it implies a small group of friends and is not fully representative of the adolescent scene. Most adolescents of the early and middle stages require large groups of many others in order to carry out their necessary comparative acts.

With the primacy of the peer in mind, we can reassess more traditional routes to understanding adolescent behaviors. We can put parent anxieties to rest and reassure them for having done (for the most part) a creditable job in rearing their children to physical maturity and cognitive advance. We can help parents to allow their adolescent's peers to take center stage as the developmental figures of his or her world. Parents struggling with outmoded concepts of "adolescent rebellion" and erroneous notions of "rejection" experience pain, and further misunder-

277

standing spreads to all parties. A new recognition of this displacement as a natural transition should help dispel the feelings of rejection that parents experience.

Professionals should bring to the attention of educators and mental health agencies the young adolescent's ongoing expenditure of psychological energies as he or she tries to adjust to new demands for independent functioning at a time when the self is merely in the process of formation. To the adolescent, agemates are the only others who seem to intuitively understand because they have the same task. Since adolescent agemates must complete their quests for identity quite independently, they cannot deeply involve themselves with one another, yet they do offer their physical company and they do provide an atmosphere for experimentation. Each is busy completing his or her own daily objective and educational tasks in the public world. Each is also involved in working out the developmental imperative to psychosocially mature and grow to adulthood. Toward these ends, adolescents must engage the comparative acts of the adolescent dialectic. They must actively take on the dynamics of the first stage of adolescence and, upon completion of a temporary self structure, proceed to the second stage, where they refine, polish, and integrate their newly discovered elements of "self." At this point, psychosocial "identity" is achieved. The adolescent does indeed know who he is, "in love and in work."

Professionals cannot target their efforts if they do not understand the primacy of the peer as the central developmental figure, rather than merely a companion for fun and games. The theory of dynamic functional interaction introduces the peer arena model of adolescent development (Seltzer, 1982). In this book findings are reported from empirical studies examining the DFI theory's basic premises. These findings are meant to assist in translating aspects of the undisclosed world of the adolescent to academicians, clinicians, and students of human behavior. It is our hope that as clinicians, academicians, and students grasp the central dynamics of adolescence and integrate this knowledge into their professions, their teaching, and their practices, the path of normative development will be facilitated, and the range and degree of adolescent social problems and self-destructive behaviors will be greatly reduced.

References

Adams, G., & Schvaneveldt, J. (1985). *Understanding research methods*. New York: Longman.

Adams, G., & Shea, J. (1979). The relationship between identity status, locus of control, and ego development. *Journal of Youth and Adolescence, 8*, 81–89.

American Psychiatric Association (1983). *Diagnostic and statistical manual of mental disorders* (3rd ed., rev.). Washington, DC: Author.

Anderson, E., & Clarke, L. (1982). *Disability in adolescence*. London: Methuen.

Anthony, E. (1983). Depression in adolescence: A psychodynamic approach to nosology. In H. Golomber & B. Garfinkel (Eds.), *The adolescent and mood disturbances* (pp. 151–165). New York: International Universities Press.

Asch, S. (1956). Studies of independence and conformity: A minority of one against a unanimous majority. *Psychological Monograph 70*, no 9, 177–190.

Auchenbach, T. (1980). *Developmental psychopathology* (2nd ed.). New York: Wiley.

Ausubel, D. (1954). *Theory and problems of adolescent development*. New York: Grune & Stratton.

Ausubel, D., Montemayer, R., & Svajian, P. (1977). *Theory and problems of adolescent development* (2nd ed.). New York: Grune & Stratton.

Ausubel, D., & Sullivan, E. (1970). *Theory and problems of child development* (2nd ed.). New York: Grune & Stratton.

Babbie, E. (1986). *The practice of social research* (4th ed.). Belmont, CA: Wadsworth.

Bandura, A. (1964). The stormy decade: Fact or fiction? *Psychology in the Schools, 1*, 224–231.

Bandura, A. (1969). *Principles of behavior modification*. New York: Holt, Rinehart & Winston.

Bandura, A. (1981). Self-referent thought: A developmental analysis of self-efficacy. In J. Flavell & L. Ross (Eds.), *Social cognition development*. New York: Cambridge University Press.

Bandura, A., & Walters, R. (1963). *Social learning and personality development*. New York: Holt, Rinehart & Winston.

Barclay, A., & Cervantes, L. (1969). The TAT as an index of personality attributes of the adolescent dropout. *Adolescence, 4*, 525–540.

Bardwick, J., & Douvan, E. (1971). Ambivalence: The socialization of women. In V. Gornick & B. Moran (Eds.), *Women in sexist society: Studies in power and powerlessness* (pp. 147–159). New York: Basic Books.

Baumrind, D. (1975). Early socialization and adolescent competence. In S. E. Dragastin & G. H. Elder, Jr., (Eds.), *Adolescence in the life cycle* (pp. 117–139). New York: Halsted.

Beck, A. (1976). *Cognitive therapy and emotional disorders*. New York: International Universities Press.

Becker, R. (1979). Adolescents in the hospital: Psychological and cognitive aspects of chronic illness—A developmental perspective. *IRS Annals of Psychiatry, 17*, 328–352.

Bell, R., & Harper, L. (1977). *Child effects on adults*. Lincoln, NE: Bison Books.

Benedict, R. (1938). Continuities and discontinuities in cultural conditioning. *Psychiatry, 1*, 161–167.

Berenda, R. (1950). *The influence of the group on judgments of children*. New York: Kings Press.

Berndt, T., & Hoyle, S. (1985). Stability and change in childhood and adolescent friendships. *Developmental Psychology, 21*, 1007–1015.

Bernstein, R. (1981). The relationship between dimensions of delinquency and the developments of self and peer perception. *Adolescence, 16*, 543–556.

Biddle, B., Bank, B., & Marlin, M. (1980). Parental and peer influence on adolescents. *Social Forces, 58*, 1057–1179.

Blos, P. (1962). *On adolescence: A psychoanalytic interpretation*. New York: International Universities Press.

Blos, P. (1970). *The young adolescent*. New York: Free Press.

Blos, P. (1979). *The adolescent passage*. New York: International Universities Press.

Bluebond-Langner, M. (1978). *The private worlds of dying children*. Princeton, NJ: Princeton University Press.

Blum, H. (1985). Superego formation, adolescent transformation, and the adult neurosis. *Journal of the American Psychoanalytic Association, 33*, 887–909.

Blum, L. (1966). The discotheque and the phenomenon of alone-togetherness. *Adolescence, 1*, 351–366.

Blyth, D., Simmons, R., & Zakin, D. (1985). Satisfaction with body image for early adolescent females: The impact of pubertal timing within different school environments. *Journal of Youth and Adolescence, 14*, 207–225.

Bowlby, J. (1969). *Attachment and loss* (Vol. 1). New York: Basic Books.

Bram, S., Eger, D., & Halmi, K. (1983). Anorexia nervosa and personality type: A preliminary report. *International Journal of Eating Disorders, 2*, 67–74.

Breakwell, G. (1986). *Coping with threatened identities*. London: Methuen.

Brehm, S. (1976). *The application of social psychology to clinical practice*. New York: Wiley.

Brim, O., & Kagan, J. (Eds.). (1980). *Continuity and change in human development.* Cambridge, MA: Harvard University Press.

Bronfenbrenner, U. (1970). *Two worlds of childhood.* New York: Russell Sage.

Bronfenbrenner, U. (1979). *The ecology of human development.* Cambridge, MA: Harvard University Press.

Brooks-Gunn, J., & Furstenberg, F. (1989). Adolescent sexual behavior. *American Psychologist, 44,* 249–257.

Brooks-Gunn, J., & Petersen, A. (1983). *Girls at puberty: Biological and psychosocial perspectives.* New York: Plenum Press.

Brown, B., Clasen, D., & Ercher, S. (1986). Perceptions of peer pressure, peer conformity dispositions, and self-reported behavior among adolescents. *Developmental Psychology, 22,* 521–530.

Brown, B., & Lohr, M. (1987). Peer-group affiliation and adolescent self-esteem: An integration of ego-identity and symbolic interaction theories. *Journal of Personality and Social Psychology, 52,* 47–54.

Burkett, S. (1977). School ties, peer influence, and adolescent marijuana use. *Pacific Sociological Review, 20,* 161–201.

Bywater, E. (1981). Adolescents with cystic fibrosis: Psychological adjustment. *Archives of Disease in Childhood, 56,* 538–543.

Carlson, G. (1981). The phenomenology of adolescent depression. *Adolescent Psychiatry, 9,* 411–421.

Carter, E., & McGoldrick, M. (Eds.). (1980). *The family life cycle: A framework for family therapy.* New York: Gardner Press.

Cattell, R. (1966). Psychological theory and scientific method. In R. Cattell (Ed.), *Handbook of multivariate experimental psychology* (pp. 1–18). Chicago: Rand McNally.

Chaim, H. (1987). Change in self-concept during adolescence. *Adolescence, 85,* 69–76.

Chassin, L., Presson, C., & Sherman, S. (1984). Cigarette smoking and adolescent psychosocial development. *Basic and Applied Social Psychology, 5,* 295–315.

Chess, S., & Thomas, A. (1984). *Origins and evolution of behavior disorders: From infancy to early adult life.* New York: Brunner/Mazel.

Clausen, J. (1975). The social meaning of differential physical and sexual maturation. In S. Dragastin & G. Elder, Jr. (Eds.), *Adolescence in the life cycle* (pp. 25–47). New York: Halsted.

Clayton, R. (1980). The delinquency and drug use relationship among adolescents: A critical review. *National Institute on Drug Abuse Research Monograph Series, 38,* 82–103.

Cnaan, R., & Seltzer, V. (1989). Etiology of truancy: An ecosystems perspective. *Social Work In Education, 11,* 171–183.

Colby, A., & Kohlberg, L. (1984). *The measurement of moral judgment.* New York: Cambridge University Press.

Coleman, J. (1961). *The adolescent society: The social life of the teenager and its impact on education.* New York: Free Press.

Coleman, J. (1965). *Adolescents and the schools*. New York: Basic Books.

Coleman, J. (1980). Friendship and the peer group in adolescence. In J. Adelson (Ed.), *Handbook of adolescent psychology* (pp. 408–431). New York: Wiley.

Coleman, J., Herzberg, J., & Morris, M. (1977). Identity in adolescence: Present and future self-concepts. *Journal of Youth and Adolescence, 6*, 63–75.

Conger, J. (1977). *Adolescence and youth: Psychological development in a changing world* (2nd ed.). New York: Harper & Row.

Conger, J., & Petersen, A. (1984). *Adolescence and youth: Psychological development in a changing world* (3rd ed.). New York: Harper & Row.

Coombs, R., Wellisch, D. & Fawzy, F. (1985). Drinking patterns and problems among female children and adolescents: A comparison of abstainers, past users, and current users. *American Journal of Drug and Alcohol Abuse, 11*, 315–348.

Cooper, C., & Ayers-Lopez, S. (1985). Family and peer systems in early adolescence: New models of the role of relationships in development. *Journal of Early Adolescence, 5*, 9–21.

Costanzo, P. (1970). Conformity development as a function of self-blame. *Journal of Personality and Social Psychology, 14*, 366–374.

Costanzo, P., & Shaw, M. (1966). Conformity as a function of age level. *Child Development, 37*, 967–975.

Crockett, L., Losoff, M., & Peterson, A. (1984). Perceptions of the peer group and friendship in early adolescence. *Journal of Early Adolescence, 4*, 155–181.

Csikszentmihalyi, M., & Larson, R. (1984). *Being adolescent: Conflict and growth in the teenage years*. New York: Basic Books.

Curran, D. (1987). *Adolescent suicidal behavior*. Washington DC: Hemisphere/Harper & Row.

Daniels, D. (1986). Differential experiences of siblings in the same family as predictors of adolescent sibling personality differences. *Journal of Personality and Social Psychology, 51*, 339–346.

Darley, J., & Aronson, E. (1966). Self-evaluation vs. direct anxiety reduction as determinants of the fear affiliation relationship. *Journal of Experimental Social Psychology, Supp.*, 66–79.

Davies, M., & Kandel, D. (1981). Parental and peer influences on adolescents' educational plans: Some further evidence. *American Journal of Sociology, 87*, 383–387.

Davis, K. (1940). The sociology of parent-youth conflict. *American Sociological Review, 5*, 523–536.

DeCatanzaro, D. (1981). *Suicide and self-damaging behavior: A sociobiological perspective*. New York: Academic Press.

DeWitt, K. (1978). The effectiveness of family therapy: A review of outcome research. *Archives of General Psychiatry, 35*, 549–561.

Dollard, J., & Miller, N. (1965). *Personality and psychotherapy: An analysis in terms of learning, thinking, and culture* (2nd ed.). New York: McGraw-Hill.

Dornbush, S., Carlsmith, J., Gross, R., Martin, J., Jennings, D., Rosenberg, A., & Duke, P. (1981). Sexual development, age, and dating: A comparison of biological and social influences upon one set of behaviors. *Child Development, 52*, 179–185.

Douvan, E., & Adelson, J. (1966). *The adolescent experience*. New York: Wiley.

Dunphy, D. (1980). Peer group socialization. In R. Muus (Ed.), *Adolescent behavior and society: A book of readings* (3rd ed. pp. 196–209). New York: Random House.

Eder, D. (1986). The cycle of popularity: Interpersonal relations among female adolescents. *Sociology of Education, 58*, 154–165.

Edwards, A. (1953). The relationship between the judged desirability of a trait and the probability that the trait will be endorsed. *Journal of Applied Psychology, 37*, 90–93.

Eichorn, D. H. (1974). Asynchronizations in adolescent development. In S. E. Dragastin & G. H. Elder, Jr. (Eds.), *Adolescence in the life cycle: Psychological change and social context* (pp. 81–96). Washington, DC: Hemisphere.

Eisert, D., & Kahle, L. (1982). Self-evaluation and social comparison of physical and role change during adolescence: A longitudinal analysis. *Child Development, 53*, 98–104.

Eiskoits, I., & Sagi, A. (1982). Moral development and discipline encounter in delinquent and nondelinquent adolescents. *Journal of Youth and Adolescence, 11*, 217–230.

Elkin, F., & Westley, W. (1955). The myth of adolescent culture. *American Sociological Review, 20*, 680–684.

Elkind, D. (1967). Egocentrism in adolescence. *Child Development, 38*, 1025–1034.

Elkind, D. (1978). Understanding the young adolescent. *Adolescence, 13*, 127–134.

Elkind, D. (1983). Strategic interactions in early adolescence. In W. Damon (Ed.), *Social and personality development: Essays on the growth of the child* (pp. 434–444). New York: Norton.

Ellis, R. (1988). Self-monitoring and leadership emergence in groups. *Personality and Social Psychology Bulletin, 14*, 681–693.

Emery, P. (1983). Adolescent depression and suicide. *Adolescence, 18*, 245–258.

Erikson, E. (1950). *Childhood and society*. New York: Norton.

Erikson, E. (1956). The problem of ego identity. *Journal of American Psychoanalytic Association 4,1*, 56–121.

Erikson, E. (1963). *Childhood and society* (2nd ed.). New York: Norton.

Erikson, E. (1968a). *Identity and the life cycle*. New York: Norton.

Erikson, E. (1968b). *Identity: Youth and crisis*. New York: Norton.

Esman, A. (1975). *The psychology of adolescence*. New York: International Universities Press.

Farrow, J., & French, J. (1986). The drug-abuse delinquency connection revisited. *Adolescence, 21*, 951–960.

Fasick, R. (1984). Parents, peers, youth culture and autonomy in adolescence. *Adolescence, 19*, 143–157.

Faust, J., Baum, C., & Forehand, R. (1985). An examination of the association between social relationships and depression in early adolescence. *Journal of Applied Developmental Psychology, 6*, 291–297.

Feather, N. (1980). Values in adolescence. In J. Adelson (Ed.). *Handbook of adolescent psychology* (pp. 247–295). New York: Wiley.

Feldman, M., & Gaier, E. (1980). Correlates of adolescent life satisfaction. *Youth and Society, 12*, 131–144.

Feldman, N, & Ruble, D. (1981). The development of person perception: Cognitive and social factors. In S. Brehm, S. Kassin, & F. Gibbons (Eds.), *Developmental social psychology* (pp. 191–210). New York: Oxford University Press.

Ferguson, G. (1971). *Statistical analysis in psychology and education* (3rd ed.). New York: McGraw-Hill.

Festinger, L. (1950). Informal social communication. *Psychological Review, 57*, 271–282.

Festinger, L. (1954). A theory of social comparison processes. *Human Relations, 5*, 117–139.

Fischer, C., & Alapack, R. (1987). A phenomenological approach to adolescence. In V. Hasselt & M. Herson (Eds.), *Handbook of adolescent psychology* (pp. 91–107). New York: Pergamon Press.

Flacks, R. (1967). The liberated generation: An exploration of the roots of student protest. *Journal of Social Issues, 23*, 52–75.

Flavell, J. (1963). *The developmental psychology of Jean Piaget.* New York: Van Nostrand.

Flavell, J. (1985). *Cognitive development* (2nd ed.). Englewood Cliffs, NJ: Prentice-Hall.

Fraser, M. (1984). Family, school, and peer correlates of adolescent drug abuse. *Social Service Review, 58*, 434–447.

Freeman, D. (1983). *Margaret Mead and Samoa: The making and unmaking of an anthropological myth.* Cambridge, MA: Harvard University Press.

French, D., & Tyne, T. (1982). The identification and treatment of children with peer relationship difficulties. In J. Curran & P. Monti (Eds.), *Social skills training: A practical handbook for assessment and treatment* (pp. 280–308). New York: Guilford.

Freud, A. (1946). *The ego and the mechanisms of defense.* New York: International Universities Press.

Freud, A. (1958). Adolescence. In *Psychoanalytic study of the child* (Vol. 13, pp. 255–278). New York: International Universities Press.

Freud, A. (1965). *Normality and pathology in childhood.* New York: International Universities Press.

Freud, A. (1966). Instinctual anxiety during puberty. In *The writings of Anna Freud* (Vol. 2, rev. ed., pp. 152–173). New York: International Universities Press.

1905 [p. 4]

Freud, A. (1969). Adolescence as a developmental disturbance. In G. Caplan & S. Lebovici (Eds.), *Adolescence: Psychosocial perspectives* (pp. 5–10). New York: Basic Books.

Freud, S. (1953). The transformations of puberty. In J. Strachey (Ed.), *The standard edition of the complete psychological works of Sigmund Freud* (Vol. 7, pp. 145–245) London: Hogarth Press. (Original work published 1905)

Friedenberg, E. (1959). *The vanishing adolescent*. Boston: Beacon Press.

Friedenberg, E. (1963). *Coming of age in America: Growth and acquiescence*. New York: Random House.

Furnham, A. (1985). Youth unemployment: A review of the literature. *Journal of Adolescence, 8*, 109–124.

Furstenberg, F., Jr. (1976). *Unplanned parenthood*. New York: Free Press.

Furstenberg, F., Brooks-Gunn, J., & Morgan, S. (1987). *Adolescent mothers later in life*. New York: Cambridge University Press.

Gaddis, A., & Brooks-Gunn, J. (1985). The male experience of pubertal change. *Journal of Youth and Adolescence, 14*, 61–69.

Gallagher, J., & Harris, H. (1976). *Emotional problems of adolescents* (3rd ed.). New York: Oxford University Press.

Gallatin, J. (1975). *Adolescence and individuality*. New York: Harper & Row.

Galloway, D. (1985). *School and persistent absentees*. Elmsford, NY: Pergamon Press.

Gargiulo, J., Attie, I., Brooks-Gunn, J., & Warren, M. (1987). Dating in middle school girls: Effects of social context, maturation, and grade. *Developmental Psychology, 23*, 730–737.

Gesell, A., & Ilg, F. (1943). *Infant and child in the culture of today*. New York: Harper & Row.

Gesell, A., Ilg, F., & Ames, L. (1956). *Youth: The years from ten to sixteen*. New York: Harper & Row.

Gilligan, C. (1982). *In a different voice*. Cambridge, MA: Harvard University Press.

Gispert, M., Wheeler, K., Marsh, L., & Davis, M. (1985). Suicidal adolescents: Factors in evaluation. *Adolescence, 20*, 753–762.

Glasser, W. (1965). *Reality therapy*. New York: Harper & Row.

Goethals, G., & Darley, J. (1977). Social comparison: An attributional approach. In J. Suls & R. Miller (Eds.), *Social comparison processes: Theoretical and empirical perspectives* (pp. 259–278). Washington, DC: Hemisphere.

Golomber, H. & Garfinkel, B. (Eds.). (1981). *The adolescent mind and mood disturbances*. New York: International Universities Press.

Goodman, P. (1956). *Growing up absurd*. New York: Random House.

Gordon, S., & Gilgun, J. (1987). Adolescent sexuality. In V. Hasselt & M. Herson (Eds.), *Handbook of adolescent psychology* (pp. 147–167). Elmsford, New York: Pergamon Press.

Gottman, J. (1983). How children become friends. *Monographs of the Society for Research in Child Development, 48,* No. 3, serial 201.

Green, R., & Framo, J. (Eds.). (1981). *Family therapy: Major contributions.* New York: International Universities Press.

Greenberger, E., & Steinberg, L. (1986). *When teenagers work: The psychological and social costs of adolescent employment.* New York: Basic Books.

Greenwald, A., Bellezza, F., & Banaji, M. (1988). Is self-esteem a central ingredient of the self-concept? *Personality and Social Psychology Bulletin, 14,* 34–45.

Grinder, R. (1966). Relations of social dating attractions to academic orientation and peer relations. *Journal of Educational Psychology, 57,* 27–34.

Grinder, R. (1975). *Studies in adolescence.* New York: Macmillan.

Grotevant, H., & Adams, G. (1984). Development of an objective measure to assess ego identity in adolescence: Validation and replication. *Journal of Youth and Adolescence, 13,* 419–438.

Grotevant, H., & Cooper, C. (Eds.). (1983). *Adolescent development in the family: New directions for child development.* San Francisco: Jossey-Bass.

Grotevant, H., Thorbeck, W., & Meyer, M. (1982). An extension of Marcia's identity status interview into the interpersonal domain. *Journal of Youth and Adolescence, 11,* 33-47.

Grunebaum, H., & Solomon, L. (1982). Toward a theory of peer relationships, II: On the stages of social development and their relationship to group psychotherapy. *International Journal of Group Psychotherapy, 32,* 283–307.

Hakmiller, K. (1966). Need for self-evaluation, perceived similarity, and comparison choice. *Journal of Experimental Social Psychology, Supp. 1,* 49–55.

Hall, G. (1916). *Adolescence* (Vols. 1–2). New York: Appleton.

Hansell, S. (1985). Adolescent friendship networks and distress in school. *Social Forces, 63,* 698–715.

Harper, D., Wacker, D., & Cobb, L. (1986). Children's social preferences toward peers with visible physical differences. *Journal of Pediatric Psychology, 11,* 323–342.

Hartley, R. (1968). Norm compatibility, norm preference, and the acceptance of new reference groups. In H. Hyman & E. Singer (Eds.), *Readings in reference group theory and research* (pp. 238–246). New York: Free Press.

Hartrup, W. (1982). Peer relations. In C. Kopp & J. Krakow (Eds.), *The child: Development in a social context* (pp. 514–575). Reading, MA: Addison-Wesley.

Hartrup, W. (1989). Social relationships and their developmental significance. *American Psychologist, 44,* 120–126.

Havighurst, R. (1972). *Developmental tasks and education.* New York: McKay.

Havighurst, R., & Neugarten, B. (1967). *Society and education* (3rd ed.). Boston: Allyn and Bacon.

Heider, F. (1958). *The psychology of interpersonal relations.* New York: Wiley.

Hetherington, E. M. (1972). Effects of father absence on personality development in adolescent daughters. *Developmental Psychology, 7*, 313–326.

Hoffman, M. (1980). Adolescent morality in developmental perspective. In J. Adelson (Ed.), *Handbook of adolescent psychology* (pp. 302–342). New York: Wiley.

Hollingsworth, L. (1928). *The psychology of the adolescent*. New York: Appleton-Century.

Holroyd, K., & Kahn, M. (1980). Personality factors in student drug use. In R. Muus (Ed.), *Adolescent behavior and society: A book of readings* (3rd ed., pp. 475–485). New York: Random House.

Horne, M. (1985). *Attitudes toward handicapped students: Professional, peer and parent reactions*. Hillsdale, NJ: Lawrence Erlbaum.

Hull, C. (1943). *Principles of behavior*. New York: Appleton-Century-Crofts.

Hunter, R. (1985). Adolescents' perception of discussions with parents and friends. *Developmental Psychology, 21*, 433–440.

Hurrelmann, K. (1987). The importance of school in the life course: Results from the Bielefeld study on school-related problems in adolescence. *Journal of Adolescent Research, 2*, 111–125.

Hyman, H. (1942). The psychology of status. *Archives of Psychology, 269*, 5–38, 80–86.

Inhelder B., & Piaget, J. (1958). *The growth of logical thinking in children and adolescents*. New York: Basic Books.

Jacklin, C. (1989). Female and male: Issues of gender. *American Psychologist, 44*, 127–133.

Jessor, R., & Jessor, S. (1977). *Problem behavior and psychosocial development*. New York: Academic Press.

Jessor, S., & Jessor, R. (1975). Transition from virginity to nonvirginity among youth: A social-psychological study over time. *Developmental Psychology, 11*, 473–484.

Johnson, C., & Maddi, K. (1985). The etiology of bulimia: A bio-psycho-social perspective. *Annals of Adolescent Psychiatry, 13*, 1–20.

Johnston, L. (1986). *Drug use among American high school students, college students, and other young adults: National trends through 1985*. Ann Arbor: University of Michigan Institute for Social Research.

Jones, S., & Regan, D. (1974). Ability evaluation through social comparison. *Journal of Experimental Social Psychology, 10*, 133–146.

Josselson, R. (1980). Ego development in adolescence. In J. Adelson (Ed.), *Handbook of adolescent psychology* (pp. 133–210). New York: Wiley.

Josselson, R. (1987). *Finding herself: Pathways to identity development in women*. San Francisco: Jossey-Bass.

Josselyn, I. (1952). *The adolescent and his world*. New York: Family Service Association of America.

Kagan, J., & Moss, H. (1983). *Birth to maturity: A study in psychological development* (2nd ed.). New Haven, CT: Yale University Press.

Kahn, A. (1987). Heterogeneity of suicidal adolescents. *Journal of the American Academy of Child and Adolescent Psychiatry, 26,* No. 1, 92–96.

Kandel, D. (1973). Adolescent marijuana use: Role of parents and peers. *Science, 181,* 1067–1069.

Kandel, D. (1975). Stages in adolescent involvement in drug use. *Science,* 190, 912–914.

Kandel, D. (1985). On processes of peer influences in adolescent drug use: A developmental perspective. *Advances in Alcohol and Substance Abuse, 4,* 139–163.

Kaplan, H., Martin, S., & Robbins, C. (1984). Pathways to adolescent drug use: Self-derogation, peer influence, weakening of social controls, and early substance use. *Journal of Health and Social Behavior, 25,* 270–289.

Kelley, H. (1952). Two functions of reference groups. In G. Swanson, T. Newcomb, & E. Hartley (Eds.), *Readings in social psychology* (rev. ed., pp. 410–414). New York: Holt, Rinehart & Winston.

Kelly, H. (1967). Attribution theory in social psychology. In D. Levine (Ed.), *Nebraska symposium on motivation* (2nd ed., pp. 192–240). Lincoln: University of Nebraska Press.

Keniston, K. (1965). *The uncommitted: Alienated youth in American society.* New York: Harcourt, Brace and World.

Keniston, K. (1971). *Youth and dissent: The rise of a new opposition.* New York: Harcourt Brace Jovanovich.

Kerlinger, F. (1973). *Foundations of behavioral research* (2nd ed.). New York: Holt, Rinehart & Winston.

Kerlinger, F. (1979). *Behavioral research: A conceptual approach.* New York: Holt, Rinehart & Winston.

Klein, J. (1986). *Truancy as a symptom of problems that an adolescent may have in establishing peer relationships.* Unpublished master's professional project, University of Pennsylvania.

Klerman, G. (Ed.). (1986). *Suicide and depression among adolescents and young adults.* New York: American Psychiatric Press.

Kohlberg, L. (1976). Stage and sequence: The cognitive development approach. In T. Lickona (Ed.), *Moral development and behavior: Theory, research, and social issues.* New York: Holt, Rinehart & Winston.

Kohlberg, L. (1984). *Essays in moral development: 2. The psychology of moral development.* New York: Harper & Row.

Kohlberg, L., & Gilligan, C. (1971). The adolescent as philosopher: The discovery of the self in a postconventional world. *Daedalus,* 1051–1086.

Kunda, Z., & Nisbett, R. (1988). Predicting individual evaluations from group evaluations and vice versa: Different patterns for self and others. *Personality and Social Psychology Bulletin, 14,* 326–334.

Labouvie, E., & McGee, C. (1986). Relation of personality to alcohol and drug use in adolescence. *Journal of Consulting and Clinical Psychology, 54,* 289–293.

Lamb, M. (1982). Paternal influences and the father's role. In J. Keating (Ed.), *Annual editions: Social psychology* (pp. 68–73). Guilford, CT: Dushkin.

Lecky, P. (1951). *Self consistency.* New York: Island Press.

Lerner, R., & Knapp, J. (1975). Actual and perceived intrafamilial attitudes of late adolescents and their parents. *Journal of Youth and Adolescence, 4,* 17–36.

Lerner, R., & Foch, T. (Eds.). (1987). *Biological-psychosocial interactions in early adolescence: A life-span perspective.* Hillsdale, NJ: Lawrence Erlbaum.

Lewin, K. (1939). Field theory and experiment in social psychology. *American Journal of Sociology, 44,* 873–884, 895–96.

Lewin, K. (1948). *Resolving social conflicts.* New York: Harper & Brothers.

Lewin, K. (1951). *Field theory and social science.* New York: Harper & Row.

Liebert, R. (1982). *The early window: Effects of television on children and youth.* Elmsford, NY: Pergamon Press.

Maccoby, E. (1980). *Social development.* Stanford, CA: Stanford University Press.

Maccoby, E. & Jacklin, C. (1974). *The psychology of sex differences.* Stanford, CA: Stanford University Press.

Maccoby, E., & Martin, J. (1983). Socialization in the context of the family: Parent-child interaction. In E. Hetherington (Ed.), *Handbook of child psychology: 4. Socialization, personality and social development* (pp. 1–101). New York: Wiley.

Mahler, M. (1968). *On human symbiosis and the vicissitudes of individuation: I. Infantile psychosis.* New York: International Universities Press.

Marcia, J. (1980). Identity in adolescence. In J. Adelson (Ed.), *Handbook of adolescent psychology* (pp. 159–187). New York: Wiley.

Masten, A. (1979). Family therapy as a treatment for children: A critical review of outcome research. *Family Process, 18,* 323–335.

Masterson, J. (1968). The psychiatric significance of adolescent turmoil. *American Journal of Psychiatry, 124,* 240–268.

Masterson, J. (1972). *The treatment of the borderline adolescent: A developmental approach.* New York: Wiley.

Matteson, D. (1975). *Adolescence today: Sex roles and the search for identity.* Homewood, IL: Dorsey Press.

Mead, M. (1928). *Coming of age in Samoa.* New York: Morrow.

Mead, M. (1942). *Growing up in New Guinea.* London: Penguin.

Mead, M. (1950). *Male and female.* London: Penguin.

Mead, M. (1972). *Culture and commitment: A study of the generation gap.* London: Panther.

Milgram, G. (1982). Youthful drinking: Past and present. *Journal of Drug Education, 12*, 289–308.

Minuchin, S. (1974). *Families and family therapy.* Cambridge, MA: Harvard University Press.

Montemayer, R. (1982). The relationship between parent-adolescent conflict and the amount of time adolescents spend alone and with parents and peers. *Child Development, 53*, 1512–1519.

Montemayer, R., & Van Komen, R. (1985). The development of sex differences in friendship patterns and peer group structure during adolescence. *Journal of Early Adolescence, 5*, 285–294.

Morrell, M. (1986). *The role of the peer reference group for 13–18 year old adolescent soft drug users: Differences between intact vs. non-intact families.* Unpublished master's professional project, University of Pennsylvania.

Mosher, R. (Ed.). (1979). *Adolescents' development and education.* Berkeley, CA: McCutchan.

Mueller, E., & Cooper, C. (1986). *Process and outcome in peer relationships.* London: Academic Press.

Munro, G., & Adams, G. (1977). Ego identity formation in college students and working youth. *Developmental Psychology, 13*, 523–524.

Mussen, P., & Jones, M. (1957). Self-conceptions, motivation and interpersonal attitudes of late and early maturing boys. *Child Development, 28*, 243–256.

Muus, R. (1982). Social cognition: Robert Selman's theory of role taking. *Adolescence, 17*, 499–525.

Muus, R. (1982). Theories of Adolescence (4th ed.). New York: Random House.

Napier, T., Goe, R., & Bachtel, D. (1984). An assessment of the influence of peer association and identification on drug use among rural high school students. *Journal of Drug Education, 14*, 227–248.

National Institute on Drug Abuse. (1983). *Preventing adolescent drug abuse: Intervention strategies* (NIDA Research Monograph 47). Washington, DC: U.S. Government Printing Office.

Neugarten, B. (1969). Continuities and discontinuities of psychological issues into adult life. *Human Development, 12*, 121–130.

Newcomb, T. (1958). Attitude development as a function of reference groups: The Bennington study. In E. Maccoby, T. Newcomb, and E. Hartley (Eds.), *Readings in social psychology* (3rd ed., pp. 265–275). New York: Holt. (Originally published 1948)

Newman, B., & Newman, P. (1987). *Development through life: The Psychosocial Approach* (4th ed.). Chicago: Dorsey Press.

Newman, P., & Newman, B. (1976). Early adolescence and its conflict: Group identity vs alienation. *Adolescence, 9,* 261–274.

Offer, D. (1969). *The psychological world of the teen-ager.* New York: Basic Books.

Offer, D., Marcus, D., & Offer, J. (1970). A longitudinal study of normal adolescent boys. *American Journal of Psychiatry, 126,* 917–1124.

Offer, D., & Offer, J. (1975). *From teenage to manhood.* New York: Basic Books.

Offer, D., Ostrov, E., & Howard, K. (1981). *The adolescent: A psychological self-portrait.* New York: Basic Books.

Owen, R., & Matthews, D. (1982). Developmental and acquired disabilities in adolescence. In Blum, R. (Ed.), *Adolescent health care: Clinical issues.* New York: Academic Press.

Parsons, T., & Bales, R. (1955). *Family, socialization and interaction process.* Chicago: Free Press of Glencoe.

Paton, S., Kessler, R., & Kandel, D. (1977). Depressive mood and adolescent illicit drug use: A longitudinal analysis. *Journal of Genetic Psychology, 131,* 267–289.

Pepitone, E. (1980). *Children in cooperation and competition.* Lexington, MA: Lexington Books, D.C. Heath.

Perry, W. (1970). *Forms of intellectual and ethical development in the college years: A scheme.* New York: Holt, Rinehart & Winston.

Perry, W. (1981). Cognitive and ethical growth: The making of meaning. In A. Chickering (Ed.), *The modern American college* (pp. 76–138). San Franscisco: Jossey-Bass.

Peterson, A. (1985). Pubertal development as a cause of disturbance: Myths, realities, and unanswered questions. *Genetic, Social and General Psychology Monographs, 11,* 205–232.

Peterson, A., & Taylor, B. (1980). The biological approach to adolescence. In J. Adelson (Ed.), *Handbook of Adolescent Psychology* (pp. 117–155). New York: Wiley.

Piaget, J. (1952). *The origins of intelligence in children.* New York: International Universities Press.

Piaget, J. (1972). Intellectual evolution from adolescence to adulthood. *Human Development, 14,* 1–12.

Piaget, J., & Inhelder, B. (1969). *The psychology of the child* (H. Weaver, Trans.). New York: Basic Books. (Original work published 1966)

Radloff, R. (1966). Social comparison and ability evaluation. *Journal of Experimental Social Psychology, Supp. 1,* 6–26.

Redl, F. (1974, October). *Something new has been added on the way to the forum.* Paper presented at the Second Annual Friends Hospital Clinical Conference, Philadelphia, Pa.

Reich, R., & Feinberg, H. (1974). The fatally ill adolescent. *Adolescent Psychiatry, 3,* 75–84.

Richards, M., & Peterson, A. (1987). Biological theoretical models of adolescent development. In V. Van Hasselt and M. Hersen (Eds.), *Handbook of adolescent psychology*. Elmsford, NY: Pergamon Press.

Robins, D., & Conroy, R. (1983). A cluster of adolescent suicide attempts: Is suicide contagious? *Journal of Adolescent Health Care, 3*, 253–255.

Rogers, C. (1951). *Client centered therapy*. Boston: Houghton Mifflin.

Rokeach, M. (1973). *The nature of human values*. New York: Free Press.

Roscoe, B., Kennedy, D., & Pope, T. (1987). Adolescents' views of intimacy: Distinguishing intimate from nonintimate relationships. *Adolescence, 22*, 511–516.

Rosenthal, M. (1981). Sexual differences in the suicidal behavior of young people. *Adolescent Psychiatry, 10*, 455–468.

Rosenthal, T., & Zimmerman, B. (1978). *Social learning and cognition*. New York: Academic Press.

Ruble, D., & Brooks-Gunn, J. (1982). The experience of menarche. *Child Development, 53*, 1557–1566.

Sanford, S., & Eder, D. (1984). Adolescent humor during peer interaction. *Social Psychology Quarterly, 47*, 235–243.

Sarafica, F., & Blyth, D. (1985). Continuities and changes in the study of friendship and peer groups during early adolescence. *Journal of Early Adolescence, 5*, 267–283.

Sarason, S., & Klaber, M. (1985). The school as a social situation. *Annual Review of Psychology, 49*, 908–918.

Savin-Williams, R. (1979). Dominance hierarchies in groups of early adolescents. *Child Development, 50*, 923–935.

Savin-Williams, R., & Janquish, A. (1981). The assessment of adolescent self-esteem: A comparison of methods. *Journal of Personality, 49*, 324–336.

Schachter, S. (1959). *The psychology of affiliation*. Stanford, CA: Stanford University Press.

Scheidlinger, S. (1984). The adolescent peer group revisited: Turbulence or adaptation? *Journal of Small Group Behavior, 15*, 387–397.

Schlachter, R. (1975). Home counseling of adolescents and parents. *Social Work, 20*, 427–428, 481.

Schmidt, R. (1972). *The reference other orientation*. Carbondale, IL: Southern Illinois University Press.

Schmitt, B. (1988). Social comparison in romantic jealousy. *Personality and Social Psychology Bulletin, 14*, 374–387.

Schonfeld, W. (1969). The body and the body-image in adolescents. In G. Caplan and S. Levovici (Eds.), *Adolescence: Psychosocial perspectives*. New York: Basic Books.

Schwartz, G., & Merten, D. (1967). The language of adolescence: An anthropological approach to the youth culture. *American Journal of Sociology, 72*, 453–468.

Sears, R., Maccoby, E., & Levin, H. (1957). *Patterns of child rearing*. Evanston, IL: Row and Peterson.

Sebald, H. (1984). *Adolescence: A social psychological analysis*. Englewood Cliffs, NJ: Prentice-Hall.

Sebald, H., & White, B. (1980). Teenagers' divided reference groups: Uneven alignment with parents and peers. *Adolescence, 15*, 979–984.

Seligman, M. (1975). *Helplessness: On depression, development and death*. San Francisco: Freeman.

Seltzer, V. (1980). Social comparison behaviors of adolescents. In E. Pepitone (Ed.), *Children in cooperation and competition* (pp. 253–291). Lexington, MA: Lexington Books, D.C. Heath.

Seltzer, V. (1982). *Adolescent social development: Dynamic functional interaction*. Lexington, MA: Lexington Books, D.C. Heath.

Shaffer, H. (1986). Observations on substance abuse theory. *Journal of Counselling and Development, 65*, 26–28.

Shaw, M. (1976). *Group dynamics: The psychology of small group behavior* (2nd ed.). New York: McGraw-Hill.

Sherif, M. (1954). Reference groups in human relations. In M. Sherif & M. Wilson (Eds.), *Group relations at the crossroads*. New York: Harper & Row.

Sherif, M. (1964). *Reference groups*. New York: Harper & Row.

Sherif, M. & Sherif, C. (1965). *Problems of youth: Transition to adulthood in a changing world*. Chicago: Aldine.

Shontz, F. (1986). *Fundamentals of research in the behavioral sciences: Principles and practice*. Washington, DC: American Psychiatric Press.

Siegle, L., & Griffin, N. (1983). Adolescents' concepts of depression among their peers. *Adolescence, 8*, 965–973.

Simmons, R., & Blyth, D. (1987). *Moving into Adolescence: Impact of pubertal change and school context*. New York: de Gruyter.

Singer, J. (1975). *The inner world of daydreaming*. New York: Harper & Row.

Skinner, B. F. (1972). *Cumulative record: A selection of papers* (3rd ed.). New York: Appleton-Century-Crofts.

Smith, T., Koob, J., & Wirtz, T. (1985). Ecology of adolescents' marijuana abuse. *International Journal of the Addictions, 20*, 1421–1428.

Sommer, B. (1984). The troubled teen: Suicide, drug use, and running away. *Women and Health, 9*, 117–141.

Spindler, G. (1974). The transmission of culture. In G. Spindler (Ed.). *Education and cultural process: Toward an anthropology of education* (pp. 279–310). New York: Holt, Rinehart & Winston.

Stefanko, M. (1984). Trends in adolescent research: A review of articles published in *Adolescence*, 1976–1981. *Adolescence, 19*, 1–14.

Steinberg, L. (1981). Transformations in family relations at puberty. *Developmental Psychology, 7*, 833–840.

Steinberg, L. (1987). Impact of puberty on family relations: Effects of pubertal status and pubertal timing. *Developmental Psychology, 23.*

Steinberg, L. & Silverberg, S. (1986). The vicissitudes of autonomy in early adolescence. *Child Development, 57,* 841–851.

Stouffer, S., Suchman, E., DeVinney, L., Star, S., & Williams, R. (1949). *The American soldier: Adjustment during army life.* Princeton: Princeton University Press.

Sugar, M. (Ed.). (1979). *Female adolescent development.* New York: Brunner/Mazel.

Suls, J., & Miller, R. (Eds.). (1977). *Social comparison processes: Theoretical and empirical perspectives.* Washington, DC: Hemisphere.

Tanner, J. (1972). Sequence, tempo and individual variation of growth and development of boys and girls aged twelve to sixteen. In J. Kagan and R. Coles (Eds.), *Twelve to sixteen: Early adolescence.* New York: Norton.

Tanner, J. (1974). Physical aspects of adolescence. In M. Kelmer Pringle and V. Varma (Eds.), *Advances in educational psychology.* London: University of London Press.

Thibaut, J., & Kelley, H. (1959). *The social psychology of groups.* New York: Wiley.

Thornburg, H. (Ed.). (1975). *Contemporary adolescence: Readings* (2nd ed.). Belmont, CA: Wadsworth.

Thornburg, H. (1982). Social characteristics of early adolescents: Age versus grade. *Journal of Early Adolescence, 2,* 229–239.

Thorndike, E. (1932). *The fundamentals of learning.* New York: Teachers College Press.

Topol, O. & Reznikoff, M. (1982). Perceived peer and family relationships, hopelessness and locus of control as factors in adolescent suicide attempts. *Suicide and Life Threatening Behavior, 12,* 141–150.

Turiel, E. (1974). Conflict and transition in adolescent moral development. *Child Development, 45,* 14–79.

Waterman, A. (1982). Identity development from adolescence to adulthood: An extension of theory and a review of research. *Developmental Psychology, 18,* 341–358.

Watson, J. B. (1925). *Behaviorism.* New York: Norton.

Weiner, I. (1970). *Psychological disturbance in adolescence.* New York: Wiley.

Wheeler, L. (1966). Motivation as a determinant of comparison upward. *Journal of Experimental Social Psychology, Supp. 1,* 27–32.

Wheeler, L., Kelley, R., Shaver, L., Jones, R., Goethals, G., Cooper, J., Robinson, J., Gruder, C., & Butzine, K. (1969). Factors determining the choice of a comparison other. *Journal of Experimental Social Psychology, 5,* 219–232.

Yankelovich, D. (1974). *The new morality: A profile of American youth in the 70s.* New York: McGraw-Hill.

Youniss, J. (1980). *Parents and peers in social development.* Chicago: University of Chicago Press.

Yudin, L. (1966). Formal thought of adolescence as a function of intelligence. *Child development, 37,* 697–708.

Zeltzer, L., Kellerman, J., Ellenberg, L., Dash, J., & Rigler, D. (1980). Psychological effects of illness in adolescence: 1. Anxiety, self-esteem and perception of control. *Journal of Pediatrics, 97*, 126–131.

Zeltzer, L., Kellerman, J., Ellenberg, L., Dash, J., & Rigler, D. (1980). Psychological effects of illness in adolescence: 2. Impact of illness in adolescents—crucial issues and coping styles. *Journal of Pediatrics, 97*, 132–138.

AUTHOR INDEX

Adams, G., 279, 286, 289
Adelson, J., 283
Alapack, R., 284
American Psychiatric Association, 279
Ames, L., 13, 285
Anderson, E., 279
Anthony, E., 279
Aronson, E., 282
Asch, S., 30, 279
Auchenbach, T., 279
Ausubel, D., 12–13, 279
Ayers-Lopez, S., 282

Babbie, E., 279
Bachtel, D., 290
Bales, R., 290
Banaji, M., 285
Bandura, A., 12, 279
Bank, B., 280
Barclay, A., 280
Bardwick, J., 280
Baum, C., 283
Baumrind, D., 280
Beck, A., 280
Becker, R., 280
Bell, R., 280
Bellezza, F., 285

Benedict, R., 4, 5, 227, 280
Berenda, R., 30, 280
Berndt, T., 280
Bernstein, R., 280
Biddle, B., 280
Blos, P., 6–8, 280
Bluebond-Langner, M., 280
Blum, H., 280
Blum, L., 280
Blythe, D., 280, 291, 292
Bowlby, J., 280
Bram, S., 280
Breakwell, G., 280
Brehm, S., 281
Brim, O., 281
Bronfenbrenner, U., 12, 281
Brooks-Gunn, J., 281, 285
Brown, B., 281
Burkett, S., 281
Butzine, K., 36, 294
Bywater, E., 281

Carlsmith, J., 283
Carlson, G., 281
Carter, E., 281
Cattell, R., 281
Cervantes, L., 280

Weiner, I., 293
Wellisch, D., 282
Wheeler, K., 285
Wheeler, L., 36, 294
White, B., 292
Williams, R., 48, 293
Wirtz, T., 293

Yankelovich, D., 294
Youniss, J., 294
Yudin, L., 294

Zakin, D., 280
Zeltzer, L., 294
Zimmerman, B., 291

Subject Index

Abstract thought in adolescence,
10–11
Academic learning, relationship
between emotional functioning
and, 251, 255
Academic problems, 240–241
Achievement, 8
Acquaintances, 143, 151
Acquired abilities, 104
Acting, 104
Active support stance, 237
Activity level, 156
Addictive behaviors, 168–169,
248–249
Adolescence:
approaches, 1–114
primary peer arena, *see* Dynamic
functional interaction model
secondary peer arena, *see* Dynamic
functional interaction model
Adolescent(s):
age-related differences of,
129–130
alternating needs of, 128–129
attributes always of interest to, 104
attributes never of interest to, 105
cause-committed, 169–170
different, 172–174
with disabilities, 174–177

discriminating, 80
without a group, 172
immigrant, 180–181
need to be together, 35–37
person-committed, 170
rate of change in, 18–20
settled, 165, 166–168
shared conditions of, 20
with terminal illness, 178–179
Adolescent Comparison Probe,
132, 133
Adolescent dialectic, 237
Adolescent imperative, 36, 39
Adolescent peer, definition of, 257
Adolescent Reference Group Index
(ARGI), 49–52, 85, 95, 185,
186–188, 229–230, 272
clues for remediation, 192–193
influence of parents and, 154
social relational world, 191–192
utilized with PAPP, 219
variations in utilization of,
188–193
Adolescent society, 13
Age-related differences and
socialization, 129–130
Alcohol, 190
peer pressure and, 14
Alcohol abuse, 168–169, 248–249